The Caravels of Christ

Gilbert Renault

THE CARAVELS
OF CHRIST

TRANSLATED BY RICHMOND HILL

G. P. PUTNAM'S SONS
NEW YORK

© 1959 by George Allen & Unwin Ltd.

FIRST AMERICAN EDITION

Translated from the French
LES CARAVELLES DU CHRIST
© *Libraire Plon, 1956*

Library of Congress Catalog
Card Number: 58-11671

CONTENTS

꘎

ILLUSTRATIONS

Following page 96

The Jeronimo Chapel, Lisbon

A cottage roof in Algarve

Spring in Algarve

The body of St Vincent is borne to Lisbon by ship

The tomb of João I and Philippa of Lancaster

Section from the Catalan Atlas of 1375

Panel by Nuno Gonçalves showing Dom Alfonso,
the future Dom João II, Dom Henrique, Isabel
of Aragon and Queen Isabel

The Tower at Belém

A window of the Chapter at Tomar

Cabral's fleet

Brazil, according to an old portulan

Vasco da Gama

The tomb of Vasco da Gama

Detail from the tomb of Inez de Castro at Alcobaça

Model of the *St Gabriel*

Model of the *Bérrio*

Dom João II

Dom Afonso V

The Caravels of Christ

ও I ও

The Presentation of the Swords

THE Portuguese province of the Algarve is separated from the rest of the country by rugged ochre mountains, and it turns its blossoming almond-orchards, its great fig-trees with heavy branches bowed down to the ground and the delicately-wrought chimneys that adorn even its humblest houses, southwards towards near-by Africa. In calm weather the sea at the foot of the cliffs of Cape St Vincent gently rises and falls as if stirred by rhythmic breathing, and its deep blue really is the colour of the South Atlantic. Nothing grows here but stunted junipers, raked by a salt-laden breeze, and dwarf shrubs with shiny greenish-blue leaves which adhere to the fingers and leave a stale musky odour on the skin.

During the reign of the Emperor Diocletian, a deacon of Saragossa was arrested, together with his bishop Valerius, and subjected to appalling tortures. His devotion and fortitude under the torment was such that his jailer was converted, and the martyr himself baptised him before he died. The name of Vincent was soon as deeply revered as that of St Sebastian, or the still recent memory of St Laurence; and in the litanies of the saints, the Church still places side by side these three names, all distinguished with the same purple.

Four centuries later the Muslim invasion burst upon Spain. Fearing that the relics of St Vincent might be desecrated by the infidels, pious persons placed them on a ship which sailed round the Peninsula, slipped through the Pillars of Hercules, and was finally wrecked on a promontory, where, according to the Greeks and Romans, the gods reposed from their toils and watched the falling sun expand until it became a hundred times larger than anywhere else in the world. In this sacred and deserted spot the remains of the saint were buried. The cape took the martyr's name of Vincent, and for four centuries more no Christian ship rounded it without dipping its sail in salutation, as men bare their heads before they kneel to pray.

Its only inhabitants were ravens, which kept ceaseless watch over the venerable relics. When in 1178, towards the end of the reign of Afonso I, the son of a French nobleman, Henry of Burgundy, and of Teresa of Leon, and founder of the kingdom of Portugal, St Vincent's bones were transferred to Lisbon, a raven was to be seen standing at the prow of the ship and another at its stern. Thereafter two ravens figured on the city's arms, and they have since been awarded its freedom, for these birds, which have seen generations of men come and go, are to be found on the heights of the castle of St George which dominates the whole estuary of the Tagus.

A little behind Cape St Vincent and to its east, a rocky spur juts into the sea like the prow of a ship. It is a single block of stone, five hundred yards long and of moderate width, and its surface resembles the deck of a ship on which a foaming wave has been transfixed for all eternity. It turns its back on the world, and fixes its stony stare on the infinite spaces of the distant horizons. To this point Prince Henry of Portugal came when he was about twenty-five to brood upon his vision.

His father was the bastard John I,[1] and his grandfather the terrible Peter the Justicer, who took vengeance on the two murderers of his beloved Inês de Castro by drawing out their hearts, one through the breast and the other through the back: he awaits the hour of the last Judgment in his stone resting-place in the Cistercian monastery of Alcobaça, facing the tomb of the 'Queen after her death'. As everyone in Portugal knows, when the terrible trumpet sounds, 'its fearful notes will echo round every tomb and summon all men before the throne of God': at that moment the two lovers will arise and join in a marriage of eternal glory.

Henry's mother, Philippa of Lancaster, bore the name of the gentle Philippa of Hainault, her grandmother, whose tears and entreaties stirred the heart of her royal husband, Edward III, when he had resolved to put to death the burghers of Calais, Eustache de Saint-Pierre and his five companions, who came before him bare-

[1] Reigned 1385–1433.

footed, in their shirts, with fetters round their necks, to bring him the keys of the conquered city.

Philippa had borne John six fine children: Duarte, the heir to the throne; Pedro, who was regent during the minority of Duarte's son, Afonso; the Infanta Isabel, who bravely succeeded Michelle of France and Bonne of Artois as the third wife of Philip of Burgundy, called 'the Good', with his troublesome train of bastards: she was the mother of Charles the Bold and she used the great influence she exercised over her husband to bring about peace with the King of France, Charles VII. After Isabel came Henry, born on March 4, 1394, in the old city of Oporto; then John, future Constable of Portugal. The youngest was Ferdinand. His mother was so weak when she was about to give birth to him that the doctors brought her a concoction to kill the child she carried in her womb, but she indignantly refused to be the murderer of her own flesh, and declared herself ready to accept the will of God. He spared her. The extraordinary virtue the young Prince would display one day in an extremity of suffering would gain him the reputation of 'Saint' among all his people.

Henry was approaching his twentieth year when his mother was stricken by the plague then raging in Lisbon. The Queen had prepared three swords, richly encrusted with gold, gems and pearls, which she proposed to present to her three eldest sons for the approaching expedition against Ceuta. She had heard them tell their father, who had wanted them to be armed knights after a tournament: 'Sire, great feats of courage, mortal danger and shedding of the blood of our foes, these are the things that open the door of knighthood to princes such as we, not the mere semblance of a splendid festival.' Queen Philippa had them call the King to her bedside, and she told him: 'They say that arms offered by women soften the spirit of true knights, but I am persuaded that the lineage from which I come entitles me to present these princes with these swords and that their resolution will not thereby be weakened.'

The sword she delivered to Duarte was the largest of the three, and the Queen named it 'the sword of Justice'. To Pedro she confided the honour and happiness of the women and damsels of the kingdom. When she saw her third son, Henry, the dying Queen's face was lit with joy and she smiled happily as she said: 'My son, you have seen the swords I have bestowed on your brothers. This third blade I have kept for you; it is strong as you are strong. I have bidden Duarte protect the people, and I have confided the defence of women and damsels to Pedro. To you, I entrust all the lords, knights, gentlemen and squires of this kingdom . . . '

'Madame,' replied Henry with bended knee, 'rest assured that so long as I draw breath I shall never forget what you have bidden me.'

A feeble light came into the Queen's eyes, and she raised her right hand and gave her blessing to the prince.

'What is the wind I hear blowing so strongly?' she asked anxiously. Her sons told her that it was the north wind.

'I believe,' she said with a last smile, 'that that is a good wind for your voyage.'

Soon after, her gaze seemed to be attracted by some object that was invisible to all those about her. But they saw her dying face transfigured and heard her murmur: 'Oh Holy Virgin, praised be thy name that thou hast descended from heaven to visit me!' Frail Queen Philippa drew the bedcover over her breast and kissed it devoutly. Soon after, she breathed her last breath.

Because of the stifling heat that overwhelmed the city the dead Queen was secretly shrouded during the night, and on the following morning, robed in great magnificence, her obsequies were solemnly celebrated. Clad in their sackcloth, the princes then went straight to the village of Santa Maria at Belem facing the beach of the Restelo on the north bank of the Tagus, off which their fleet lay at anchor. After a discussion the King decided, in response to Henry's earnest urgings, that the expedition should sail on the following Wednesday, July 25, 1415, the feast of the Apostle St James the Greater, venerated throughout the Christian world for his relics at Santiago de Compostela in Galicia.

'The fleet was a most wondrous thing to behold,' says Gomes Eanes de Azurara, the author of the *Chronicle of the Feats of Guinea*. 'In the morning it seemed like a forest stripped of its leaves and fruit, and then suddenly it became like a splendid orchard gleaming with green leaves and many-coloured flowers; pennants and banners were without number, and of many forms and colours. And it was as though the voices of strange birds were heard singing in their grove, for innumerable instruments were heard playing in each ship, of many kinds and their sound was heard all that night.'

❧ 2 ❧

The Bells of Sines

THE Master of the Order of Avis, from which his dynasty was to take its name, had ascended the throne after a bitter struggle. In order to save his country from the threat of occupation by the ruler of Castile, he had been forced to stab to death in the palace itself the Galician Andeiro, the scandalous favourite of King Ferdinand's widow, the beautiful Queen Leonor.

Once proclaimed Governor and Defender of the Realm, the Bastard of Avis won the support of all the populace, which stoically endured the cruellest sufferings in the closely invested city of Lisbon, until finally the besiegers were decimated by plague and forced to retire. But the Castilians did not give in. Chosen King by the Cortes of Coimbra, John came face to face with the enemy on August 14, 1385, on the plain of Aljubarrota. The Spanish army consisted of 20,000 horse and 10,000 infantry: John had only 2,000 lances and 4,000 foot, with 800 crossbowmen. Yet by the skill of his pious Constable, Nun'Álvares Pereira, he routed his adversary, establishing the independence of Portugal in the most striking and decisive fashion.

The King of England, Richard II, had sent to his aid a handful of archers trained in the square tactics of which the French had had such bitter experience at Crecy some forty years earlier: from this episode derives the alliance, based on the treaty of peace and friendship of June 16, 1373, between Ferdinand and Edward III, which still unites Great Britain and Portugal. It was concluded at Windsor on May 9, 1386, and affirms 'between the two hereinafter mentioned kings now reigning, and their heirs and successors, and between the subjects of their two kingdoms, an inviolable, eternal, solid, perpetual and loyal bond of friendship, alliance and union, not only

17

between these two and their heirs and successors, but also on behalf of their realms, lords, possessions and subjects, vassels, allies and friends, wherever they may be, so that each shall have the obligation to assist and give succour to the other against all those, now living or yet unborn, who shall seek to violate the peace between the two contracting parties, or shall make bold to offend their estates in any way soever.'

These were fine phrases, but England was far off, and John knew that for the moment he could rely only on himself to rear the structure of his kingdom and consolidate it.

Thus when his three eldest sons, themselves thirsting for glory, approached him to propose that they should attack the Moorish town of Ceuta, he began by turning a deaf ear. They insisted, but his only response to their pleas was a great burst of laughter: it seemed to him pure madness to risk his hard-won crown in such an exploit. But the young princes were true to their stock. Such a rebuff did not dismay them, and they returned to the charge with redoubled ardour. The King's spirit was troubled and he turned to his confessors: Would the conquest of Ceuta be considered as a service to the glory of God, yes or no? The churchmen, Master Frei João Xira and Dr Vasco Pereira, replied in the affirmative: their assurances weakened the resistance of the cautious monarch, but they did not suffice completely to convince him. Under the seal of the greatest secrecy, he took aside the wisest and most experienced of his counsellors and sounded them one by one. He also took the advice of his eldest son, who, as heir to the throne, had the right to be heard. They all expressed agreement with the men of God, and John thereupon summoned the princes and informed them:

'You think doubtless that I have not given speed to the matter on which you approached me, and this bears witness to a lack of enthusiasm on my part. If so, you are much mistaken: although my age is much more than yours, I challenge you to show a greater resolution than I to perform this deed. But I, who have seen many things in the course of my life, am able to weigh certain obstacles that are still hidden from your eyes. They tell me that the taking of Ceuta will be a service to God: this is well, and I should therefore undertake it. Yet it remains to decide whether I have the resources to do so. . . . Touching this, I find great doubts, and shall mention

18

five of them to you: they can be taken singly, for each is strong enough to prevent the accomplishment of this design, and I shall tell them to you so that you may realize their weight.'

There was, firstly, the question of money. 'I have not the treasure that will be needed and I do not know how I may come by it. Should I seek to raise it from my people by increasing the taxes, I shall draw great displeasure on myself and at the same time dispel the secrecy that is necessary if our enterprise is to succeed.'

Secondly, Ceuta was distant: an attack would require many men, a great amount of arms, equipment, artillery and an enormous quantity of supplies. And for the transport of the men, the beasts, and the equipment, 'there would necessary be a great fleet of many great ships, without counting small ones of which I do not even speak. Where shall you find great ships in my realms? As for me, I do not see how we shall find them.'

Thirdly, the threat of Castile still hung over them: 'I would have to be able to leave at least some forces on the frontiers, and if I do this, I should not have sufficient for my purpose; for the city of Ceuta is very large and very strong. In order to besiege it and take it, I should need many men, since otherwise the expedition would be a source of shame never to be forgotten.'

Fourthly, 'even if God gave me victory, as I readily believe, the taking of this town will bring me more loss than gain, for after the conquest of Ceuta the kingdom of Granada would be much easier to reduce; and what will it profit me if the kingdom of Granada falls into Castilian hands? On the contrary I shall only lose by it, for I know full well that the Castilians hate us; and doubly so now, since the defeats we have inflicted upon them. . . .'

Fifthly, 'my last reason seems to me to be of great moment, since a wise man, before he commit himself to an undertaking, should study it from every aspect and as profoundly as he may, and not only as to its present effects, but also to those it may have in the future. He must contemplate not only the contrary effects that may immediately arise, but also those which may occur later. If it should please God to aid us to take this town, what honour or renown shall we derive from its conquest if, once accomplished, we cannot maintain or defend it? And concerning this I have grave doubts. . . . Furthermore, the Moors who are in the town of Ceuta will have graven in their hearts the memory of the offence and wrong done them by our victory. In order to seek revenge, they will load their ships with the flower of their young men and descend on the people of our Algarve, who, being defenceless in their homesteads, will be deprived of their lives and property. . . .'

The King paused before concluding:

'Consider then what will be the advantage to us of such great expense, so many efforts and cares, and so slender a hope of victory! Glory and honour would escape us if we could not hold the town, and I do not see how we can keep it and govern it. It is my opinion therefore that we should forget these designs, for the last reason I have given is sufficient, without speaking of the other four, which are no less strong, to prevent the achievement of what we all desire. If you do not think my reasons are just, bring me your objections, and I will weigh them according to right and reason.'

The princes were discomfited, and held their peace. But they were tenacious, and returned to their father to try to convince him. As Prince Henry insistently raised the question of Granada, the King disposed that they should discuss it more.

'It appears to me, sire,' said his son, 'that whatever we do in this world must be founded on three principal things, which are the past, the present and the future.

'As to the past, I recall that at the time when God, by his grace, was pleased that you should be King, you held then only a small part of this town of Lisbon, for the castle held out against you. It was the same at Almada, Sintra, Torres Vedras, Óbidos, Santarém, and almost everywhere else in the kingdom. Yet God has shown you the way by which all these castles have come into your hands, and they today render you homage and obedience with no loss or sacrifice on your part.

'Wherefore in this present should you expect less of God than he has bestowed upon you in the past? Even if the kingdom of Granada should fall under the domination of the crown of Castile, with God's aid you will have the power to frustrate the designs of your enemies if they should seek to do you harm. It would indeed be much easier for you to do these things now than formerly, for many reasons which I need not repeat to you, since you are fully aware of them.

'At this present I see that the taking of Ceuta would be a service to God. I know your faith and your Christian spirit, and my reason tells me moreover that you should not refrain from war with the infidel for fear that its result may be favourable to the King of Castile: even if he were our greatest enemy, this could only be by chance since he, like ourselves, professes the Christian faith, while the infidels hate us from their innermost hearts.

'Touching the future, I do not think that the taking of Ceuta can in any wise bring about the breaking of the treaty of peace and friendship you have lately concluded with the kingdom of Castile. On the contrary, by the greatness of this exploit the Castilians shall perceive the stoutness of your subjects' hearts and the marvellous power at your command to perform such a feat: they cannot then fail to reflect that the winning of Ceuta will facilitate the conquest of Granada for them. Should they refuse to recognize the evidence, I would still scarcely fear their illwill. In any case the conquest of Granada will be difficult, and in seeking to maintain it, the Castilians will have other things to do than to pick quarrels with us. And above all, our Lord God, knowing your good will and the excellence of your inclination, will always be with you; and like the prophet, you shall say: "Since God is with me, I need not fear what men can do to me." '

King John was so delighted with this reply that he embraced his son laughing with joy, and gave him his blessing.

'Well,' he said, 'I need no other arguments than these to bring me to a conclusion I had already foreseen. I am persuaded that no virtue can attain perfection save through practice: this is true of any occupation, and especially that of a knight, which requires at once the exertion of the body and of the soul. Thus if the nobles and other valiant men of this kingdom find no way in which to exercise their power, they will do one of two things: either they will quarrel among themselves and stir up strife like that which brought about the decadence of the Romans, or they will wreak such havoc on the people of Castile that the peace may be broken, and this I cannot on any account accept. It appears to me then that, even if the conquest of Ceuta were of no profit to us, this reason alone would suffice to convince us of the usefulness and need of the hardships and expense that this undertaking will entail. As to the difficulty of keeping and maintaining Ceuta once we have conquered it, I leave this care to our Lord God, for as he is mighty enough to make small things great, he can, through his divine grace, give us the means to govern and keep this town.'

The King smiled at Henry and added:

'So, with the aid of God, I resolve to begin this enterprise and pursue it till the end. And since God has willed that you and I should be together at the moment when this resolution is taken, you shall be the messenger whom I entrust to carry the news to your brothers and you may inform them of my intention as I have told it to you.'

The Prince knelt before his father in a transport of joy, kissing his hand and stammering words of thanks.

According to the Book of the Three Kings 'God says: "Aid thyself, and I will aid thee: or otherwise, I will fail thee." ' In order to win Ceuta, it was necessary to take every precaution. Nothing was known of the plan of the town, the thickness of its walls, the disposition of its towers and its powder-magazines, and all this information was indispensable for the use of the artillery. It was desirable also to know the anchorages, the prevailing winds, the system of observation practised by the enemy to guard the coast. Was the sea deep enough off-shore so that they might open fire effectively from the ships before landing. As the King pondered on these questions, he put them to his court, and no one could supply the answers. John proceeded at leisure in order to impress his sons with this lesson of prudence. It was only when they seemed on the point of giving way to discouragement that the wise monarch unmasked his batteries.

'A great stratagem has occurred to me,' he said, 'which I have a mind to employ. The Queen of Sicily, if I may believe the request she has made of me, is not inclined to remain a widow, and she has written to ask if it is my pleasure that she should marry you, Duarte. . . .'

Joan of Naples had recently succeeded her brother Ladislas: she was nearly fifty and her reputation was not of the brightest. Duarte, a handsome youth of twenty-three summers, may well have blanched at the shock.

'We shall spread the report,' the King went on, 'that I am sending the Prior of the Hospitallers and Captain Furtado on an embassy to this gentle dame whom I shall propose to unite to Pedro. . . .'

He gazed upon his second son before adding:

'I am quite sure that she will refuse. But the negotiation will not be unprofitable, for my ambassadors will twice have the opportunity to pass in front of the town of Ceuta and to observe and study the points I need to know.'

And this was done. Two galleys were equipped wth enormous splendour, and also with artillery so that they might defend themselves in case of need. From prow to poop they were aflutter with oriflammes and banners, and they were covered with awnings in the colours of the royal house. This had never been seen before, and it made such an impression that the fashion remained.

'When all was ready,' says Azurara, 'the ambassadors took leave of the King and the galleys departed. After leaving Lisbon in all their splendour, they cast anchor before the town of Ceuta, where they made pretence of resting before they resumed the voyage. And the Prior, as he sat on the deck of his galley, calmly and at leisure, like a prudent and peaceful man, attentively observed the arrangement of the town and noted all he needed to know. The captain, for his part, scanned the beaches, seeking the places where these were least rocky and which offered the most favourable landing-point for an army. And when night had fallen, he stealthily left his galley, and was rowed in a small boat round the port, studying the anchorages and all the matters which the King required to know. Next day, having completed their observations, the ambassadors raised the anchors and proceeded with their voyage.'

The precautions taken by King John recall exactly those which preceded the landing of June 6, 1944, leading to the liberation of France. Experts who had come secretly from England gathered all the information that was needed on the beaches of lower Normandy, and this, together with the reports of the clandestine Free French movement, enabled the allied forces to approach with the minimum of loss. But, as we shall see, the Portuguese also instituted another practice which is no less modern.

As King John had foreseen, Joan rejected the offer of his second son, for she had hoped to unite the crown of Portugal with her own by becoming the wife of Duarte, his heir. Pedro, a handsome stripling in the flower of his youth, breathed a sigh of relief.

'Sire,' declared Afonso Furtado crisply when he was brought into the royal presence, 'I bring you only one reply: you will find at Ceuta an excellent landing-place and a splendid anchorage which you may safely enter whenever you will. With the grace of God, the town will soon be in your hands.'

'Such is my hope, if it please God!' replied the King devoutly. 'But I would have you speak to me of the anchorage and all the other matters which I bade you observe.'

'Sire,' replied the stubborn captain, 'I shall tell you nothing more, save that you may go, and that you will find everything as you desire it. I can add that you will not only take this town, but many other places besides, which, as soon as you hold Ceuta, will readily fall into your hands and will long remain in those of your descendants.'

The King grew red, a sign that his patience was wearing thin. But Afonso Furtado pretended not to notice.

'Sire, this I know from a marvellous occurrence that took place when I was a young man, and I have always remembered it because of singular proofs that have already shown it to be true; and so that you may understand, I shall recount it to you. . . .'

King John, with an air of resignation, allowed his captain to continue.

'Your father, King Pedro (God rest his soul) sent my father on a mission to a foreign land, and as I desired to see new countries, my father took me with him in the hope that I should learn from the experience. We landed at a port in Africa, not far from Ceuta, and I did my best to observe everything that seemed worthy of note. I sat myself down not far from a fountain that flowed into a fine pool and took much pleasure in watching the horses come down to drink, for there were many of them and I remember how much I was struck by their outstanding beauty. There was an old man . . .'

The story promised to be a long one, and King John sighed; but Afonso Furtado proceeded:

'An old man, whose flowing beard and bent figure showed him to be well-stricken in years. He approached me and after observing me attentively, he asked me what country I was from, and I told him that I was a Spaniard. He pressed me to know of which of the Spains I was a native. "I was born in the city of Lisbon," I told him. "And in what kingdom may that city be?" he asked. "In the kingdom of

Portugal," I replied. "And what King reigns in that kingdom?"
"A very good King called Dom Pedro, the son of the most excellent
Dom Afonso, who fought in the battle of the Salado and defeated
the Moors and did great havoc among them. Dom Pedro is a just
King and he loves his people. . . ." '

King John nodded his head. It was almost a gesture of encourage-
ment; at least Furtado interpreted it as one.

' "Tell me," went on the old man, "how many sons has this King?"
"Three," said I, "the first is Prince Ferdinand, the second Prince
John, and the third Prince Denis." "Has he no others?" asked the old
man.

'I said that he had not, but the Moor bade me consider well. I did
not think of you, Sire, for you were only a tender babe. Then
suddenly I remembered your birth; I said: "Friend, it is true that
the King has another son, only an infant, called John. I had forgotten him, for among us, bastards are not held in such honour as
lawful sons." '

Here Afonso Furtado broke off the flow of his anecdote. The King
was silent; reassured, Afonso Furtado continued:

' "Ah!" exclaimed the old Moor, "that is as I feared!" and he gave
a hollow groan, and dropped his head and wept. I stood amazed at
this, and as his tears continued to flow, I begged him to tell me the
cause of his woes. For a long time he refused to confide in me, until
at length, as I continued to press him, he said: "Friend, these tears
of mine are of little moment in comparison with the deed that makes
them flow. These tears you see are not shed for any present woe . . .
no, my grief arises from the foreknowledge I have of the evils that
will befall my friends and fellow-countrymen. And since destiny
has brought you to this spot, listen, and I shall tell you what I know.
This King Dom Pedro who now reigns over you has but a little time
to live: his days are numbered, and after him, his eldest son, Ferdin-
and, will come to the throne. He will marry a wife who will give rise
to great troubles after his death. Through her, Dom Pedro's other
sons will depart for Castile, where they will end their days. And the
youngest son of Dom Pedro who is now despised in comparison with
his brothers shall be like a spark from which a great fire is born, for
the day will come when, after avenging the disgrace of his dead
brother, he will be chosen by the people to ascend the throne. He

will have great strife with the kingdom of Castile, but he will always emerge victorious. He will also be the first King in Spain to have possessions in Africa, and he will be the source of the downfall of the Moors. And in days to come he or his sons will come to this fountain to water their horses." '

"And is that the whole of your story?' asked King John.

'All, sire. But consider: I who have heard these things have seen all that was prophesied turn out just as the old man foretold and in the order in which he foretold it. I cannot therefore doubt but that the town of Ceuta will fall into your power, and so I repeat that you shall find everything exactly as you desire: beach, anchorages, all.'

The King burst into hearty laughter, like one filled with contempt for such old wives' tales. His merriment over, he became serious again, and reminded his captain that if he had entrusted him with a mission it was because he had expected him to give a good account of himself and he therefore begged him to present the information he had gathered. But Afonso's pride had been wounded and he refused to open his mouth. Thereupon King John turned towards the Prior of the Hospitallers and ordered him to recount all he had discovered about the defences of the town of Ceuta.

'Sire,' replied the Prior, 'I shall say nothing of what I have seen until you order four things to be brought—two bags of sand, a ball of thread, half a bushel of beans, and a bowl.'

Mystified by this strange request, King John all but gave way to anger. Then he contained himself and laughed with all his heart.

'Think you not that we have had our fill of foolery with the captain's prophecies?' he said. 'A truce to these triflings, and tell me plainly what you have seen.'

'Sire,' replied the Prior calmly, 'it is not my practice to jest before your Highness, as God is my witness. I repeat that I can tell you nothing till they have brought these four things hither.'

The King was now truly angry, and turned to his sons:

'See what sage discourse these wise men ply me with! I ask them to give me the news I have sent them to discover and one talks astrology while the other prepares to perform a conjuring trick before me! Is it possible that a valiant captain and a learned Prior should act in such a fashion?'

The princes urged the two companions to reveal what they had learned without more ado. But Afonso Furtado refused to be drawn from his sulky silence, while the Prior swore by his faith that with the best will in the world he could not give his report until he had the objects he had demanded. There was no remedy but to humour him, and to retire from the room, where he demanded to be left alone. After a long spell, he at last reopened the door, saying: 'Now you see the result of my observations. Ask what you will.'

'With the sand,' writes Azurara, 'the Prior of the Hospitallers had copied the hill of Almina and the whole town of Ceuta as it is, rounding out the hills and valleys, and Aljazira and the mountains of Ximeira in their exact places. The thread followed the line of the wall, and the beans were poised upon it, so that the whole was very perfectly rendered.'

The ingenious Prior had in fact invented the principle of the panoramic model, without which no army staff today could elaborate its plans. To his sovereign he displayed the thickness of the walls on the side of the town facing the sea, the position of the towers and their height, and the points most suitable for attack by main force. King John, now quite appeased, congratulated him warmly on his handiwork and concluded that circumstances were favourable. There were, he thought, only two quarters from which opposition might still be met: the Queen and Dom Nun'Álvares Pereira, Constable of Portugal. The princes went at once in search of Dona Felipa, and when she had heard them she duly sought audience of her spouse:

'Sire,' she said, 'the boon I come to crave is not such as you might expect to issue from a mother's lips. I do not ask you to spare our sons toils and dangers, but to deprive them of merrymaking and pleasure. . . .'

King John was delighted with the Queen's words, and at once gave orders for the felling of timber to build the galleys and foists he would need. Carpenters and caulkers were at once engaged, and orders were given for the collection of all the copper and silver that were to be found, and to procure further supplies of these metals abroad. João Afonso, the governor of the exchequer, was sent to draw on the revenues of the city, and forthwith arranged with the master of the mint for the furnaces to be made ready. The King sent his admiral, Micer Carlos, to gather all the equipment that would be required, and the secretary of state took steps to draw up a roll of all able-bodied men who were available for active service.

These preparations naturally did not pass unnoticed, and the people were filled with curiosity to know what expedition was being planned. The representatives of friendly powers in Lisbon and merchants of all nations left no stone unturned to discover the secret, but their efforts were in vain. Only Ruy Diaz de Vega, the ambassador of Ferdinand I of Aragon, guessed that its object must be either Gibraltar or Ceuta. The princes strained at the leash, impatient to cover themselves with glory: eighteen months had passed since they had laid before their father the scheme that was so dear to their hearts and it seemed to them that everything still remained to be done.

In order to consult with the Constable, who lived in retirement on his estates, where he had acquired the fame of sanctity, Dom João organized a great hunting party. Thus the interview took place without arousing any attention. The King told Nun'Álvares of all that had taken place and added that he would undertake nothing without first having obtained this advice.

'I believe that this plan is not yours, nor that of anyone else in the world,' replied the conqueror of Aljubarrota. 'It can only have been revealed by God himself. . . .'

The court now moved to Santarém, and the princes urged their father to set the expedition in motion. He promised to call his council in June to fix the date of departure. On the eve of the discussion, Prince Henry said to his father:

'Sire, seeing that your preparations are about to bear fruit, I have come to beg two boons of you before all your plans are completed.

'The first of these is that I may be one of the first to land, when with God's aid we cast anchor before the town of Ceuta. The second is that you will permit me to be the first to mount the royal scaling ladder as soon as it is set against the wall.'

'My son,' replied the King with a smile, 'may God bless you as I bless you for the earnest of your good will you have just given me. It does honour to your name. For the moment I shall not reply to either of your requests, but I promise to do so at a more proper place and time.'

King John was not without apprehension as to the welcome his plan might receive from the Council. But the Constable, who had rejoined him at Torres Vedras, assured him:

'See that you do not put the plan forward as some new thing,' he advised. 'Make it known as a matter you have already pondered on and have decided to be just and right since your motive for undertaking it is to serve God. Do not ask your counsellors if they think the expedition reasonable, but only what is their opinion about the best way to execute it. If you will command me to be the first to speak, I will see to it that when they have heard me none of them shall make bold to oppose our plans.'

This was done, and the counsellors heard the Constable offer the King his services and support. Then Duarte, the heir to the throne, spoke, and was followed by his two brothers. João Gomes da Silva, a veteran of Aljubarrota famous for his spirit and good humour, swept away any lingering doubts with a burst of laughter as he cried: 'As to me, sire, all I say is this: "Up and over, greyheads!" '

It was not sufficient to cloak in mystery the purpose of preparations which now roused the whole country to a fever of speculation and agitated the host of official and unofficial foreign observers who swarmed in the streets of Lisbon. In order to keep the secret it would be necessary, thought King John, to put the seekers of information on to a false scent. The astute monarch found the pretext he needed in complaints against the Count of Holland voiced by Portuguese merchants who had often suffered robbery and extortions as they crossed his territories.

King John chose Fernão Fogaça, Prince Duarte's steward, to go in his name to Count William and threaten him with war unless he engaged forthwith to put an end to these abuses. The date of the expedition against Ceuta had now been fixed for St John's Day of the following year, and Fogaça was duly supplied by the King with letters of credence and confidential instructions. On his arrival he begged the Count to grant him an audience, very discreetly informing him that he desired to speak to him alone and that his public utterances were intended merely to disguise the real nature of his mission.

Count William, filled with perplexity, agreed secretly to receive the King of Portugal's envoy. Fogaça requested him to accept the challenge that was about to be delivered with a display of indignation, and assured him that King John would ever after show his gratitude for it. The play was so well acted that Fogaça was loaded with abuse and driven from the Count amidst general consternation, while heralds bade the people prepare for war. King John was delighted and quietly hastened his preparations.

'The stir of toil was such,' says Azurara, 'that on a still day the noise from Lisbon could be clearly heard in the villages of the Ribatejo. It was indeed a beautiful sight to behold how the strand was thronged day and night by caulkers and other craftsmen busily engaged on the caravels and ships of all kinds, while butchers flayed oxen and cows, quartered the carcasses, salted the meat and packed it in barrels and tubs. The fishermen and their wives cleaned and cured fish and dried it in the sun. The great hammers of the mint struck away night and day so thunderously that it was impossible to hear oneself speak, even by shouting, in their vicinity. The coopers were given not a moment's respite, for endless staves and barrels were needed for wine, meat and other provisions. Tailors and clothiers never ceased weaving, cutting, sewing, making liveries of various shapes and colours according to the orders of the nobility. The whole day long carpenters were nailing chests containing bombards, cannon, and all the other multifarious equipment for the artillery. In the ropewalks ropes, cables and rigging and all forms of hempen cord were ceaselessly wound for the ships, both Portuguese and foreign. . . .'

Men whispered that the war with Holland was no more than a pretext. There were well-informed persons who asserted that the King was preparing to send his daughter, the Infanta Isabel, to England to marry an English prince and would help him to conquer France. Not at all, declared others, who, according to themselves, were even better informed: the great expedition is intended for the recovery of the Holy Places! No, no, that's quite off the mark, retorted King John's agents, who intensified the mystery by spreading a different tale abroad—Don't tell a soul! The King has decided to go and fight the Antipope and depose him!

Learning that the Kings of Castile and Aragon had received the assurances they had sought, and hearing that many French and German lords were to take part in the expedition, the Moors of Granada now became intensely alarmed.

'I know not on what score the King of Granada is troubled, since he knows nothing of my plans,' King John told their ambassadors. 'Tell him that I have no cause to give him any undertakings, for I have no intention to cause him harm. And now you may take your departure when you please.'

The Granadines were discomforted and sought to make an ally of the Queen, promising on behalf of the wife of their sultan to present the Infante Isabel with the finest bridal dress ever possessed by any princess, Muslim or Christian.

'It is true,' replied the wise Philippa, 'that Christian Queens are not so isolated from affairs that they may not at times put before their husbands requests for such things as they desire, but their petitions must of necessity be of such a nature that they can readily be granted, and any princess who acted otherwise would be thought imprudent and indiscreet. Tell your Queen that I thank her for her good wishes, but that she may dispose of the robes of which you speak as best pleases her, for with God's help my daughter will not lack what she needs for her marriage. Why do you not seek the good will of my lord the King? If your request is justified, he will readily grant whatever you desire.'

Thus rebuffed by the sovereign and his spouse, the sedulous Muslims attempted to seduce the heir to the throne by means of a gift which any prince in the world would have thought magnificent.

'Noble people in my country are not in the habit of selling their good will for silver,' replied Duarte. 'If they did so they would be called merchants, not lords or princes. Even if your King offered me his kingdom I could not accept it, for I shall never ask my father for anything but what is reasonable and just. But why should he be disturbed? Of what is he afraid?'

The Granadines went home 'not very satisfied with the answers they were given', returned to their own country and reported to their king that they had come from a land bustling with activity, where all, noble and commoners alike, burned with desire to take part in an expedition without even knowing against whom it was directed.

One day Prince Henry saw approaching what seemed to be a phantom of the past, surrounded by ghostly squires and white-bearded men at arms. It was the noble warrior Ayres Gonçalves de

31

Figueiredo, stooping in his antique mail. Henry could not repress a smile, for he knew that the knight was approaching his eightieth year. As the old man kissed his hand, he said: 'Surely a man of your years has earned his repose after so many hardships and battles!'

The ancient warrior was nettled, and replied:

'I know not if my limbs have lost their power, but I assure your highness that my will is as stout today as it was during all the fights I have fought in your father's service. For me there could be no greater honour than to be at your side in this undertaking in the hour of my death.'

Two impoverished squires, not much younger than the valiant Ayres Gonçalves, were told by the prince:

'It is enough that you have done what you have in the course of your lives in my father's service. I am indebted to you for your good will, but it seems to me that at your age you have earned your repose, and that you should not hazard yourselves. . . .'

'We have no need of repose!' the two old warriors replied simultaneously.

'But what am I to do? All the arms I had are already distributed, and I have none left to bestow upon you.'

'A brave man never sells his arms even if he is in distress. Though there have been times when our pay has fallen short, our arms have never left our side. Give us our rations, and we shall see to the rest.' Stirred by their proud reply, the Infante had the two men reimbursed, finding their arrears of pay from his own resources.

'Ah,' cries Azurara, 'how regretfully did the spirits of those good people who were then dying of plague bid farewell to their bodies! Not merely with the natural regret that seizes every soul that leaves its house of flesh, but with a special sorrow at departing from this world without having seen the end of this enterprise! I do not know if I speak as a pagan, but I think verily that in those days the dead would desire that their bones were once more clothed in flesh so that they might rise from their tombs and accompany their sons and relatives. I say too that though the living were full of joy the souls of those who already shared in the divine splendour exulted even more since they already knew the whole truth!'

When the fleet appeared off the straits of Gibraltar, the people on shore were filled with amazement, for they had never seen so many sail together on the sea. At night-fall, the inhabitants of Tarifa said to one another: 'Surely these are phantoms.' Their governor, a Portuguese by birth, replied: 'I believe that this array belongs to my lord the King of Portugal, and none other.' 'No, no,' cried others, 'if all the trees in Portugal were felled for timber, and all the Portuguese turned carpenters, they could not in a lifetime build so great a multitude of ships.'

'You shall see,' replied the governor. 'What you think are phantoms are real ships laden with brave and well-armed men. They bear the standard of Portugal and will soon appear before your eyes.'

At dawn, emerging from the mist-shrouded sea, there came a trumpet-sound that the people of Tarifa took for celestial music. Then suddenly the sun shone out, and the vast fleet passed in slow majesty before the walls of the town.

'My son,' said King John to Prince Henry, 'I remember the boon you asked of me when we were still at Lisbon. The time has come for me to give you my reply. You asked to be among those who are first to leap ashore. This I grant you, but it displeases me that you should go otherwise than as the chief of my captains.'

As he spoke, his face became radiant with joy, such was the hope he placed in the Prince.

'The sun shot his beams on the side of the ships,' says Azurara, 'and the people on shipboard began to speak to one another with blasts of their whistles, or shouted the names of their friends across the water. They polished their arms, and tried them on to see that nothing was wanting. Some with tools under their arms or hammers in their hands offered to rivet armour, others tried the leather laces of their pourpoints. Some, bethinking themselves of their sins, sought their priests in order to show God the great penitence that was in their hearts. Others wielded their axes to see that nothing would impede the freedom of their motions, or drew their swords from their scabbards and flourished them to prove that they were well ground. . . .'

'Ah!' they cried, 'my trusty blade! How well do you cleave when God wills, despite armour of iron and coat of mail! Today we shall see how you bite the flesh of these dogs who cannot bear the weight of breast-plates.'

Some hungry ones broached the kegs containing their choicest

33

provisions, and summoned their friends, saying: 'Let us eat, for today's meal may be the last in our lives. . . . And if by God's grace the victory falls to us, then we shall not lack supplies.'

In the distance the Moors could be seen running along the ramparts to show that they did not fear the Christians. At the moment when Henry awaited only his father's signal to leap into the boat that would carry him to the shore, his chaplain Martim Paes took a newly consecrated host in his hands, and holding it aloft for all to see, cried:

'Brothers and friends! I think that no man can expect a good outcome from what he undertakes unless he well knows the purpose of his action. Perhaps you who are gathered around me do not fully understand the reason why you are here. . . . Know then that you have come to serve our Lord Jesus Christ, whom I hold here before you all, and that it is for love of him that the King, our Lord, has launched this enterprise.'

Now the Moors were flocking to the shore, defying those on the ships with shouts and interjections. Unable to bear their abuse, João Fogaça, the Count of Barcelos' squire, jumped into a boat and bade the rowers ply their oars: Rui Gonçalves was the first to reach the strand. The Moors rushed upon him, but he laid about himself with his good sword to such effect that he soon cleared a space for Prince Henry who, as he approached, bade the trumpeters sound the assault. About a hundred and fifty Christians had now landed, and they vigorously attacked the enemy and drove him back towards the gate of Almina. Striking and thrusting, Vasco Anes Corte-Real entered the town, closely followed by the Prince with all the rest upon their heels. There was a warrior fighting furiously a few paces away, and in him Henry recognized his brother Duarte. He saluted him, and thanked God that he had so good a companion in the fray. 'And O Lord,' he added, 'I thank thee a thousand times for thy good will in coming to our aid.'

'But,' as Azurara discreetly adds, 'the moment was not a fitting one for the exchange of much discourse, for spears and stones were not idle. The battle continued, and the Christians pressed the Moors back towards the gates of the town, wounding and killing without mercy. Among the Moors there was one great threatening fellow who fought naked and used no other weapon but stones; yet such was the strength of his arm that each seemed to be propelled by a cannon or catapult. When the Moors were driven back to the very gate, he turned on the Christians, bent down, and flung a stone which struck Vasco Martins of Albergaria and carried away the visor of his helmet. The very sight of this giant inspired terror, for his whole body was as black as jet and his teeth very long and white, and his lips full and fleshy. But despite the violence of the blow he had received Vasco Martins was not discomfited, and speedily repaid the Moor in kind. Scarcely had the man recovered his balance when the Portuguese transfixed him with his lance. As he fell lifeless, his companions were seized with panic. . . .'

The first royal standard that floated above the town was planted on the walls by Prince Henry. On seeing it, King John sounded the signal for those still on the ships to land and rejoin the rest. These captains and lords were disgruntled. They could be heard complaining: 'We shall arrive too late, and our glory will be the less brilliant. The others have already entered Ceuta!' News was brought to King John that the princes and their half-brother, the Count of Barcelos, were within the gates, each fighting in a different place. It was not in his nature to show gladness or sorrow before others, but the lords around him saw him laugh joyfully when he heard that Duarte had secretly rejoined Henry so as not to miss the assault. He himself remained seated, for two reasons. Firstly because his leg, wounded long ago, still pained him, and secondly because it did not befit his dignity to enter the fray: he would await the time to storm the castle, when he would lead the onset in person.

Of all those who had accompanied the Prince only seventeen were left. 'The rest were gradually disbanded as he advanced, either distracted by their desire for booty, or driven by the heat of the sun to seek refreshment at the wells, their bodies, fed on salt foods, streaming with sweat. Others were soft and would not long withstand the toil of battle. So, with his seventeen companions, the Prince sustained a bitter fight for two hours and a half. Many Moors were mortally wounded by his blows, and one of his squires, named Fernão Chamorro, was so gravely wounded that he fell to the ground, apparently lifeless. The Moors tried to seize his body, while the Prince and those about him sought to defend it. Then Henry suddenly set about the enemy with such fury that his adversaries were forced to abandon the street and take refuge under the gate, the Prince still pressing on and laying about him without quarter. Of his seventeen companions only four were now to be seen. . . .'

It was doubtless at this moment that a false report of the young Prince's death was brought to the King. Dom João did not blanch, but said only: 'What of it, provided that he died as a soldier should?'

The Prince was still alive, and soon gave good proof of it. The gate that stood open before him was let into a wall of great thickness surmounted by a double range of battlements so that it could be defended simultaneously from both sides. Behind it rose a tower with a second gate, followed by a third at the end of the road leading to the castle.

When they saw the Prince pursuing their fleeing companions with his bare blade in his hand the Moors tried to crush him with heavy stones dropped through the machicolations, but they were unable to reach him. Followed by his four Portuguese, Henry crossed the threshold of the third gate, and so decided the day. At the moment when the King gave the order for the final assault on the castle, it was empty of defenders.

In the church of Ceuta, now restored to Christianity after having served as a mosque for seven centuries, a solemn mass of thanksgiving was celebrated on Sunday, August 25, 1415. King John knighted his three sons and those of his men who had shown themselves worthy of the honour. In order to reward Henry's valour, the King would have admitted him before all the rest, but the Prince in his modesty shrank from the distinction, which, he said, belonged by right to his eldest brother Dom Duarte, thus respecting the order laid down by their mother in the swords.

'It was indeed a wondrous sight to behold the three princes,' exclaims Azurara. 'They were all three tall and well built, and their armour was brilliant and richly adorned, and their blessed swords hanging from their belts. . . . Before them went trumpets and drums, and I think that there was no man who did not take pleasure in beholding them, and more than any other the King their father.'

Despite his triumph Dom João was full of care. He was not mistaken when he foresaw that it would be even harder to hold Ceuta than to take it. Of all those whom he sounded none seemed anxious to undertake the responsibility of governing it. While the question was being discussed in the council, a group of young fidalgos, or noblemen, were amusing themselves by playing the game of 'choca', which consists of hitting a ball with a stout stick. Dom Pedro de Meneses was proclaimed the winner with the customary shout of *aleo!* Hearing that the session over which the King was presiding still continued to drag on, Dom Pedro went to seek him and jestingly offered to defend Ceuta against the attacks of the Muslims with the stick he still held in his hand. The King thought the offer a good one, and took the bold Meneses at his word, creating him Count of Viana and appointing him on the spot captain of the town of Ceuta with a garrison of 2,500 men. As a further proof of his approval and confidence he forewent the usual oath of allegiance. The choice was not a bad one: for twenty-two years, from that day until his death, Pedro de Meneses defied every onslaught of the Moors, who twice besieged the city by land and sea. 'Aleo' became his war-cry and is included in the device of his family.

The glorious conquest of Ceuta opened the way to the long series of exploits which conducted the armies of Portugal stage by stage to the very shores of China. Moreover, it established, at the dawn of the fifteenth century, the starting-point of one of the greatest changes in universal history. Two bells, long ago stolen by the Moors from the Portuguese town of Sines and now recovered by Prince Henry, who knew that they were hidden at Ceuta, rang out on that Sunday in August 1415 to summon Christians to the Mosque, which Master Fr João Xira and the grand chaplain Afonso Eanes had newly restored to the worship of the true God. Their peals not only called the faithful to the celebration of the mass ordered by King John: they also rang the knell of Muslim power, and likewise that of the fortune of the Mediterranean towns which had drawn their wealth from trading with the enemies of the faith. Seized from the old Portuguese city where Vasco da Gama was first to see the light of day, they now announced the rising of the curtain that was to unfold the hidden regions of the earth before the eyes of a dazzled Europe.

≯ 3 ≮

The Virgin Prince

IT is said that Prince Henry's first expedition to discover the sea-route to India dates from before the expedition to Ceuta, and that his navigators rounded Cape Non, or Não, whose very name is the Portuguese negation and so symbolizes the opposition of the mysterious powers of the Dark Sea to seamen who dared to defy them. The Prince would then be only eighteen, a tender age, yet sufficient when genius is supported by faith.

In those years Europe was emerging from the middle ages and active with conflicting aspirations. The spirit of the Crusades, which seemed to have expired for ever on the death-bed of St Louis, still survived in noble hearts. The Prince was aware that a century and a half before the extraordinary Catalan, Ramon Llull, had foreshadowed the conquest of the Muslim empire from Ceuta, whose conquest would be followed by the circumnavigation of the African continent, leading to the shores of India. He knew too that the Venetian Marino Sanuto had striven tirelessly to persuade Christendom to launch a general assault against Islam, to be followed by the creation of a common fleet to secure the dominion of the islands and coasts of the Indian Ocean. The ancient dream of Peter the Hermit, Gautier sans Avoir, Godefroy de Bouillon, Tancred, Richard Coeur de Lion and so many others burgeoned with fresh vigour in the Prince's soul. This Christian, whose whole life was exemplary, realized that it was necessary to substitute the territorial expansion of the gospel for the mere conquest of the Holy Places. In his mind the surest way to recover the Holy Sepulchre was to plant the cross on those shores from which the infidel drew his power, and to send after it new apostles of the Gospel. The attainment of India by a sea-route, the exclusion of Islam from the wealth of the east by the

38

closure of the mouth of the Red Sea and her consequent collapse from privation, the winning of a great empire that should be a Christian domain for the young Portuguese nation, newly reassured of its independence and unity, a century before the reconquest of Granada by Spain, the bringing to Lisbon of the vast traffic in the wares of the Levant—all this would one day be called the 'Plan of the Indies', conceived in its entirety by an adolescent prince who also devoted himself single-mindedly to its achievement, constantly subjecting his natural enthusiasm to the most rigorous and methodical self-criticism. He must be considered one of the greatest geniuses of his age, if not the greatest.

There was also Prester John.

A tradition whose origin is lost in the mists of time maintained the existence of a Christian sovereign in the East. Some placed him in the kingdom of Tartary, while others believed that he held sway in Cathay or among the mountains of Persia, where the apostle St Thomas had met his martyrdom. Wherever he reigned, it was generally accepted that he was the mightiest monarch on earth. In the popular imagination he was thought of as the descendant of Melchior, Gaspar and Balthasar, and he was fabulously represented in the semblance of one of the Magi. His robes were woven by a salamander and laundered only in fire. At his court he was served by seven kings who were surrounded by sixty dukes, three hundred and sixty viscounts, and such a quantity of knights and gentlemen that none had ever been able to take count of them. A magic mirror set before his throne enabled him to observe at every moment all that happened in the remotest corner of his realms. Thirty archbishops sat at his right hand and twenty bishops at his left. In his kingdom whoever scratched the surface of the earth would come upon the miraculous stone that restored sight to the blind or made its wearer invisible at will. Poverty was unknown and no one had ever killed or robbed his neighbour: no lips had ever uttered the slightest untruth there.

Many of the crusaders confirmed the existence of Prester John on their return from Palestine. But they held that his kingdom lay in Ethiopia. The unknown frontiers of this land stretched as far east as the Red Sea, in the vast area between the Nile and Astaboras, where of old Jews and Phoenicians had sought cinnamon, myrrh,

ivory and gold-dust. It was surrounded by the Ichthyophagoi or
Fish-eaters, the Creophagoi, who touched no meat, and the Cheno-
lophagoi, whose diet was of tortoises; the Elephantophagoi with
their boundless voracity, the Strouthiophagoi, whose weakness was
for the meat of ostriches, and the Ophiophagoi, who commonly
consumed the flesh of serpents. Along the Red Sea dwelt the Troglo-

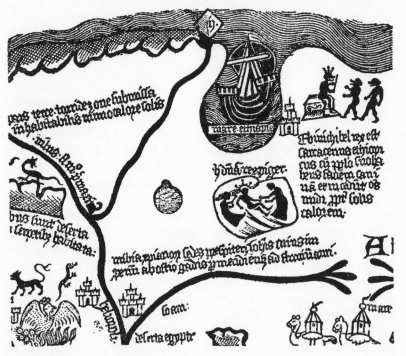

Fig. 1. The kingdom of Prester John. Fragment from a map that was once
in Cardinal Borgia's library and is now in the Vatican

dytes, in the land of Adulai. The kingdom of Prester John was
formed out of the ancient empire of Meroé, which in the days of the
Trojan war had had a quarter of a million warriors. It had given
birth to King Sabacon, the founder of the XXVth dynasty, King
Sua, the ally of Hosea, King of Israel, against Shalmaneser, and
King Taraka, all three of whom had ruled over Egypt. To the east of
Meroé were the abominable Blemmyes, repulsive headless beings

whose eyes and mouths were in their breasts. To its west were the Nubians or Acridophagoi, who devoured roasted locusts; to its south the Sembriles, with their capital at Axam. In those distant forests Pygmies were often found, and they were so small that they could be seen harvesting stalks of wheat with little axes one by one as if they were trees.

Prince Henry was attracted by the beauty of the legend, but his practical spirit drove him directly to the point. Since it was certain that none of the Christian princes of Europe, all busily engaged in rending one another asunder, would second him in his enterprise, why should not he seek to establish the existence of the mysterious oriental sovereign who shared his faith and could scarcely refuse to make alliance with him and do battle with the Infidel lodged at his very gate?

Twice every day the tides of the sea came beating against the promontory of Segres as they had done for thousands of centuries. To the Prince their waves seemed to whisper or beat, or thunder, according to the temper of the oceans, these words: 'Portugal! Portugal! Your destiny lies not among the mountains of the east, for all your glorious victories, but on my flowing plains whose infinite spaces I shall reveal to you. . . . Portugal! Portugal! Your plough is not only the share drawn by the straining ox, but also the rapid prow of the ship cleaving the double furrow of foam from which new worlds shall spring! Oh, Portugal, beloved land poised like a garden between the sky and sea, I behold your Prince gazing motionless and silent upon me and his countenance is brooding on the great ambition that will one day open the very gates of India! Do you know what wares your ships will then bring to your shores? Listen, and I will say. From the shores of Africa where the sun goes down and from those where the dawn breaks you shall draw gold and slaves and ivory, with ebony and amber; from the Red Sea seed-pearls, from Aden madder; from Socotra aloes; from Arabia incense and myrrh; from Ormuz, the precious carpets and fiery steeds of Persia; from Bahrein, the most perfect pearls; from Hindustan, sugar, alum, wax and opium; from Chaul, silk; from Onor, Bransalor and Manganor ginger, saltpetre, iron, precious woods; from Cananor, Calicut, Cranganor and Cochin, pepper, whose every grain is today weighed in gold; from Narsinga, diamonds; from the

Maldives, wine, coral and amber; from Ceylon, the most splendid rubies, the most perfect sapphires, the purest topazes and pearls of the finest orient, and from Ceylon too the great fighting elephants for which all the ports of India compete, the finest cinnamon and the best brazil-wood for the finest dyestuffs. . . . Let us go even beyond. . . . From the coast of Coromandel, your ships shall bring the finest cloths, white or dyed bright colours, and skeins of scarlet thread; from Bengal, cotton stuffs, rice and sugared fruits; from the kingdom of Pegu, the rubies most sought after by merchants, and musk and gum lac which is also found at Tenasserim; from Malacca, the universal emporium of all the east, more treasures of all sorts than your stores can even hold; from the great island of Sumatra, gold and silk, with pepper again, and aloes, camphor and gum benjamin; from Java, more pepper, which you shall make a common spice in Europe; from Borneo, camphor, tortoiseshell, gold, pearls, diamonds; from Macassar, gold and sandalwood; from the isle of Amboina, cloves and plumes from the fowl called 'birds of paradise'; from the isles of Banda, the nutmeg; from Solor and Timor, red or white sandalwood, of the most delicate sort that can be found; from Siam, brazil-wood, lead, saltpetre, silk, leather; from Annam, the most precious woods; from the kingdom of Cathay, that other world, musk, rhubarb, silks, heavier and richer than the damasks of Syria, porcelain, lacquer and jade. . . . Further still, at the uttermost end of the earth, lie the islands of Jypen-Khoué or Cipangu, whence your ships shall return laden down with wrought silverware, with silks, lacquers, gold–dust and seed–pearls. . . .'

The Prince listened to the voice of the sea, which was but the echo of his dreams. It still sounded in his ears and filled his soul with a burning yet suppressed ardour as he returned to his '*vila*', the township he called his '*Tercena naval*', from the Arabic word 'darsana', or arsenal. There he bent once more over his maps.

'Of the finished state of this township,' writes Azurara, 'I cannot speak at length, for at the time when this book was being written, it still possessed only its outer walls, like those of a stout fortress, and a few houses. But the work was being pressed on without respite. Men said that the Prince intended to build a town there for the trade of merchants, a place where ships coming from the east to the west could cast anchor and find stores and pilots as they do at Cadiz, where the haven is much less good than here. . . . And I have heard it said too that as soon as the building of the town was begun the Genoese offered to buy it at a great price; and as everyone knows, they are men who only risk their wealth when they have great hopes of gain. . . .'

The Prince drew his information from various sources in the Arab countries. The Muslim traders of Oran, Bougie, Tunis, Tlemsen, Fez, Safi regularly visited the markets of the east from Aden and

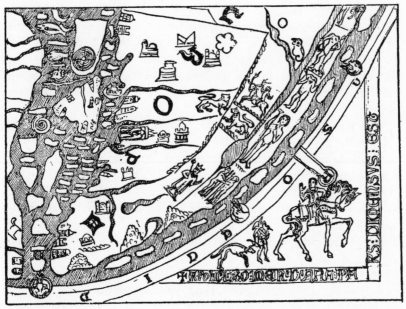

Fig. 2. Africa according to a world map of the end of the thirteenth century

Ormuz to Calicut and Malacca, the port of transit for all the trade of the Sunda islands, the peninsula of Indo-China, China and Japan. The information patiently culled from these sources was carefully compared with that obtained from Jewish merchants, who were also busy in these parts. Also from Oran, caravans from black Africa contributed their quota of news. Master Jacome of Majorca (or Jahuda, the son of the Jew Abraham Cresques, the author of the celebrated Catalan Atlas) noted meticulously on his charts all information that was considered worthy of credence. The Prince had secured his assistance for a goodly sum of gold and had had to press for years before obtaining it. Under his master's eyes the Majorcan followed out the network of tracks that crossed the sands of the dessert, joining Ceuta to the land of Negroes and the Country of Gold or stretching by way of the Red Sea and Persian Gulf to Bagdad and Ormuz. Thence, said Master Jacome, ships set sail for the shores of India and even reached the archipelago that stands across the gateway to the China Sea. The Jew had learned from his father the means of ascertaining the time by the observation of the Pole Star, and his training in the Ptolemaic system had taught him to believe that the land of Africa stretched out towards the east, forming the western coast of the lake whose waters bathe the shores of India and which the ancients called the Erythrean Sea. Prester John ruled over this coast, according to the Jew of Majorca.

The Jew was not only skilled in the making of charts; he had no rival in the manufacture of astrolabes and other instruments used in navigation, unless it were the Genoese Antonio da Nola, whose knowledge the Prince greatly esteeemd. The Venetian navigator Alvise da Cadamosto was likewise received at the 'Vila do Infante', as was Valarte or Wollaert, a vassal of the King of Norway and a specialist in the navigation of the seas between Scandinavia and the coasts of Iceland and Greenland, the great 'green' zone of the frozen regions of the icy north. There was also at the '*vila*' a merchant of Oran for whom the trading relations of the kingdoms of Calicut and Malacca held no secrets, and finally enigmatic and sharp-featured persons with ebony skins who acknowledged the sovereignty of the ruler of Ethiopia.

In order to maintain these followers, to build and equip his ships, to pay their captains and crews, the Prince could draw upon the resources of the Order of Christ founded by King Denis a hundred years earlier. But he well knew that his treasury would never suffice to carry through the grand plan to which he had devoted his whole life, and he therefore proposed to seek the gold-dust said to be found on the west African coast. This would permit him to build new ships to sail even further, to India, whose wealth seemed to represent not an end in itself, but the means of encompassing the rim of the hated Crescent. In the fifteenth century the Muslim empire alarmed the Christian world much as the vast Soviet block now overshadows the destiny of the 'Atlantic' world. The day was approaching when on May 29, 1453, the fall of Constantinople would open the road into Hungary and even Vienna to the Turkish advance. Without the application of the Prince's plan, which would shake the power of Islam to its very foundations, what would become of Europe?

Nor was Henry prevented from proving himself first and foremost a Portuguese and a European afterwards. While France and England were locked in a struggle which would be known as the Hundred Years War, the kingdoms of Castile and Aragon were paralysed with internal troubles. Venice, Florence and other Italian towns were blinded by their fruitful traffic with the lands of the Levant, just as in our own time there are those who do not fear to trade beyond the Iron Curtain or with Mao's China. The Prince realized that his policy would give his country an incalculable advantage over other nations. He incarnated the past and the future, the mysticism of a crusading knight, and the cold reasoning of a man of that Renaissance brought to the west in the baggage of the refugees from ancient Byzantium; and he was prepared to surrender everything to his plan, the last of a long series of schemes elaborated over a period of sixty years throughout the Christian world and all aimed at reaching India to overthrow Islam and the only one to be crowned with success. The Prince was determined to sacrifice his person, his family and his wealth, as he freely sacrificed the most lawful of human joys. When Pope John XXII gave his approval to the statutes of the Order of Christ he imposed on its knights the rule of St Benedict and the constitutions of Cîteaux, and Henry submitted to them entirely, with body and soul.

'He possessed,' Azurara tells us, 'great force of character and a keen intellect. His desire to accomplish great deeds was unparalleled. The sins of avarice and voluptuousness never entered his heart. As to the latter, his restraint was such that during his whole lifetime he preserved the most perfect chastity and his body was still virgin when it was laid to earth. What shall I say of his greatness, sublime above all the princes of the earth! I believe that of all uncrowned princes he had the greatest number of servitors and men of the greatest quality. He welcomed all those who had some merit in their own country, and especially those foreigners whose fame might justify the expense of bringing them to him. He surrounded himself constantly with men from the most varied and often distant lands, and they all considered this a great wonder. No one left him without receiving great benefits at his hands.'

'His heart was great and his talents sublime,' as Cadamosto confirms. 'He gave himself wholly to the service of our Lord and Master Jesus Christ in the war against the infidel, and always refused to take a wife, and preserved his chastity. . . .'

From his mother, Philippa, he had inherited a fresh complexion, soon tanned by the sun. He was rather tall and strongly built, and his person inspired a respectful awe in those who set eyes upon him for the first time. When he was seized with anger, which was rare, he was terrifying to behold.

'Each of his days was devoted to diligent toil,' Azurara continues. 'It would be impossible among all the nations on earth to find a man better able to dominate himself. Countless were the nights when his eyes felt not the touch of sleep, and he so mortified his flesh that he seemed to have given a second nature to it. . . .

'He was a man of excellent counsel and of great authority, wise and possessed of a faithful memory. He was slow in the accomplishment of certain things, perhaps because his humour was somewhat phlegmatic, or because it was his will to be so for a reason that men did not know. His manner was quiet and his words calmly delivered. In adversity he was constant and in prosperity prudent and humble. . . .

'He was never seen to display hatred or ill-will towards any man, even when he had just reason to complain of him: rather was he reproached for excessive clemency in the application of justice, for he dealt equally with all who came before him. . . .

'He touched wine for only a short period in his life during his early youth. Afterwards he never drank it again. He had always a great attachment to the common good, to which he devoted a large part of his labours, and he readily engaged in undertakings that cost him dear for the advantage of all. He joyfully dedicated himself to the practice of arms, especially against the enemies of the holy faith, for he desired to remain at peace with all Christians. He was generally beloved, and did good to everyone without ever seeking to harm any. His speech was always courteous, and his replies did honour to the rank of those who spoke with him without lessening his own. No unseemly or indecent word ever passed his lips. He obeyed all the commandments of the holy church, and attended the offices with great devotion: in his chapel these were celebrated with as much pomp and solemnity as in any college of a cathedral church. He venerated holy things, honouring the ministers of the faith and loading them with benefices. He was seen to fast during almost half the year, and the poor never left his presence empty handed. I should certainly never find a Christian or a regular to compare with him. . . .'

An ascetic—not content with fasting vigorously, he also wore a hair-shirt—and a mystic—he spent his leisure in prayer at the foot of the altar—he was an exceptional being who yet remained human under every circumstance. For twelve years he tirelessly despatched his captains southwards with the mission of turning the famous Cape Bojador whose low, sandy silhouette crouched like a sinister figure among treacherous deeps, but the terror of the crews at what they thought was the edge of the world was so deep-seated that none felt their hearts stout enough to venture beyond Cape Non among the shallows and mists of the Dark Sea. The Prince never grew angry, but 'listening graciously to the accounts of his captains, he rewarded them just as well as if they had fully executed his wishes'. But he made them ceaselessly repeat the same voyage and insisted ever more on the need to round the terrible headland.

He was well aware that their fears were not assumed, and that in some sense they were well founded. A French Admiral, Jurien de la Gravière, has described the inhospitable shore that filled them with such terror: it is a coast of steep cliffs or sand-dunes skirted by reefs at water-level. When the west wind howls, the troughs of the waves are as much as fifteen yards deep and their roaring can be heard miles out at sea. From October to April the land is continually enveloped in a thick fog and constantly beaten by heavy seas, and the great Canary Isles current assisted by the dominant winds, the north-east trades, though it favours the outward voyage to Africa, fiercely opposes the return journey to Europe.

In the course of the year 1433 the Prince fitted out a *barcha* which he placed under the command of his squire Gil Eanes. Filled with the same fears that had held back his predecessors, he failed to pass the Canary Islands, which Portuguese seamen had reconnoitred a century earlier under the reign of Afonso IV, the Brave. Henry made no criticism of his squire, but a year later he ordered him to fit out the same vessel. Taking him aside, he urged Gil Eanes to do his utmost to pass the accursed cape.

'You will not find there any danger that cannot be surmounted by the hope of reward,' he said. 'Indeed, I am amazed by these fancies that fill all your heads when you are faced with things that are still so uncertain. . . . Were they based on the least authority, however

Fig. 3. A *barcha* (from a sketch by Admiral João de Oliveira)

slight, I could well excuse you. But I am astounded that you should set store by the opinions of a few captains whose only seamanship has lain in hugging the shore to Flanders or in ports that can be entered by anyone who has never handled a compass or read a chart. Have no fear then of what they may say when you undertake this journey! With God's grace you shall bring back honour and profit.'

Even though the Prince himself sought to moderate his remonstrances, they carried great weight in the hearts of those who incurred them. Gil Eanes swore never to appear again before his master until he had accomplished the enterprise, and he kept his word. In proof of his success, the squire brought back to Henry a plant with flowers resembling what are called in Portugal 'St Mary's roses': it grew in Guinea, the Land of the Negroes.

In the following year, this time accompanied by Afonso Gonçalves Baldaia, he went even further south, reaching a point marked on modern maps as Cape Garret, where he found nothing before him but a desert 'with no houses, and no trace of men or camels'. In 1436, pressing still further south, Baldaia gave the name Rio do Ouro or River of Gold to a deep bay lying between two shores of yellow sand which he took to be the mouth of a river. The name Río de Oro is today applied to the part of the Sahara that stretches from Cape Non to Cape Blanco, which now belongs to Spain. Baldaia sent two knights ashore, and on their approach a score of Moors armed with assegais took flight and hid among the rocks, where they could not be found.

Continuing his way towards the south, Baldaia came upon a cape surmounted by a rock, which from a distance resembled a galley: he called it the Galley-stone, '*Pedra da galé*', or on modern maps Piedra de Galea: here he turned back. At this point there was a lull in the progress of the expeditions, by decision of the Prince.

The great King John, still in full possession of his mental powers and of his will, had died three years before, on August 14, 1433, the anniversary of his birth and of the great battle of Aljubarrota. Holding that a king should breathe his last in the finest palace of the chief town of his realms, he had himself borne from the village of Alcochete on the Tagus to his palace of the Alcáçova at Lisbon, then newly decorated with great magnificence. The chronicler Rui de Pina informs us how he required the princes to escort him from the palace to the cathedral, where he prayed before the body of St Vincent. At the moment of death, 'being already alone with the religious and ministers of his conscience he brushed his hand across his face and noticed that his beard had grown. He at once gave orders that it should be shaved, saying that it was not fitting that a king whose face would be beheld by so many after his death should present an unkempt and displeasing appearance.' He died in his seventy-seventh year, the forty-eighth of his reign, 'and the whole kingdom was clad in sackcloth and weeds of black wool'.

The general outlines of Prince Henry's plan were now clearly settled. Eighteen years' work had established a solid bridgehead at Ceuta; his squires João Gonçalves, nicknamed 'Zarco' from his pale blue eyes, and Tristão Vaz Teixeira, had discovered the island of Porto Santo, and later, in company with Bartolomeu Perestrelo, that of Madeira, which came to form an invaluable way-station on the great ocean route to the south. The exploration of the African coast, the first stage on the sea road to India, was now well launched. In the following year, a decisive step forward would be taken with the second expedition of Gil Eanes.

Rui de Pina describes Duarte, the successor to the late King, with his 'straight hair, his round and rather lined face, his light beard and dreamy eyes'. Henry's eldest brother piously suggested to the Bishop of Evora that at the close of the ceremony of his coronation a few pieces of tow should be burnt to remind him of the small worth and short duration of the glory and pomp of the world.

'I think, sire,' the Bishop prudently replied, 'that your thoughts and your knowledge of these truths will suffice, and that there is at present no need for this symbolic act.'

The new King was in his palace at Almeirim when his youngest brother, Ferdinand, whom he loved tenderly, approached.

'Sire,' said the young Prince, 'all the world knows your great desire to prove your love towards us, your brothers, by maintaining us in the state of honour and greatness to which we were born and which we merit. But this care lays upon you a burden which may be beyond your resources. I can well understand that the Princes my brothers should rejoice in your benefits, for they have earned the right to enjoy them. But for my part, I cannot be satisfied with this: though I have all that I need for my wellbeing I feel the thirst for honour, and I desire to prove by my deeds that what I have is due to me.'

This discourse disturbed Dom Duarte, but before he could open his mouth, the young Prince went on:

'Your kingdom, Sire, was great enough to serve as a cradle for us and to satisfy us while we were still growing. Now it is too small for us all to reach the height that befits us. For this reason, and because you have sons for whom you must soon provide according to their station, I ask it as a favour, sire, that you shall give me your blessing and permit me to leave this kingdom, which now enjoys tranquillity and is at peace with the neighbouring and distant kings, and go wherever God and my destiny shall call me. I have so far achieved nothing, and I see here no opportunity to accomplish such things as will allow me to deserve the name of son to a father such as ours, or brother to such brothers as mine.'

The King was on the point of protesting, but the Prince concluded the speech he had carefully rehearsed.

'My object is to offer myself to the Holy Father or the Emperor, or even to the court of France, in countries whose size offers me the hope of earning some recompense for my efforts. In this way I shall relieve you of part of your expenditures and of your cares, while, if God wills, I shall obtain the glory for which I yearn and the profit that befits me. If at any moment of my life you have need of my services and I learn of it, rest assured, sire, that even were I then Emperor of Germany or Greece, I would return at once to serve you as a faithful vassal out of the love I bear you and the loyalty I owe you.'

Dom Duarte did not doubt that Henry was behind this strange proposal and he urged him to persuade Ferdinand to abandon his adventurous plan.

'Sire,' replied his brother coldly, 'in this matter, as in all else, I shall do as you bid me. Yet I must say that Ferdinand, in bringing this request to you, has asked nothing to which he is not entitled. Why should the son of a father such as ours and the descendant of our ancestors pass away his life without accomplishing any action worthy of praise, and capable of rewarding him with the glory that is lacking in an existence of idleness? I cannot reproach him for his discontent. . . .'

The moment had come for the recluse of Sagres to reveal his inmost thoughts. In his eyes the methodical exploration of the African coast which he had undertaken more than twenty years before required, in addition to the possession of Ceuta, the conquest of the ports and fortresses held by the Moors in North Africa, and first and foremost that of Tangier, which faced the southernmost point of Europe.

'Our father,' he reminded the King, 'knew in his wisdom that many kings and princes who enjoy too long an idle peace are ill-prepared for war and are wretchedly defeated at the first reverse of fortune. In your kingdom Prince Ferdinand and I have no responsibility towards wife or child: grant us then permission to go to Africa. With our servants and the Knights of the Order of Christ and the Order of Avis who belong to us we shall fight the infidels and so do service to God. You, as the chief author of the enterprise, shall receive all the praise and all the merit. I know that in this way the Prince our brother will be satisfied and will cause you no more anxiety or care, while the men of your kingdom will remain well practised in the exercise of arms, as you yourself must desire.'

The King objected, referring to his people's need of rest after so many exertions and fatigues and the sorry state of his exchequer, still depleted by the expenditure required to maintain the garrison at Ceuta. His brother Dom Pedro and his half-brother the Count of Barcelos, first Duke of Braganza, supported his objections. But Henry did not accept defeat. Knowing Duarte's great regard for his wife, he made an ally of Queen Leonor by jointly with Ferdinand adopting her second son, who would thus come to inherit all his uncle's possessions. Now burning with the desire to depart for Africa, he exchanged his device: '*Talant de bien fere*', 'Will to do well', for the three letters I.D.A., which some took for his initials (Infante Dom Anrique) and reproved his pride. But others knew that the letters referred to the ambition blazing in his heart: *ida* in Portuguese means 'departure'.

His plan required 14,000 men, but cortes, meeting at Évora, were hesitant. 'Suppose, sire,' said Dom Pedro, 'that you were to take Tangier and even Alcácer and Arzila: I wonder what you would do with them! There is no possibility of settling these places, when the kingdom is depopulated and short of men. Even to attempt such a thing is like changing a good cloak for a torn jacket. . . .' But Henry finally got his army, though he was to have at his disposal no more than 2,000 horse, 1,000 crossbowmen and 3,000 foot.

He led the assault on Tangier on September 13, 1437. The town was defended by seven thousand warriors led by Sala ibn Sala, a leader well known for his valour. The Christians were disturbed by an ill omen: when the standards were unfurled, Prince Henry's was broken at the staff and the wind tore the cloth to shreds. The attack proved fruitless and it was necessary to call for additional equipment from Ceuta. For ten days, the Christians faced the infidels in murderous affrays, and every day more defenders rallied to help the besieged town. On September 30, Henry saw his scouts come galloping in: the enemy's army was approaching, and it numbered no less than 10,000 horses and 90,000 foot. The Prince arrayed his troops in order of battle: next day, the enemy attacked and was repelled.

The second assault on the town was no more successful. As he sallied forth, the Prince learned that the rulers of Morocco, Fez, Velez, Lazaraque and Tafilelt were hastening towards Tangier at the head of 60,000 horse and several hundred thousand warriors. On October 9 the Moors appeared from all directions and the battle was engaged. It soon became a bloody struggle. Henry's horse was killed under him, but the valiant Knight of Christ never ceased to fight. That day the enemy was worsted, but the Christian camp was left with supplies for only two days and the infidels barred the road that led to the ships.

Their next attack lasted seven hours and was seven times renewed. The Portuguese were reduced to eating the flesh of dead horses, which they cooked by burning the panniers of dead carriage animals. There was no water left in the camp. At last a truce was made. The enemy agreed to allow the Christians to return to their ships on condition they left behind their horses, cannon and equipment, that they surrendered Ceuta with all the captives held there, and that they undertook to keep the peace for a hundred years, by land and sea, throughout the land of Barbary. As a guarantee that they should depart freely Sala ibn Sala would deliver his own son to the Portuguese, and as a pledge for the surrender of Ceuta, Prince Ferdinand would remain in his hands.

Henry warmly urged his companions to consent that he should take his young brother's place, declaring that once the army had been liberated, he would refuse to allow himself to be ransomed. His freedom was, he said, a small thing in comparison with that of Ceuta, and he cared nothing if he died. But his council would not allow this to be done, and Ferdinand was handed over.

Despite the provisions of the treaty, hordes of Berbers savagely attacked the Christians as soon as they left their camp, and the latter only regained their ships by clearing a way at the point of the sword. As soon as he arrived at Ceuta the Prince took advantage of the enemy's failure to observe his plighted word to denounce the agreement. He bade ibn Sala return Ferdinand at once in exchange for his own son. The Moor, says Azurara, 'regretted that he could not obey Prince Henry and advanced reasons to which Dom Fernando gave his approval'.

On his return to Portugal, Henry retired to Sagres, declaring that he would never appear at court until he should bring back his brother. Knowing the King's grief, he feared to present himself before him, fearing lest Dom Duarte should bid him renounce Ceuta. But he was constrained to meet him, and this interview took place at the village of Portel.

'The King found Prince Henry firmly determined that Ceuta should under no circumstances be returned to the Moors,' says Rui de Pina. He declared that such a thing was, first, an act that would be contrary to the service of God; second, that as the infidel had not honoured their bargain, the Christians were not bound to keep their part of it either. He assured his brother the King that his object in pressing to take Ferdinand's place as a hostage in Moorish hands was to assure that the town of Ceuta should never be delivered to the enemy. To keep it, he would joyfully have surrendered his liberty and his life.

Exhausted by constant self-reproach, the King died shortly after, on September 9, 1438. The news was brought to Dom Fernando in his prison at Fez. 'I tell you,' he said, turning to his companions in wretchedness, 'that if it is true that the King is dead, my life and my captivity will end together.'

Realizing that it was now unlikely that the Prince would be ransomed, the Moors took vengeance on their prisoner by forbidding him to leave the airless and unlit cell, swarming with vermin, to which he was consigned. Even this was not enough; the unhappy Prince was later shifted to the eunuchs' latrine, and left huddled in a space so confined that he could scarcely stretch his limbs: there he remained fifteen months until his death. The Muslims opened his corpse and extracted the entrails, replacing them with salt, myrrh and laurel in the hope of offering it for ransom if the opportunity should ever arise. Then the wretched body was borne on a board by other Christian prisoners to the gate of the town, where it was suspended naked by the feet from the battlements of the outer wall.

৯ 4 ৫

Portugal, The Standard-bearer
of Christ

'I SEE no reason why these caravels should not sail anywhere in the world,' the Venetian navigator Cadamosto observed. 'I believe that they are the best sailers that ever travelled on the sea.'

This was also the Prince's opinion, and these ships owed a great deal to him, for he never ceased to improve them by taking advantage of the lessons of experience drawn from every expedition he organized. For his first voyages he had chosen stout sailing ships of medium tonnage, like the *Talhim*, in which Baldaia had reached Rio do Ouro. But he had speedily realized that he needed vessels capable of navigating in shallow waters and, especially, able to strive with the constant contrary winds which opposed their return journey northwards.

In the days of Dom Fernando, King John's predecessor, the Portuguese navy was divided into two *frotas* or fleets, one of *naus*, or ships, and the other of *galés*, or galleys. The *nau* was a heavy, tall-sided ship, driven solely by sail. The *galé* was lighter, long, narrow and low, and depended on a combination of the force of the wind and the exertions of rowers: it was a characteristically Mediterranean type of ship, with a spur at the prow above or below the water line. This prow was later lengthened and curved outwards so as to permit the crew of an attacking ship to leap easily on to the enemy at the moment of boarding. Thus converted into a '*galera*', the *galé* was used exclusively for war, and its length was extended to 135 or 140 feet, though its beam remained invariably eighteen feet.

The western '*nau*' was distinguished from that in use in the Levant. The former possessed a massive and heavy bulk and the

55

two extremities, each of which was curved back, carried a two-storeyed castle. They were fitted with a mast, a crows' nest and a square sail carried on a rig. The *naus* of the Levant were equipped with a large mast near the prow and a smaller one amidships. They had a length of about 108 feet, not including the overhang of the castles, and beam of about forty; they could transport up to fifty horses at a time. Their triangular sails were replaced by black cloth at nightfall so that they could remain concealed from the enemy in case of emergency.

The *barcha* was a tall ship of northern European origin used for the carriage of merchandise. The *barca*, a smaller vessel, was used for coastal or river traffic. After Gil Eanes had rounded Cape Bojador in a barcha, it became clear that more substantial ships with a greater cruising-range would be required, and the Prince gave preference to the *barinel*, which like the galley, made provision for the use of oars. With a *barinel* Baldaia reached a point 120 leagues beyond Bojador. But this type of ship was slow and heavy to handle, and consequently the caravel was evolved.

The caravel doubtless originates from the Moorish *caravo*, which itself derives from the Greek χάραβος; and the diminutive suggests that it was originally of smaller dimensions. The first caravels were indeed no bigger than coasting craft. Perfected by the seamen of the Algarve, they had only a shallow draught and were lighter and more manageable than the *barineis*. Henrique found them even more attractive in that when carrying only a lateen rig, which enabled them to head five or six points into the wind (or 55 to 65 degrees), they could be made to sail on a bowline and so to make the return journey from the land of Negroes on the contrary winds that prevailed. In his *Life and Deeds of King Manoel* Dom Jerónimo Osório describes them as follows:

'They have no topsail and their yard-arms are not fixed at a right-angle to the mast, but suspended at an oblique angle, being lashed near the mast head with four thicknesses of a hawser. The sail is triangular and its lower edge comes down almost to the level of the ship's gunwale. The yards are rigged from the ship's deck, and are of the thickness of spars at the lower end but taper as they go upwards. The Portuguese use ships of this kind for naval warfare, since they are extremely fast. It is easy to move the lower end of the

Fig. 4. Two-masted caravel

Fig. 5. Two-masted caravel (according to Juan de la Cosa's map of 1500)

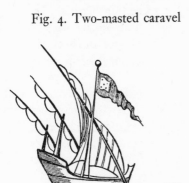

Fig. 6. Portuguese three-masted caravel (according to Juan de la Cosa's map of 1500)

Fig. 7. Portuguese three-masted caravel (according to Kunstmann's atlas of 1516)

Fig. 8. 'Round caravel' (according to the fifteenth century *Livre de Duarte de Armas*)

Fig. 9. 'Round caravel' (from a sketch by Admiral Gago Coutinto)

yards forward and by simply crossing the ship they can be shifted from left to right or from right to left in a trice, according to whether the sail is to be cleared or run off the cleats by which it is held to the lateen-yard. The sails thus open at one corner according to the direction from which the wind is blowing, and they are soon fully extended. All winds are favourable to them, and even with a breeze from the side they will sail on a bowline exactly as if they had a following wind. For the ship to sail in the opposite direction all that is necessary is to reverse the rig, and this is rapidly done.'

As the voyages became longer, the caravels grew correspondingly larger, and they finally reached two hundred tons and carried one or two round sails at the mizzenmast, and even on occasion had four masts, of which the foremast was rigged with square sails and the rest with lateens. These were the 'round caravels' or 'fleet caravels', which played the same part as the despatch-boat of modern times and were known as 'warning-ships'.

It has been said that the expeditions down the African coast undertaken by the Portuguese—and even that of Bartolomeu Dias, who first rounded the Cape of Good Hope—were made on ridiculous skiffs. This is not true. The vessels commanded by the captains of Prince Henry, and of Afonso V and John II, were stout and perfectly equipped for the task for which they were designed. The fifty-ton caravels commanded by Dias had the same displacement as a modern craft with a net tonnage of over two hundred. Within the means at his disposal, the Prince never needlessly risked the lives of his crews, and he left nothing to chance.

It has also been stated by those who have followed Baron Humboldt that Portuguese nautical science owed almost everything to the researches of the famous German astronomer Regiomontanus, or Johann Muller, the author of several learned works of which the earliest are the *Ephemerides astronomicae* and the *Tabula magna primi nobilis*, both published at Nuremberg in 1475. It is sometimes added that Muller's astronomical calculations were brought to the service of the Portuguese by one of his pupils, Martin Behaim von Schwarzbach, in about 1480. We shall shortly see the extent of Behaim's supposed science. As to Humboldt's assertions, they have been completely demolished by the discovery by Joaquim Bensaude in the Royal Library at Munich of the *Regimento do estralabio e do quadrante pera saber ha declinacam e o logar do soll em cada huum dia e asy pera saber ha estrella do norte* ('Rule of the astrolabe and the quadrant to tell the declination and position of the sun for each day and so to tell the north star'). In view of the instructions for an earlier period contained in this book, it seems reasonable to suppose that it was composed with a view to Vasco da Gama's voyage in 1497, though it was doubtless not printed at Lisbon until after 1509, when it appeared from the press of Hernão de Campos. Its estimate of the ecliptic, or the orbit which the sun appears to describe round the earth in a year, is 23° 33', while Regiomontanus bases his reckonings on 23° 30'. Moreover, according to the eminent Portuguese archaeologist, Commander Quirino da Fonseca, a study of the declination tables in this book shows that they were calculated for 1449, when Regiomontanus was only thirteen years of age. No one acquainted with the precautions taken by the Portuguese to keep their discoveries and results secret will be surprised at the delay in publication, which would probably not have occurred at all but for the 'accident' which placed this precious document in the hands of the Catholic Monarchs, the rulers of Spain.

In the words of Professor Mário de Vasconcelos e Sá, 'tenacity allied to temerity, and both fortified by spirit, intelligence and courage' alone permitted the Portuguese mariners to achieve these astounding explorations spread over a whole century and leading to the revelation of two-thirds of the earth's surface to old Europe. These qualities were all present in the highest degree in the Prince himself.

His first captains were simple sea-dogs, who required to be patiently instructed in the complicated laws of astronomy. Prince Henry knew the *Books of the lore of Astronomy of King Alfonso X of Castile* written in the thirteenth century by the learned Rabiçag of Toledo. The second volume of this work contains the *Book of Astrolabes*, which describes plane and spherical astrolabes and gives full instructions for their construction and use. In the third volume, we find the *Book of the Quadrant*, with a description of the method of measuring the height of stars above the horizon. Assuming that the sun is always to the south of the zenith, the book shows how to apply the astrolabe for the purpose of finding the latitude, based on the height of the sun observed at mid-day. It may be observed that the astrolabe, the invention of which is ascribed to the Chaldeans, was already used by Hipparch and that the quadrant had been introduced into Europe by the Arabs.

The teachings of Rabiçag were intended for astronomers, and not for sailors. But two years before the daily tables of Regiomontanus were published at Nuremberg, the Jew Abraham Zacuto printed at Salamanca, at the request of the Bishop of the town, his *Almanach Perpetuum Celestiam Radix*, first written in Hebrew (1473). Unlike the *Ephemerides astronomicae* which followed it and contained no tables of declination, this work was not intended solely for astronomers, but also for mariners, who would find in it all the charts required for navigation. Zacuto was called to Portugal in 1492 by King John II and remained there for five years: his book was to be published at Leiria in a Latin translation executed by José Vizinho, a member of the 'mathematical board' set up by the monarch.

When the *Ephemerides* appeared, Prince Henry had been dead fifteen years. Soon after, his captain, Pedro de Sintra, discovered a land of wild and mountainous appearance, frequently assailed by violent storms, during which the rolling of the thunder was often mistaken for the roaring of lions. He called it Serra Leoa, the 'Mountains of the Lioness': this is the Sierra Leone of today. The equator was less than ten degrees distant. Since Gil Eanes had rounded Cape Bojador in 1434, Prince Henry's caravels had advanced nearly 1,500 sea-miles to the south, conquering league by league a hostile sea and league by league recording the outline of the unknown shore it bathed. Nuno Tristão explored Cape Branco, the 'White Cape', in 1441, and in 1443 reached the isles of Arguim and of the Herons (as Garças). In 1444 Lançarote found the islands of Naar and Tider, while Tristão pressed on to the estuary of a river which marked the end of the desert and which, following the geographical notions of the day, was thought to be a branch of the Nile: this was the Senegal. Stirred by the announcement of this discovery, Denis Dias urged the Prince to entrust him with the command of a caravel, though he was no longer in his first youth, and he sailed towards the place Tristão had named the 'Land of Negroes', thus distinguishing it from the 'Land of Azenegues', or Saharan Moors, who lived on the right bank of the river. When they saw Denis' ship, these negroes,

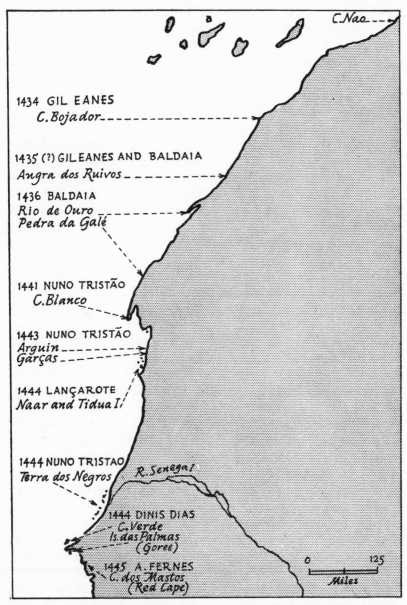

Fig. 10. Progressive reconnaissance of the African coast from Cape Bojador to the Cape dos Mastos (Red Cape) from 1434 to 1445

the Jaloffs, mistook it for a large bird or a gigantic flying-fish. Four of them, bolder than the rest, paddled up to it in their canoe, but they hastily took flight when they saw on board the caravel creatures they would have thought human by their faces, had not their skin been white.

'Our navigators,' says Azyrara, 'went their way. A little further on they saw more canoes filled with natives, who sought to return to the bank, being seized with terror at the sight of these astonishing and unknown creatures. This opportunity was more favourable than the first, and four of the negroes were captured by the Portuguese. They were the first ever to be captured by white men in their own country, and no history or chronicle contradicts this fact. This was a great honour for our Prince, whose power was so great that he could send his servants so far from our own land and take captives among people close to the land of Egypt.'

Some two thousand years earlier, a Carthaginian seafarer named Hanno had ventured into the same region, and his men had pursued 'savages' whose body was 'covered with thick fleece'. The distant forerunners of the Portuguese succeeded in capturing three 'women' who fought so stubbornly to defend themselves that they were killed: their skins were removed. These were in fact gorillas, which the Carthaginians had taken for human beings.

Since Gil Eanes had brought the 'roses of St Mary', the Prince had been presented by his captains with various specimens of what they found on this coast whose memory had so long been lost to Europe and which persisted so surprisingly in extending ever further southward without ever bending towards the east as the best cosmographers, imbued with the teachings of Ptolemy had supposed. Baldaia had brought back to Henry Azenegues or Blackamoors, who, being only simple pagans, were easier to convert to Christianity than the Muslims (Prince Henry was ever careful of the eternal salvation of his seamen and had obtained from Pope Eugene IV a bull by which plenary indulgence was granted to all who were surprised by death in the course of his voyages). The same Baldaia brought his master a bag of gold-dust and ostrich eggs, which were turned into omelets by the cook at Sagres and found delicious by the guests. One João Fernandes, who agreed to remain on the shore of Rio do Ouro, lived for seven months among the Azengues, Berbers and Arabs, and was able to give Henry information about their customs and the routes taken by the caravans which left the depths of Guinea and brought gold and ivory to Ceuta.

Denis Dias' four negroes came from the Isle of Palms, later the island of Goree, opposite Dakar, and from a promontory covered with such luxuriant vegetation that the Portuguese had named it Cabo Verde, or 'Green Cape'. In 1445 Álvaro Fernandes went even beyond and discovered another promontory which he called the 'Cape of Masts' (Red Cape on modern maps). Then came the discovery of the Casamance river and the Bissagos islands. The Cape Verde Archipelago was explored in 1457.

From the year 1448 onwards there occurred a slackening in the frequency of the expeditions. Henry had made use of more than fifty caravels in less than thirty years, despite the interruption caused by the campaign against Tangier. The cause of the suspension lay doubtless in the internal situation in Portugal. When King Duarte died, he left as his heir a six-year-old boy, Afonso, entrusting the regency to his brother Pedro. His widow Queen Leonor opposed Dom Pedro, and the conflict between them came to a dramatic end in the battle of Alfarrobeira in 1449, in which the Regent perished. But by now the true outline of Africa was already becoming known and the Dark Continent was no longer terra incognita. As Henry surrendered his soul to God, his expeditions were already approaching the equator.

The pilot, whose skill enables him to fix a rhumb-line, to measure accurately the altitude of the sun, to calculate the degrees of longitude and latitude, to make full use of the scientific information that comes his way, a specialist still unknown in Europe at the outset of the fifteenth century, was a creation of what may be called the 'school of Sagres'. The further the discoveries penetrated southwards, the more needful it became to separate the duties of the captain of the ship, who was also its military leader, from those of the navigator. The Prince was the first to draw this essential distinction. By patiently moulding a new type of seaman, he was to provide his country with the human instrument that would permit it to plough the seas to the very shores of China.

The knowledge, ability and inflexible will of this man of genius could scarcely have sufficed to ensure the success of his undertaking

63

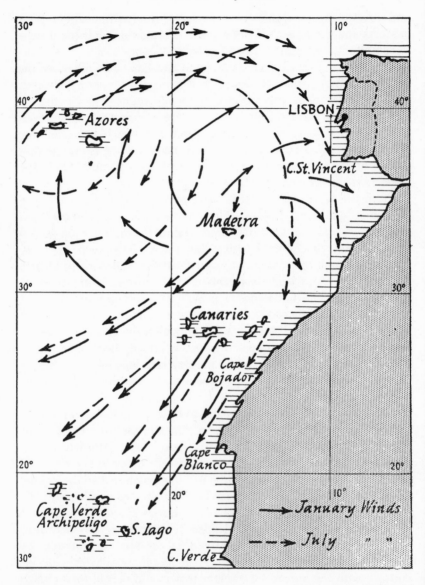

Fig. 11. Prevailing winds in the area between Portugal and the C. Verde Islands

but for his profound faith in his mission. And this faith would have remained vain had not the Portuguese people, from its kings to its humblest fishermen and peasants, been forged of a steel tempered in a long series of battles and ordeals, and especially by the hardness of their daily struggle for existence. Prince Henry's Portugal was a very poor country, enclosed within narrow frontiers which had remained almost unaltered since the thirteenth century. Its population was barely a million. Fifty years after the Prince's death, it was to experience its Golden Age, but this gold was the fruit of a long period of testing in the pitiless crucible of experience. King Manoel's account-books shows that it was at once delivered to the mint.

Arnold Toynbee has written that the westernized world of our own times is properly the work of the pioneers of western Christianity. Of all these pioneers, Portugal was the earliest in date and remains the first by the vastness of the area it discovered. If King Manoel the Fortunate had reigned over five million subjects, there is every reason to suppose that the face of Asia would today be very different, for Portugal would have had at her disposal enough soldiers and seamen to extend and maintain her astonishing conquests and enough priests to support a missionary effort that would have resulted in the evangelization of India and China. This latter prospect was the fuel that sustained for forty years the flame that burned in Prince Henry's heart.

One word in the Portuguese vocabulary suffices to define the spirit of its people with its admirable qualities of sobriety, patience, tenacity, tirelessness in toil and resistance in the face of hardships. The word is '*Saudade*', which expresses not only the sense of regret in absence, as the dictionaries say, but also and especially hope allied with unconquerable melancholy, the expression of a destiny that could never be fully achieved, enthusiasm tinged with sadness, gentleness ever on the verge of turning to sudden violence: it stands also for good faith, often naïve, yet not without prudence and even astuteness. Above all it stands for loyalty, courage and the nostalgia of a legitimate pride that no reverse or catastrophe can ever abase. In the thick of the battle of Alcazar-Kebir, when on August 4, 1578, Portuguese power was laid low and the pick of the nation perished, a gentleman cried out to young King Sebastian who, streaming with blood, still fought like a lion: 'What are we to do?'

'Die!' replied the King, scarcely pausing between one stroke and the next. 'Is there no hope then?' his companion insisted, now losing heart. 'Yes, of heaven!' And 'Christ's captain' disappeared for ever as a swirl of enemies encompassed him on every side.

When on Thursday, November 13, 1460, at his beloved *vila* of Sagres, facing the ocean now for ever reflected in his motionless gaze, Henry returned to God the soul which he had put to such good service, he knew that he had left his inheritance in good hands. His temporal possessions, consisting of the islands of Terceira and Graciosa in the Azores, were bequeathed to his nephew Dom Fernando, according to his promise, while the revenues of the island of Madeira passed to the Order of Christ. But all this was a small thing by comparison with his true patrimony, a spiritual heritage that benefited not only his own country, but the whole Christian world.

In the eyes of this tireless scourer of the seas and visionary of genius, every league won from the unknown was merely a stage towards a distant horizon. The half-hearted and the sceptical believed that it would continue to withdraw, mirage-like, for ever, but the Prince was certain that beyond it India would one day be attained. Now aged sixty-six, the ascetic who would be known to the world as 'the Navigator' from the many ships he had sent out to discover a way in which he so obstinately believed, had died at his post, cleaving to the rock of Sagres. It had not been God's will that he should see the fulfilment of his dream, but that only adds to his greatness. The dream would survive him, growing in consistency from year to year until it was finally dazzlingly justified in reality. As his century was about to expire, his frozen hand would from the depths of his tomb turn a decisive page in the history of mankind.

❧ 5 ❧

Mina

THE Prince's spiritual heritage offered two alternative routes to his successors. Although they appeared to diverge, they were as before designed to complement one another, tending towards the same end, the destruction of Muslim power, with the empire of India and the domination of the seas of the Orient as the prize for the conqueror.

The first of the two routes led round the southernmost extremity of Africa, which Henry thought would be found immediately below the equator, where the great lake that washed the shores of India and of the kingdom of Prester John would presently be entered. The second route was the direct road to Prester John, but it remained impracticable until the Muslims were ejected from their strongholds in North Africa, whence they constantly threatened the Algarve and the coasts of Spain and the sea-traffic of the Mediterranean. Whilst the caravels pursued the methodical exploration of the African coast, the army would attack the enemy from Ceuta.

King Afonso's tastes inclined him to wage war on the African mainland. He had already offered his uncle Henry, still vigorous despite his sixty-four years, the chance to take a brilliant revenge for his check at Tangier by storming the town of Alcácer-Saghir, on October 23, 1458. Duarte de Meneses was made captain of the place, and soon found the opportunity to prove his worth by resisting a siege lasting fifty-three days led by the King of Fez in person and attended, it was said, by a hundred thousand warriors. This exploit filled the hearts of the Moors with such hatred of Meneses that when he fell in battle his body was torn to pieces. Only a single tooth of the unfortunate captain was discovered, and it was placed symbolically in the magnificent tomb which perpetuates his memory in the church of São Francisco at Santarém.

On August 14, 1471, Dom Afonso set sail from Lisbon with a fleet of 400 ships and 30,000 men, including the flower of the Portuguese nobility. Prince João, the future John II, was at his side; although the young heir to the throne was only sixteen, he had recently been joined in holy matrimony with his cousin Leonor, the daughter of Dom Fernando, Duke of Viseu, Prince Henry's heir. Five days later, they cast anchor before Arzila, a rich Moorish city whose inhabitants engaged in continuous raids on the Christian shore of the straits of Gibraltar, winning much booty and causing great bloodshed. On August 24, by the lifeless bodies of Dom João Coutinho, Count of Marialva, and Dom Alvaro de Castro, Count of Monsanto, the Prince was knighted in the former mosque, now converted to Christian use. The King wept as his eyes rested on Marialva's corpse, and he told his son: 'May God make you as perfect a knight as he who lies lifeless before you!'

Filled with his natural generosity, King Afonso refused to take any part of the immense booty of 800,000 gold dobras, but distributed it entirely among his gentlemen and soldiers. The prisoners included two wives of the King of Fez, who had arrived too late to succour the town, as well as a young son and daughter of the same potentate. The wives and daughter were used as currency in order to ransom the poor remains of Prince Ferdinand the Saint, whose remains were brought back to the monastery of Our Lady at Batalha. As to the boy, the King decided to keep him as a pledge for the observance of the truce newly concluded with his father, which assured Portugal of the uninterrupted possession of Ceuta, Alcazar and Arzila for twenty years The conquest of this last place led to the fall of Tangier, whose inhabitants were filled with panic and fled, carrying their possessions with them. King Afonso was able to enter the place, so long coveted by the Portuguese, without spilling a single drop of blood. He then assumed the title of 'King of Portugal and of the Algarves on both sides of the African Sea', indicating his control of the entry of the straits: history was to bestow on him the title of 'the African'.

The victorious monarch did not neglect the exploration of the coast of Guinea. On the morrow of Prince Henry's death, he had all the charts and instruments accumulated by the Prince in his *vila* brought secretly to Lisbon in order to remove the precious treasure of information from prying eyes. There was good reason to believe that the Venetians, Florentines and Genoese were particularly wide awake. If Columbus was born in Genoa, he did nothing to dispel its doubtful reputation.

In 1462, at the instigation of Cadamosto, the King had given orders for the preparation of two caravels, to be commanded by Henry's old squire, Pedro de Sintra. As we have seen, this expedition was to lead to the discovery of the coast now called Sierra Leone. Pedro showed his love for the man who had been his master and whom he now mourned by bestowing the name Cape Sagres on an impressive promontory covered with splendid trees, whose highest point was shaped like an enormous diamond. The two caravels pressed on even further, reaching a charming little grove with the sea at its feet: this place was called 'St Mary's Wood' and is approximately at the site of Monrovia, the capital of Liberia.

In the month of November 1469 when all his resources were absorbed in preparations for the expedition against Arzila, Dom Afonso had recourse to a provisional solution which was to prove an excellent device for reconciling the continuity of the voyages of discovery with his African policy. He granted the discovery of the Guinea coast for five years to an honest Lisbon merchant, Fernão Gomes, who undertook to pay the treasury an annual rent of 200,000 reis, to sell to the crown all the ivory he could obtain from the negroes at the price of 1,500 reis a hundredweight, and to discover a hundred leagues of new coast each year, counting from the last point reached by Pedro de Sintra. At the end of the concession Gomes would deliver the five hundred leagues of newly explored coast to the crown. As a special and highly valued privilege, he received permission to buy each year one civet-cat, an animal greatly prized by apothecaries and manufacturers of perfumes.

Gomes fully justified the confidence the King had shown in him. Whilst the King was conquering Arzila and Tangier, the merchant's ships, commanded by two gentlemen, João de Santarém and Pero de Escolar, assured the kingdom of a source of wealth which would prove essential for the financing of future expeditions. In Portuguese *mina* is both 'mine' and 'spring', and when the captains bestowed this name on the coast that was to become the head-quarters of the gold-trade with the natives, Gomes' captains were thinking only of the supply of pure fresh water found there. This is today the Gold Coast.

Still acting on behalf of Fernão Gomes, Fernão do Pó went even further. After having explored the coast of the region that has become our Cameroons, he discovered an island which he thought so beautiful that he called it 'Formosa': it now bears the name of Fernando Po and belongs to Spain. Further south, Vasconcelos

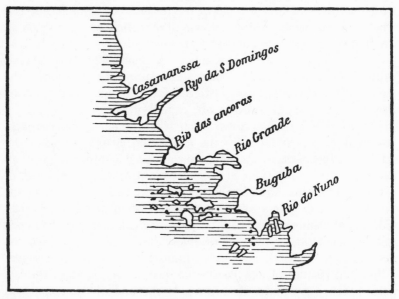

Fig. 12. The rivers of 'Guinea' according to Portuguese maps of 1471

sighted on St Thomas' day the island he christened São Tomé: that of Príncipe, or Prince's Isle, was discovered shortly before.

Gomes' pilots expected to double the southernmost point of Africa at any moment, and their disappointment was great when Lopo Gonçalves found that the great cape he had newly discovered and which is now called Gonçalves Lopez (his Christian name having been converted into a surname) was followed by an indefinite prolongation of the coast, towards the south. Gonçalves had won the distinction of crossing the equator, and Rui de Sequeira, a knight of the King's household, went two and half a degrees beyond it, reaching a headland which he named St Catherine, it being the day of the virgin saint of Alexandria. In 1474, when he was only nineteen, Prince John became the superintendent of the explorations of these African shores, as the contract concluded with Fernão Gomes expired. Gomes had very honestly placed the great fortune he had made in his trade with the Guinea coast (which had earned him the name of 'Gomes of Mina') at the service of the crown to assist in the financing of its expeditions against the Moorish towns. He also made his personal contribution, fighting under the orders of his Prince, who rewarded him by conferring on him the honour of knighthood at Tangier.

Prince John's first thought was to confirm the arrangements made of old by his great-uncle Henry, and to extend them. He made the trade with the Guinea coast a royal privilege and forbade any private intervention except with the special authorization of the crown, under pain of death and the confiscation of all the offenders' property. It remained lawful however for all to seek their fortune anywhere else overseas on providing adequate assurances.

In Castile, the King, Henry IV, had recently died after a tumultuous reign which was generally considered a great misfortune. Nine years earlier the nobles had solemnly deposed him in favour of his younger half-brother Alfonso, and when he had done battle with the rebels in 1468, the result had been indecisive. When Alfonso died, a year later, the nobles turned towards the King's sister, Isabella, the wife of Ferdinand of Aragon. She had refused to rebel against her brother and would do no more than accept the title of Princess of the Asturias, which made her heiress to the throne with Henry's consent. But on his death-bed Henry retracted, and recognized as his legitimate daughter a child of eleven, Juana, whose real father was rumoured to be the royal favourite Beltrán de la Cueva, whence she was commonly called 'La Beltraneja'. Henry declared Afonso V of Portugal defender of his kingdom, requiring him to marry the child Juana. This led to war between Afonso and his rivals, Isabella and Ferdinand.

These two had watched the growing trade between Lisbon and Mina with jealousy and concern, and they did not fail to stimulate rival trading expeditions to the same region, ignoring the claims put forward by the young Prince John. In 1475 alone they sent some thirty ships to Mina. One of these, a Flemish vessel piloted by a Castilian, appearing off that coast with its supposedly inexhaustible supply of gold, had the misfortune to be stranded on the shore on the return voyage. Its crew of thirty-five was cut to pieces on the so-called Slave Coast, and the simple savages ingenuously confessed to

Fig. 13. The rivers of the Guinea coast according to modern maps

the Portuguese that they celebrated this windfall by making a hearty meal of the victims.

In 1478 Ferdinand and Isabella expressly authorized the seamen of the active little Andalusian port of Palos, situated at the mouth of the Río Tinto, not far from the Portuguese frontiers, to traffic by land and sea in the wares they brought back from Mina, and in the following year a new expedition was organized; but the Portuguese Prince had fitted out a fleet which seized the Spanish ships and their cargo. In 1480, the Portuguese captain Diogo Cão brought into Lisbon several ships which he had seized in the area his Prince had closed to foreigners. Among them was the Mondanina, with a French merchant called Eustache de la Fosse on board: a little later he was to publish the tale of his misadventures. Prince John's retort to the Castilian demonstrations was what might be expected from such a Prince. He had already given proof of his extraordinary energy. On his advice, the King issued an edict enjoining the captains of ships sailing from Lisbon to the Guinea coast to attack any vessels from Spain or elsewhere and to throw overboard any members of the crew who were not killed in battle, taking no prisoners. This ferocious order was signed exactly a month after the peace-treaty signed at Toledo on March 6, 1480, in confirmation of the treaty of the Alcáçovas on September 4, 1479, which had put an end to the hostilities between the two countries.

By the provisions of this treaty Afonso V accepted that the marriage he had contracted at Plasencia with Juana, subject to the receipt of the dispensation rendered necessary by their relationship, was null and void. He abandoned, and undertook never to resume, the title of King of Castile and Leon, which he had not neglected to add to that of King of Portugal. On their side Ferdinand and Isabella expressly renounced their claims to Portugal, hitherto considered as forming part of Spain. The unfortunate Beltraneja paid the score: she was confined to a convent to meditate at leisure on the vanity of human greatness. It was furthermore stipulated that as soon as Prince John's heir Afonso should reach his seventh birthday (in three years' time) he should be affianced to his cousin Isabella, the eldest daughter of Ferdinand and Isabella, two years his junior. The marriage would be celebrated when Afonso reached the age of fourteen.

A further clause of the treaty of the Alcáçovas referred to the line of demarcation which should separate the zones of influence of Portugal and Spain. In view of their ancestral claims, Ferdinand and Isabella demanded recognition of their ownership of the Canaries, and this was satisfied; but in return they acknowledged that the whole coast of Guinea from Cape Non to the Indies, with all the adjacent seas and coasts, already discovered or yet to be

73

discovered, should belong for ever to the King of Portugal and his heirs. This was the object of Prince John.

Less than eighteen months after the signature of the treaty of Toledo he acceded to the throne at the age of twenty-six. Endowed with a powerful intellect, a strong and clear will, perfect self-control and a remarkable physical constitution joined to invincible courage, he was to equal the greatest kings Portugal had known, and none of his successors can be compared to him.

His thoughts had never ceased to be occupied by the plan of his great-uncle Henry. One of his first actions was to order the restoration of the fortress of Arguim which his father had neglected after having ordered it to be built. He also decided on the erection of a fortress on the coast of Mina. His advisers sought to dissuade him from the plan, pointing to the unhealthiness of the site, its extreme remoteness, and the savagery of the natives with their pronounced taste for human flesh. The young King listened politely to them, but persisted in his design.

'He gave orders that all the wood and stone needed for the doors, windows, cornerstones, towers and other requirements should be cut and made ready so that when they arrived in Mina there was nothing to do but assemble them,' writes his chronicler Rui de Pina. 'Also great quantities of mortar, tiles, flooring-bricks and nails and tools, as well as an abundance of foodstuffs, were sent out, together with all that was needful for the building. Six hundred men were ordered to prepare to depart, and they included a hundred masons and carpenters and a hundred and fifty soldiers to defend and assist in the works.'

The Mina coast did not enjoy a good reputation. Those whom the King proposed to make commanders of the undertaking avoided the honour on a variety of pretexts, and the only one who offered his services was a treasury-official called Fernão Lourenço. But Prince John refused to give up. He thought of Diogo de Azambuja, who had been his father's comrade in arms and whom he loved and esteemed sincerely, as he had demonstrated in the presence of his whole court. The good Diogo had recently married his daughter and had come to court to present the young couple to the monarch. There was such a press about him in the great ball-room that he could hardly stand on his single sound leg, and the King came down the steps from the throne and took the old knight by the hand, obliging him to take his place by his side. 'Come and take shelter here, and let the rest think what they will!' the King said, loudly enough to be overheard by all. Bidden by King John, Azambuja accepted the dangerous mission without hesitation, 'his face lit with joy and his heart filled with courage'.

On December 12, 1481, the eve of St Lucy, Azambuja left Lisbon at the head of nine caravels and his company included Bartolomeu Dias: two transport vessels laden with wood and stone had already departed to await him in the bay of Bezeguiche, where Dakar now stands. Having carefully explored the coast in order to ascertain the best point for building his fortress, he finally cast anchor on January 19, 1482, before a port called Duas Partes where there was a high plateau which could be easily defended and would certainly be healthier than the coast. The proximity of a large native village showed that there would be no lack of water or supplies: the anchorage was good, and all the stone that was needed could be obtained from the cliffs.

On the following day, the feast of St Sebastian, Diogo went ashore clad in silk and brocade. Surrounded by his men in their best rig, he had mass said under a tree and bestowed the name of the holy martyr on the valley.

'After they had eaten, he had a rich platform set up, on which he sat with the leading members of his company and made ready, amidst the playing of trumpets and drums, to receive the chief of the place, whom the negroes called King. His name was Caramansa, and he approached our people surrounded by a great clamour of conches, horns and bells, which constitute their musical instruments. He was accompanied by an infinite number of negroes armed with bows and arrows, assegais and shields. Their leaders were followed by naked pages carrying wooden stools. The King was naked except for chains of wrought gold and other baubles which he wore about his arms, legs and neck. An infinite number of long gold pendants and bells hung from his hair and beard.'

Azambuja descended from his platform, and went out to meet his visitor. As a token of peace, Caramansa touched the end of his fingers and bit them, murmuring: 'Bere, bere', in proof of his desire of friendship.

'When this ceremony was over and they were all seated, with a negro who acted as interpreter before them, Diogo de Azambuja asked for silence and began to speak. He declared that, because of the reports the King his master had received of the good relations between the Portuguese and the people of Caramansa and the trade there was between them, his Highness had sent him to those parts to conclude a treaty of peace and friendship that should last for ever.

'The place, said Azambuja, had been chosen among many others on that coast, to become the emporium for many valuable wares and its trade would enrich all the inhabitants of the country. Many other Kings and lords had sued for the privilege, but the King of Portugal had decided to reserve it for Caramansa's people, in whom he had special confidence. It would be necessary to build a stout house to hold the goods, and Caramansa and all his subjects would always be assured of finding aid and protection from it. . . .'

'Until now,' replied the negro King, 'the Christians we have seen were few, and they seemed poor and dirty. Those we see today are far otherwise, and especially the captain, who, to judge by his air and his garments, must surely be son or brother to the King of Portugal.'

'No, indeed!' exclaimed Diogo. 'I am neither the son nor the brother of the King, my Lord, but one of the humblest of his vassals. The King is so great and so powerful that there are in his realms at least two hundred thousand men more important than I.'

This reply astonished the negroes, who displayed their wonder by smacking their bodies loudly.

'To judge by the appearance of the Christians who are about you and the way in which you speak in the name of your King,' said Caramansa, 'I think that you do not hide the truth and that you do not mean harm. I therefore give you permission to build the house. When you have built it, if you keep your promises, I shall do all I can to please the King of Portugal. But if you break your promises, I and my people will leave our houses and our land and go to another place, for we do not lack straw and wood to make another village.'

Azambuja protested that Christians never lied and that it was their custom to do even more than they promised. He assured Caramansa that the King of Portugal would make his kingdom the richest and most populous and flourishing on the whole coast. The chief and his followers seemed satisfied.

'The captain at once went off with his masons to decide the place where the fortress should be built. They chose a hill top where there were rocks which the natives worshipped and regarded as holy. On the same day, Diogo de Azambuja divided the work into various departments, placing each under a responsible leader, and decided that the task should be begun the following morning. He prepared a present for the negro king: it consisted of many metal bowls, bracelets and cloth, and one João Bernaldes was sent to deliver it.'

At daybreak next day, they began work. Azambuja desired to have a tower which could be used for defence: it would be necessary to move the rocks to prepare its foundations. This infuriated the negroes, who drove off the workmen with spears and arrows. Diogo learned that Bernaldes had still not carried out his mission.

'He therefore ordered that the present should be conveyed to Caramansa without further delay and added other items, since the urgency of the moment required it. When the negroes saw this fine present, their anger turned to joy and they offered no more opposition to the operations of the Christians. The latter prudently finished their tower before beginning the rest of the works. In order to make a palissade they had to demolish some native huts, but the negroes made no objection after being given some more presents, and they and their wives even helped to pull down their own dwellings.'

After twenty days the main works were complete, at a cost of several lives, for the workmen had difficulty in standing up to the climate. Azambuja gave the fortress the name of the Castle of St George, out of devotion for the patron saint of Portugal. A royal decree, issued at Santarém, awarded the place the privileges of a Portuguese town.

'When all the goods brought in his ships had been bartered for the wares of the country (which has a great abundance of gold), Diogo de Azambuja chose sixty men and three women to stay with him and sent the rest back to Portugal with the merchandise he had bought and an account of all they had done since their arrival. He spent two years and seven months in the fortress, and during that time he governed the town and made laws. He made peaceable agreements with the negroes to the honour and profit of the King, and at the end of his service, the King recalled him, without any petition on his part, and rewarded him generously for his services, as he well deserved.'

While the brave Diogo was carrying out his delicate task so loyally and with such success, great changes were taking place in Portugal. While still heir to the throne, Prince John had been disturbed by the excessive ease with which his father gave way to the demands of the nobility. Lavish to the point of prodigality, Afonso distributed so many honours and revenues that the royal patrimony was seriously reduced. Scarcely had he been proclaimed King when he summoned cortes at Évora, declaring that the oath to be taken to him would assume a new form, at once humbler and less ambiguous. His lords must swear to receive their prince 'above and below, by night or by day, at any hour and season', which by interpretation meant that the towns and castles they held by royal favour could not be transferred except under the royal seal or until the monarch had relieved the beneficiary of his homage and vassalage. The oath stipulated that the vassal took it 'without artifice, dissimulation, fraud, deceit or restriction of any kind', and the formula was to be signed, then sworn kneeling, the King holding his vassal's hands.

One who felt himself directly aggrieved and insulted by the monarch's demands was the most high and mighty lord, Ferdinand II, Duke of Braganza, a direct descendant of King John I, since his grandfather, the Count of Barcelos, was the son of the conqueror of Aljubarrota by Dona Inês Pires, a lady of his court. He was the brother-in-law of the King and considered himself his equal, for he held fifty cities, towns and castles, and could summon three thousand horse and ten thousand foot, and exercised enormous influence among the nobility. When John demanded that the titles and privileges of the nobility should be examined one by one, and not confirmed in a block, as his father had done, the Duke sent one of his gentlemen to his castle at Vila Viçosa to bring the necessary documents. The messenger was aided in the search by one of Ferdinand's treasurers, who discovered among his master's papers a strange correspondence between the Duke and the court of Castile: it included a secret treaty, dated only a year before, in which the Duke appeared as the agent of Ferdinand and Isabella.

The treasurer had the precious bundle of papers conveyed to King John, and when copies had been taken it was restored. Not only Ferdinand, but several other notables, including the Count of Montemór, the proud Duke's brother, were involved in the affair. The King decided to await a favourable moment before striking at the greatest most powerful and wealthiest of all his subjects. He knew that he could rely on the support of the people, for the representatives of the third estate had complained in *cortes* of the abuses of justice perpetuated by the nobility and certain high dignitaries of the church. John's inquiries had resulted in the suppression of the '*adiantados*' or lords-lieutenant of the provinces of the kingdom, who frequently obeyed no interests but their own (conduct which in Portuguese popular speech is still described as '*insolente*'). These officials were replaced by *ouvidores* or royal justices, while the *corregidores*, officials appointed by the crown to assure the execution of justice, were henceforth empowered to enter the domains of the nobility in order to inspect their administration of justice.

The opportunity for which John was waiting was presented in 1483 at Évora, when the return from Spain of the young Prince Afonso, then only eight years of age, was being celebrated. In view of the possibility of a new war, the Portuguese had feared that the heir to the throne might be held as a hostage in Castile: John had learned that Ferdinand and Isabella had sent a secret messenger to Braganza to persuade him to refuse to render military service to the Portuguese crown.

After two days of merry-making, Ferdinand went to take farewell of King John. The letter begged him not to leave the town in view of the suspicions that attached to him and announced before the whole court that Braganza was to be tried. The Castilian embassy which had come with Prince Afonso was still present in Évora, and the news of Braganza's arrest caused his brother Montemór to flee post-haste to Castile, thus admitting his complicity.

When Ferdinand was confronted with twenty-two charges, he could not conceal his agitation. He appeared before twenty-nine judges above whom sat King John in person. After twenty-two days of discussion, the court gave its verdict and sentenced the Duke to be beheaded in the main square of Évora, all his possessions being confiscated. When the executioner had decapitated Braganza, he

79

brought down his axe on a lay figure of Montemór, whence a spurt of red liquid represented the blood of the traitorous and fugitive Marquis.

Another who had shared in the plot was the young Dom Diogo, Duke of Viseu, brother to the Queen and brother-in-law to the Duke of Braganza. In view of his youth the King spared him, but the warning did not prevent him from foolishly conspiring with a group of noblemen to murder his benefactor. Warned that an ambush was being prepared, John summoned the ungrateful Prince to his castle at Alcácer, and had him conducted to his own chamber. He closed the door, and when it was reopened, the body of Viseu was discovered 'stabbed without many words by the King's own hand'.

King John's throne was thus assured and the guilty so rigorously punished that their accomplices offered no more trouble. He was now free to work for the execution of the schemes and ambitions to increase the greatness and prosperity of his kingdom. His policy was expressed in his motto: *Por tua lei e por tua grei*—'By thy law and for thy people'. He was inflexible in the application of his laws and did not cease to toil for his people. But for a pointless accident his son would have become the most powerful sovereign on earth: King of Portugal and of the Spains, Lord of Africa, the New World and the Indies.

❧ 6 ❧

The Discovery of the Congo

ONE day when the King was at table, there was a discussion about Guinea. As tempers rose, King John cut short the argument, saying that no ship with a round sail had ever come back from Mina, and that no ship but a caravel would ever make the return journey.

'By your leave, sire!' exclaimed Pero de Alenquer, who was the most famous pilot of his day. 'I will warrant to take any ship Your Majesty cares to entrust me with, whatever its rig or draught, to Mina and bring it safely back.'

'Nonsense!' cried the King. 'I am no novice in these matters, and I tried it before your time. Think of the two hulks I sent down there with wood and store to build the castle of St George. Did you ever see those ships come back?'

The pilot replied that no one knew what had become of the hulks, but he obstinately maintained that he was ready to try the experiment whenever the King desired. King John brusquely declared: 'Fools are always sure they can do everything, to hear them talk, but when it comes to the test they do nothing.'

Crushed by this retort, Pero took his leave of the Prince and departed. But after his meal, King John sent for the poor pilot and shut himself up with him.

'I beg you,' he began, 'to forgive my rudeness in gainsaying you a little while ago. My reason for doing so was that it is necessary that men should believe the legend that no ship but a caravel can return from Mina. You were right in taking the contrary view, but I wish you not to speak of it again. I shall now give you a piece of information which I beg you not to divulge. The two hulks which I entrusted to Pedro de Évora to transport the material required for the castle of St George were old and almost useless, and Diogo de Azambuja

81

destroyed and burned them on my orders so that the spies who surround us should report that they had been lost on the return journey.'

King John was not without experience of the spies to whom he alluded. The main object of the diplomatic missions maintained by the Italian republics and the Spanish court in Lisbon was to obtain by devious methods maps and astronomical tables prepared by the Portuguese cosmographers and itineraries based on the reports of Portuguese pilots. The latter, apart from such verbal indiscretions as they might commit in good faith, observed the instructions to maintain secrecy enjoined on them by their captains, at the royal command. The same directive required that the works of chroniclers and historians should be rigorously censored and expurgated of any statements which might illumine Venetians, Florentines, Genoese or Castilians about the progress of the Portuguese discoveries. King John proposed to preserve for himself, or rather for his own country, the profits of his own labours and those of the expeditions undertaken in his father's time, and more remotely by his great-uncle, Prince Henry. This applied also to the observations made by his other great-uncle Dom Pedro in the course of extensive travels which kept him away from Portugal for ten years, from 1418 onwards. In the course of his visits to London, Paris, Rome, Venice, Constantinople, Alexandria and Cairo, as well as Jerusalem, Sinai, Mecca and Medina, Pedro had seen much and spoken to many people. In a condensed account of his travels he had minutely described the conduct of trade between India and the Mediterranean whose repercussions extended to the Germanies and the countries of the north. King João remembered also that his father's first care on the morrow of the death of the Prince Henry had been to bring to Lisbon the maps, particulars and nautical instruments, which had accumulated as the result of Henry's forty years of toil in his *vila* of Sagres. The description of this invaluable collection was omitted from the inventory of the dead Prince's property.

Moreover, John's experience as superintendent of the 'parts of Guinea' already known or still to be discovered had taught him to keep his achievements secret. He was sure of the silence of Fernão Gomes, the former concessionary of Mina, who had given his King so many proofs of his loyalty. The discretion of Gomes' captains was no less certain, and the same was true of the pilots, who included Martim Fernandes and Alvaro Esteves: this last was one of the most notable in Portugal. King John felt the same degree of confidence in the crews, and indeed in his whole people, for national sentiment, still unsure in so many European countries, rose in Portugal from a unity that had existed for more than three centuries.

In building the castle of St George at Mina, King John had thought not only of the gold-trade. In his mind the place would also serve as a point of departure for the states of Prester John situated on the far side of Africa, on the edge of the expanse of sea which divided it from India, as Master Jacome had shown Prince Henry.

As soon as the fortress guaranteed the security of the trade, caravans from Timbuctoo and Uaden, laden with gold and ivory and followed by interminable lines of slaves, began to move in a ceaseless stream towards Mina. After loading, the assembled caravels would sail out on a course that led first due west, and then turned towards the north, before veering eastward again at the level of the Azores. This itinerary, known as the 'return from Mina', had been carefully planned to deceive spies, as well as to protect ships from the attacks of pirates, who were known to lie in wait for their rich cargoes.

This traffic included numbers of slaves. Much as we may deplore this, slavery was then still practised: if current information is to be trusted, it exists even today under cover of pilgrimages to Mecca. On their arrival in Lisbon, slaves and merchandise were transferred to the 'Casa da Mina', the centre for registration and transactions: when later Portuguese power was installed in the Indies, the 'Casa' became the 'House of India and Mina' and was later known simply as the 'India House'.

King John had not merely destroyed the two hulks placed under the command of Pedro de Évora. In order to mislead those who spied on the arrival and departure of his ships at Lisbon, he openly despatched from time to time round-sailed ships on the voyage to Mina. They were escorted by captains of caravels who had secret orders to send them to the bottom, and were thus seen to depart and known never to have returned. Thus the rumour was spread that only caravels were capable of undertaking the voyage, and in order to give further currency to it the King forbade the sale of these ships to foreigners, under the severest of penalties.

By his bull of January 8, 1454, Pope Nicholas V had thus defined Prince Henry's purposes: '. . . to render the ocean navigable as far as the Indies in order to succour western Christendom against the Saracens, and to subdue these last and likewise the pagan peoples still uncontaminated by the Mohammedan pest.' The King knew that every discovery which carried him further on the way to India would serve to strengthen his power, which drew from the church the concept of a divine right. This was indeed necessary, for the great lords had never ceased to combat royal authority and to frame conspiracies against it. King John's genius enabled him to perceive that the accomplishment of Henry's plan would raise the ruler of Portugal from the rank of *primus inter pares* and make him a King in the full sense of the term, that is to say, arbiter and master of the destinies of the Nation for which he stood, outside of and above all rivalries and partialities. His successor, King Manoel the Fortunate, was to give full expression to this new definition of royal power.

Like Henry, John realized that the wealth derived from the Guinea coast represented no more than an approach to the infinitely vaster and more varied riches of the East and Far East, which constituted the power of Islam. He also foresaw that as soon as his ships established direct communications between Lisbon and India, the commercial hegemony then shared between Genoa, Barcelona, Marseilles, Florence and Ragusa (the last under the protection of Venice, which had seized the lion's share) would all become an appanage of Lisbon. This calculation was so exact that Venice, in her desperate struggle to preserve a tottering supremacy, would soon seek an alliance with the infidel in the hope of barring the way to Portuguese navigation.

Following the example of his great-uncle, the young King proposed to range on his side every possible advantage that could at the time be taken into account. In this his own naturally inventive spirit played its part. Having observed that caravels were handicapped in fighting by their inability to carry a large number of cannon, he decided after many experiments to equip them with wide-breached bombards which, by firing almost at sea-level, could cause great havoc even against much larger ships. When his captains informed him that the observation of the Pole Star, which was indispensable for the determination of latitude, became impossible as they approached the equator, he summoned a meeting of experts who carried forward the work of Rabiçag and devised a method of calculating latitude from the height of the sun at mid-day.

Until that time the captains had marked each stage of the progress on the route of discovery by setting up a simple wooden cross made on the spot, or by carving their names and the date of their visit on trees. King John decided that the signs to point the way on the long road to the Indies should henceforth be made of more lasting material, and he ordered the cutting of stone pillars twice the height of a man, which would carry a stone cross bedded in lead. The top was hewn in the form of cube or block, one of the faces of which was carved with the royal arms, while the others bore an inscription in Latin with the Portuguese translation proclaiming 'which King had sent the ships to make that discovery, and on what date, and which captain had set up this monument'. All this was called a *padrão*, or commemorative pillar. Many of these stones must have kept silent guard on the shores of East and West Africa and in India long after the death of those who set them up on newly conquered shores.

Diogo Cão, the son and grandson of good and trusted servants of King Afonso and John I, was the first to be supplied with them. Setting out in the spring of 1482, he took on provisions at the fortress of Mina and pursued his way southward, passing Cape Catarina, which marked the furthest point south of the equator so far reached. He mounted his first 'padrão' which he called St George, on the left bank of a river that flings itself into the sea with such spirit, as the chronicler João de Barros tells us, that fresh water is found twenty leagues from shore. Diogo called it the 'Poderoso' or Mighty River. This was the Congo, known to the natives as the Zdani, and to the Portuguese as the 'River of the Padrão' and later, the Zaire.

'Having set up his stone pillar, Diogo Cão considered that in view of the size of the stream, its banks must be thickly populated. He sailed up it for some distance, and perceived a crowd of natives who thronged to the shore. They were exactly like the people already found on the coast, very dark in colour with frizzy hair. But although he was furnished with negro interpreters from the various lands he had visited, he had none who could understand the tongue of these people. Diogo Cão at length succeeded in making himself understood by gestures and thus learnt that their King dwelt several days' journey inland. As the people were peaceable, the Portuguese captain decided to send several of his men with them to take a present to the king, instructing them to return within a short time.

According to João de Barros, Diogo Cão's expedition went no further. It appears, however, that the voyage was continued to a large cape much further south, called Cabo do Lobo, or Cape Wolf. Meanwhile, three rivers, the Madalena, Fernão Vaz and Paul, had been discovered, as well as the bay of St Mary: its high cliffs resembled the walls of a Portuguese stronghold and were called the Castle of Alter Pedroso.

At Cape Wolf, Diogo Cão erected the *padrão* of São Agostinho, which has been found almost intact except for the cross and is now preserved at Lisbon. It stands almost seven feet high and weighs about a thousand pounds. On the face opposite to that which bears the royal shield of King John an inscription in Portuguese states that: 'In the year of the creation of the world 6681 and of the birth of Our Lord Jesus Christ 1482 the most high, excellent and mighty Prince, King John the Second of Portugal, has ordered the discovery of this land and the setting up of these pillars by Diogo Cão, a squire of his household.'

It is possible that Cão stopped at the mouth of the Congo on his return journey in order to pick up his emissaries. But there was no news of them, and he held on board four negroes, explaining to their companions that the King of Portugal wished to see them and that he would bring them back after fifteen moons, leaving his own men behind as proof of his word. Let us admire in passing the resignation of the messengers whom Cão was unable to forewarn of his decision and who were obliged to endure their misfortune in patience for so long a time in so distant a land, and at the mercy of a King who, furious at not having been consulted, was on the point of having them executed.

On his return journey, Cão enjoyed exceptionally favourable winds, since he regained Lisbon at the beginning of spring 1484. The King loaded him with honours, which at first glance seemed disproportionate to the small results of the expedition. Cão was rewarded with a pension, knighted by the King and received the right to bear a coat of arms showing two rocks on a green field, each crowned by a silver pillar or *padrão* bearing a blue cross, the whole surmounted by two pillars in the form of a St Andrew's cross. This symbolism evidently meant that the two *padrões* set up by the brave Diogo Cão were thought to mark the end of the African continent and that Cão himself sincerely believed it to be the case. Beyond Cape Wolf—now known as St Mary's Cape, in latitude 13° 26′ south, he had observed that the coast turned sharply to the east and he supposed that the sea on which he gazed was the Indian Ocean. In his 'Prayer of Obedience' read before the Holy Father on December 11, 1485, King John informed Pope Innocent VIII of the sensational discovery, assuring him that in the previous year the Portuguese had almost reached the promontory at which the 'Gulf of Arabia' began. The map of Cristoforo Soligo, now in the British Museum, which probably dates from 1486, reflects this erroneous supposition.

Cão again left Lisbon in the autumn of 1485, taking with him the four negroes, whom the King had been delighted to welcome. João de Barros tells us that they were of a noble race and extremely intelligent, and that 'they had readily learnt all Diogo Cão had taught them on the journey, and on arriving in Portugal they were capable of answering many questions'.

'When Diogo Cão reached the bar of the river Zaire he was greeted by the negroes with great joy, for they saw how well treated and cared for their compatriots had been, and how contented they were. In obedience to King John's instructions, Diogo Cão sent one of these four negroes, accompanied by others of the country, to the King of the Congo with a message informing him of his return, together with the four negroes.'

He must certainly have been greatly disappointed to find that the coast, after sweeping far to the east, resumed its southward course. But his courage did not fail him, and he set up a last pillar 'at an altitude of 22 degrees' at a point today known as Cape Cross: he was at least nine hundred miles short of the Cape of Good Hope. It is said that he died at the limit of his voyage, but João de Barros is probably right in stating that he visited the negro King on his return journey.

'When this King had listened to Diogo Cão and had received the presents sent to him by King John II, he was so proud of them and so delighted that he did not know how to express his pleasure and gratitude. He was so jealous of Diogo Cão's friendship that he would not leave anyone else with him. And at this time, as the Holy Spirit began to enter the soul of this pagan King, he questioned Diogo Cão about matters concerning the faith and became passionately interested in them. When Cão returned to Portugal, the King of the Congo sent in his company one of the negro lords who had already made the journey, called Caçuta; and he also sent several young people as a sort of embassy to ask King John to do them the favour of sending priests to baptise him and all those of his kingdom. He also asked the King to arrange for the baptism of these young men, who were the sons of the chief lords of the Congo, and to instruct them in matters of the Faith, so that they in turn might teach it later in their own country. He further begged as a favour that masons and carpenters be sent to build churches and oratories like those of Portugal, together with farmers and oxen, so that his people might learn to profit by the fruits of the earth, and also Portuguese women, who might teach the natives how to knead bread, for he would be very happy, for love of King John, if everything in the kingdom of the Congo should resemble Portugal. . . .'

The present the good negro King sent to the captain as an offering for King John consisted only of ivory and palm-leaf cloth, which constituted the sole wealth of his country. But King John was none the less content, and even more so by the pious desires of the natives. He himself led Caçuta to the baptismal font with the greatest display, and the Queen was godmother to the neophyte, who was christened John and took the surname of Silva from his godfather, the King's chamberlain.

There was no dissimulation in the joy of the King, whose discoveries were chiefly designed to bring these idolatous people under the standard of Our Lord Jesus Christ. But his bitter disappointment may well be imagined when he learned that, contrary to what the reports of Diogo Cão had given him to suppose, the south-east passage that led to the 'Gulf of Arabia' was still to be discovered. This would explain the obscurity surrounding the name of the captain whose report demonstrated that the extremity of the African continent lay far beyond the point hitherto supposed and that the approach to India was therefore still further off. But King John's self-control was too great for the depth of his bitterness to be revealed, and it was characteristic of the man to have made such a brave show for Caçuta's baptism.

On the southern shore of the Congo, at about a hundred miles from its mouth, some rocks near the cataracts of Yellala bear distant witness to the arrival of Diogo Cão and his companions, whose names are inscribed there beside the royal arms and the cross of the Order of Christ. Nearly four centuries later, David Livingstone was amazed to discover that the ruler of the Congo professed the Christian faith, that there were no fewer than twelve churches in his kingdom and that thousands of natives knew how to read, some of them as much as a hundred and thirty miles from the coast.

An important compensation for the King's disappointment was now brought by another captain, João Afonso de Aveiro, who had accompanied Diogo de Azambuja on the expedition of 1481 to the coast of Mina. He had been sent by King João to explore the interior of the country behind this coast, which acknowledged the rule of the King of Benin. In 1486 Aveiro brought back the news that this ruler desired to receive priests and to be instructed in the Christian religion (in the hope that these religious, whom he expected to be wizards, would rid him of his numerous enemies): he was further able to inform the King of Portugal that according to the accounts of the natives there existed a mighty ruler, the most powerful known, twenty moons' march away to the east. All other kings were his vassals and venerated him, and his name was Ogané.

'It was,' says João de Barros, 'a very ancient custom that whenever a King of Benin acceded to the throne, he sent an embassy with rich gifts to Ogané, informing him that the preceding King had died and that he had taken his place, and begging Ogané to confirm his rights. In token of this confirmation, Ogané would send him a wand and a sort of copper helmet like those used in Spain: these were his sceptre and crown. And at the same time he would send a cross, also made of copper, to be hung about his neck and worn as a sacred object. This cross was of the same shape as those worn by the Knights of the Order of St John. Without these insignia the people did not consider the King to be duly consecrated and refused to allow him the right to govern. While the embassy remained at Ogané's court the ambassadors never beheld this ruler: they saw only the silk curtains behind which he was concealed, and when they were about to leave, they were shown one of his feet at the bottom of the curtain in token of his presence. . . .'

King John called for the maps which had been drawn after his captains' voyages. Twenty moons' march would be about 250 leagues. In the light of what was known of the outline of north-east Africa as far as the Red Sea, this distance corresponded to the location of the kingdom of Ethiopia, as Master Jacome of Majorca had defined it for Prince Henry. The King had also heard it said that Prester John never revealed himself to strangers, but was hidden behind silk curtains. . . .

'Having studied all these things, which stimulated even more his desire to discover India, he decided to despatch that very year twice as many ships as hitherto to explore the African coast to the south, and also to send men overland in order to bring to completion a quest which filled him with hope.'

As commander of the new expedition by sea, King John chose Bartolomeu Dias, who had already accompanied the mission of Diogo de Azambuja. His pilot would be Pero de Alenquer. John entrusted the land-journey to an officer of his household called Pero da Covilhã, who had already successfully executed several very delicate missions: he would be assisted by Afonso de Paiva.

The King ordered Pero to discover the land of Prester John and to bring him news of this Prince, and also to determine the part of India from which cinnamon and spice were brought to the Venetian ships at Alexandria. 'He insistently urged Pero da Covilhã to perform this service for him, and he undertook to do so.'

❧ 7 ❧

Prester John

KING JOHN was aware that the letter supposedly addressed to Manuel I Comnenus, Emperor of Byzantium, by the fabulous ruler who had haunted the imagination of the west since the twelfth century was a forgery: he did not believe in the robes woven by a salamander and laundered only in flames, or in the magic mirror, the seven Kings, the host of archbishops and bishops or the table cut from a single block of precious stone about which thirty thousand guests could gather at one sitting. Long before, legend had given way to the more modest truth. Its outlines were already known to Prince Henry, and it still held immense possibilities. Prester John did exist: he was a living reality.

In 1316 some Dominicans sent by Pope John XXII had wandered as far afield as Ethiopia, the vast land of 'men with burnt faces'; they had made several conversions there, and one of them, Jean de Sévérac, had accurately identified the monarch of the country: 'imperatore Æthiopiam, quem vos vocatis Prestre Joham'. In 1402 an embassy claiming to have been sent by the Prester reached Venice, and in 1427 Abyssinians appeared at the court of the King of Aragon: eight years before the death of Prince Henry, some had been seen in Lisbon. Some said that Prester John was a Nestorian, while others held that he followed the opposite heresy and was a monophysite (and they were right): what mattered to King John at that moment was that he was a Christian, even though his beliefs were distorted by heresy.

The information gleaned by João Afonso de Aveiro in Guinea showed that the influence of the King of Ethiopia reached as far as the kinglets of the Atlantic coast. It was therefore necessary to win his friendship in order to establish a connection between the castle of St George at Mina and the great sea lake across which Arab shipping transported the wealth of India. The geographical situation of the allied kingdom would permit the Christians to attack the Sultan of Cairo's Egyptian dependencies in the rear, and at the same time to bar the entry to the Red Sea, through which the spices, gold and precious merchandise of the orient passed. By holding the Red Sea it would be possible to block the enemy in his lair. Later on, attempts could be made to show Prester John that if Nestorius was wrong in maintaining that there are two distinct persons in Christ, his opponent Eutyches was no less in error in affirming that the single person could contain only one nature.

While Prince Henry was in many respects a man of the crusades, King John belonged to the renaissance. This did not prevent his being sincerely and profoundly Christian. He knew nothing of Macchiavelli, for the simple reason that the latter only wrote his *Treatise of the Prince*, a quarter of a century later: it is however possible that the subtle Florentine who in 1497 (two years after King John's death) became secretary of the republic, having previously held the offices of Chancellor of the Second Chancery *dei Signori* and of secretary to the office of the Ten Magistrates of Liberty and Peace, had the opportunity to read through recent archives in which the name of the King of Portugal constantly appeared. Macchiavelli's recommendation to those who had charge of states was to insist constantly on the principles of justice, good faith and clemency, but also to have recourse to arbitrary power, deceit and cruelty whenever they thought necessary. If this cynical counsel was inspired by reading the reports of the ambassadors or spies maintained by the Florentine Republic in Lisbon, he must have misjudged the real character of King John. When this great Prince struck it was with the hand of justice; and his extraordinary ingenuity never degenerated into ill-faith or perjury: although he showed himself ruthless in protecting the fundamental interests of his state, he never gave way to cruelty. He had begged the judges at Évora to spare the Duke of Braganza, though he humbly acknowledged before them that he could not oppose the rigorous course of justice: when after an exhausting trial lasting twenty-two days, he heard each of the twenty-nine judges successively pronounce the Duke guilty of high treason and deserving of death, the young King could not prevent the tears from rushing down his cheeks. He had pardoned his brother-in-law the Duke of Viseu, who was undoubtedly involved in the plot against his throne, and only decided to punish him when he incurred new guilt by preparing an attack upon the royal person. By slaying his would-be murderer with his own hand, King John avoided the mud of an investigation which would have besmirched the Queen.

England may rightly be proud that the excellent Prince Henry was the son of a Lancastrian Princess, whose blood ran also in the veins of his great-nephew: an English writer has, however, pressed the claims of parentage a little too far in finding resemblances between the Portuguese ruler and the Prince who, fourteen years after his death, was to become Henry VIII. It is true that John loved hunting, falconry, dancing, physical exercises, and especially swimming. It is true that he was thick-set, broad-shouldered and red-complexioned. It is also true that when he became angry his eyes grew bloodshot and his appearance inspired terror. But it is hardly necessary to compare the lives of the two Princes to realize that these are only superficial resemblances. Henry seems by his arbitrary love of power, his duplicity and his brutal cruelty, to have taken Macchiavelli's newly published work as his bedside-book: there may be added his cupidity and his love of debauchery—King John would never have exposed himself to incur the risk of excommunication; had he ever been visited with so dire a penalty, he would have behaved like an obedient son of the church and implored the pope's pardon.

In order to discover King John's true nature it is only necessary to have recourse to the magnificent panel in which Nuno Gonçalves has shown him, still as a young Prince, before his great-uncle Prince Henry. He has the same air of mystical melancholy as Henry, and nothing in common with the expression Holbein has given to Henry VIII in his famous portrait: the crass materialism in which the crowned Bluebeard is steeped is enlivened only by a wicked gleam shining in the corner of his eye. There can be no doubt that if King John's embassy to Prester John had a practical and definite purpose, it was, in the King's mind, primarily to make contact with a sovereign whose faith was fundamentally the same as his own.

Pero da Covilhã enjoyed the King's fullest confidence. As a reward for his services, the King had made him a squire and he had also been included in the royal body-guard, the formation of which had been rendered necessary by the late plots against the royal person. He spoke Spanish fluently, and had been entrusted with the task of secretly following the movements of the accomplices of Braganza after they had taken refuge beyond the frontier: he had no less discreetly visited Fez and Tlemsen, where he had learned to express himself in Arabic. His new mission, which was evidently the most important of all, was prepared with the great care which the King habitually bestowed on all his plans, by a committee of well-tried experts: it included the grand chaplain Dom Diogo Ortiz, King John's private physician, Master Rodrigo das Pedras Negras, and Master Moses, the future translator of Abraham Zacuto's *Almanach* under the name of José Vizinho. A 'carta de marear' or itinerary was drawn up for the traveller, and it was accompanied by a plan copied from a mappamundi on which he was to record the location of each stage in his journey and the places he visited in the realms of Prester John. He also received from the hands of the King a letter accrediting him to the Prester, and 400 cruzados for his and his companion's expenses, as well as letters of introduction 'so that they might be succoured in any danger through which they might have to pass, for the King of Portugal was well known everywhere', as the chronicler Fernão Lopes de Castanheda assures us.

Leaving Santarém on May 7, 1487, Pero da Covilhã and Afonso de Paiva reached Barcelona on Corpus Christi. There they changed some money to pay for their passage to Naples, where the sons of Cosimo de' Medici arranged passages for them on a ship to Rhodes, then the property of the Knights of St John of Jerusalem, who had newly repulsed a second attack by the Turks. Two Portuguese religious sheltered them on the island and facilitated their departure for Alexandria, where they arrived without difficulty in the guise of merchants. At Cairo, passing as Arabs, they joined a group of Moors from Fez and Tlemcen, who were making the pilgrimage to Mecca and from whom they parted at Tor, near Mount Sinai. A ship carried them to Suakim, the port of Nubia, where they embarked for Aden. There they separated. Whilst Afonso de Paiva went to take the King's letter to Prester John, Pero da Covilhã took passage on a Muslim ship which was about to profit by the monsoon to sail for the coast of India. The two Portuguese agreed that whichever of them reached Cairo first should await the other there.

Covilhã landed at Cananor, the centre for the ginger trade, and reached Calicut, which astonished him. Gold and precious stones poured across the counters of its many merchants, who possessed great quantities of pepper. In those days this was an article of inestimable value which could bring fortune or ruin to European traders. Pero carefully took note of all he saw, not only of the mounds of riches spread out before his gaze, but also of the configuration of the town and its approaches, as the King had instructed him. Muslim ships, brought in on the north-east monsoon, arrived from Aden or Ormuz, laden with merchandise from the West or from Persia: when the monsoon changed, they took their departure carrying the spices of India, porcelain brought from China, the gems of Ceylon and a thousand wares gathered together at Malacca.

Covilhã also saw Goa, ruled by the Muslim sultan of Bijapur. There he found a ship which was sailing for Sofala, the centre of the gold-trade on the east coast of Africa. He visited the great Island of the Moon, the name given by the Muslims to the place baptized São Lourenço by the Portuguese and known to us as Madagascar. There he had the good fortune to find a passage to Ormuz, a town situated at the meeting-place of the Persian Gulf and the Gulf of Oman. According to the Muslims, Ormuz, Aden and Malacca were the three keys which opened the treasure-chamber of the world; some compared Ormuz with a jewel set in the great ring of the universe. Having completed his Odyssey, King John's emissary took the road to Egypt.

The King of Portugal's intelligence service operated with extraordinary efficiency. Just as Covilhã 'who now knew many things for the King's ear' was preparing to leave Cairo, where he was weary of waiting for Paiva, two Jews from Lisbon found him by some mysterious subterranean channel of which we know nothing. They were Rabbi Abraão and José de Lamego, and they brought a letter from the King which showed that John was impatient to receive Prester John's reply. He urged his good and trusted servant to see that the mission to Abyssinia was carried out, in case it should not already have been executed, sending a written report on all that he hed seen during the course of his travels by the hand of José de Lamego, and escorting Rabbi Abraão as far as Ormuz, where he had business.

The good Pero had left a wife in Portugal, and expected her to have borne him a son since his departure. Despite his anxiety to embrace them, the faithful squire put the royal service before any other consideration, and did not for a minute think of offering the excuse that in view of Paiva's long delay he must already have seen Prester John. He wrote a long description of all he had seen and heard for King John, and drew the positions of Calicut and Cananor on the map, showing the best route for anyone approaching them from the west was to follow the east African coast as far as Sofala and make there a direct crossing to Calicut. Then, having handed his letter to José de Lamego for delivery to the King, Covilhã left with Rabbi Abraão for Aden, whence they travelled together to Ormuz. 'Pero da Covilhã gave the Jew a new letter to present to the King on his return, and left him.' His adventures were only beginning.

We now know that Afonso de Paiva had reached Cairo in the hope of finding a way of reaching the kingdom of Prester John and had died there with his mission still unachieved. The fate of Rabbi Abraão is unknown, but it is extremely likely that the shoemaker José de Lamego succeeded in delivering to the King the precious report confided by him to Covilhã.

From being an enquiry agent, Covilhã had risen to be an unofficial ambassador: he had no credentials, since King John's letter had disappeared with its bearer. But this consideration did not cause Pero to tarry. From Ormuz he went to Jedda, the port of Mecca, where he performed his devotions as the good Muslim he was supposed to be. Then by way of Medina, he crossed the Hejaz, doubtless with a caravan, and reached the gulf which separates the Arabian coast from Mount Sinai. At Tor he found a ship which conveyed him to Zeilah, a town on an island on the Somali coast in the Gulf of Aden. It drew its prosperity from gold-dust and dragon's blood—a palm-resin much sought after by apothecaries of the time—elephant-tusks, sheep, and slaves, who were sold at Moka, the port of the Yemen. The heat on the island was sometimes so intolerable that its inhabitants left it and took refuge on the mainland.

Beyond the land of the Danakils rises a range of high mountains which guard the entry to the kingdom of Ethiopia. Pero scaled the foothills, and the great heights closed in behind him: only in the last

The Jeronimo Chapel, Lisbon, in which Dom Manoel, Vasco da
Gama, and Luiz de Camoens are buried

Photo: A. Santos d'Almeida

A cottage roof in Algarve

Spring in Algarve

The body of St. Vincent is borne to Lisbon by ship. Reproduced from a miniature given by Dom Manoel to the officials of the Câmara

The tomb of João I and Philippa of Lancaster in the monastery of Batalho

Section from the Catalan Atlas of 1375

Panel by Nuno Gonçalves in the Lisbon Art Gallery, showing the King, Dom Afonso, kneeling; behind him is his son, the future Dom João II, and behind Dom João is Dom Henrique 'The Navigator'. Kneeling on the left is Isabel of Aragon; and standing behind her, Queen Isabel, daughter of the Duke of Coimbra

Photo: Edit. d'Histoire et d'Art

The Tower at Belem

A window of the Chapter at Tomar, the work of João de Castilho and the most striking product of the Manuelian style. Surmounted by the cross of the Order of Christ, its decorative motives include corals, seaweed, chains, nets, shells and the trees used in the construction of ships

Cabral's fleet, from the sixteenth century 'Livro das Armadas'

Brazil, according to an old portulan

Vasco da Gama

The tomb of Vasco da Gama in the Jeronimo Chapel at Lisbon

Photo: Edit. d'Histoire et d'Art

Detail from the tomb of Inez de Castro at Alcobaça

Model of the *St. Gabriel* made by Comm. Baldaque da Silva

Model of the *Bérrio* made in the naval yards at Lisbon

Dom João II

Dom Afonso V

years of King Manoel's reign did the fate of King John's ambassador become known.

King Manoel the Fortunate came to the throne in 1495, and, continuing the work of his predecessor, strove in turn to establish relations with the elusive Prester John. He confided this difficult task to Padre João Sanches, who was accompanied by João Gomes, and a guide, Sid Muhammed, a Tunisian Moor. The three men left in one of the ships forming part of Tristão da Cunha's fleet, on April 5, 1506. Eight years later, on February 24, 1514, a strange individual called Mateus, who described himself as the brother of the Coptic patriarch of Cairo, appeared before King Manoel, to whom he had been sent by Afonso de Albuquerque, then Governor of India. This was Prester John's ambassador. His journey had been crowded with obstacles and had taken him four years. He produced a letter of credence written by Queen Helen, the grandmother of the young Emperor of Ethiopia, who was then regent:

'In the name of the Father, Son and Holy Ghost, one God in Three Persons, grace and blessing on our beloved brother King Dom Manoel, Lord of the Oceans, dictator and oppressor of the Infidels and Muslim unbelievers, may Our Lord Jesus Christ grant him prosperity and victory over his enemies! May he extend his empire through the intercession of the messengers of Christ, the four Evangelists, John, Luke, Mark and Matthew! May their sanctity and their prayers guard him from all evil!

'We desire to inform our beloved brother that his two emissaries, coming from his high and noble house, have reached us. One is called João, and says that he is a priest; the other is called João Gomes. They have said: we desire supplies and men. For this purpose we have sent as our ambassador Mateus with instructions to go to one of the ports of India under your control, and to tell you that we can send mountains of supplies and as many men as there are grains of sand in the sea!'

Continuing in the same style, Queen Helen concluded:

'With Mateus, our ambassador, we send you a cross made of the wood on which Our Lord was crucified. This wood was brought to me from Jerusalem and I have had two crosses made of it, one for myself and one for you. The wood is black, and has a little silver

97

ring attached to it. We could have sent you much gold, but feared lest the Moors should steal it on the way.

'If you accept, it would give us great joy that your daughters should marry our sons, or better still that your sons should marry our daughters. There is no more to say, except to wish that the grace and salvation of Our Redeemer Christ and Our Lady the Holy Virgin may rest on your empire, your sons and your daughters, and all your house! Amen. However, we may add that if our two peoples were only one, we could fill the world: but we have no power by sea. May Christ Jesus aid you, for what you have done in India is assuredly a miracle!'

Dom Manoel received the venerable Mateus as if he were sent from heaven, and knelt before the fragment of the Holy Tree brought by this messenger for whom Europe had waited for so many centuries. The chronicler Damião de Gois tells us that the King's eyes were filled with tears. He thanked God for the mercy of this gift and for the safe arrival of the letter brought from a country so remote from Europe by the ambassador of so great a Prince as the King of Abyssinia. . . . Dom Manoel at once wrote to the Holy Father to inform him of the result of this fortunate embassy, and the sovereign Pontiff's heart was filled with joy.

Having kept Mateus at his court for a full year, Dom Manoel entrusted him with the task of conveying presents to Prester John. The Abyssinian watched the embarkation on the galiot in which he was to sail of a monumental bed with covers of the finest cloth at least four yards long and exquisitely decorated posts carrying curtains of blue and yellow silk, the whole surmounted by a figure representing an Emperor on his throne crowning the Queen with his own hands while four trumpets rang out. This couch devised for the comfort of the King of Kings was covered with six soft mattresses stuffed with the finest wool to be found in Portugal. The pillows were made of the same wool and embroidered with gold thread. The same pattern was repeated on the bedspread in yellow damask and black velvet, surrounding the royal arms.

The table was not forgotten, together with all that was necessary for its service: there was the finest inlaid wood, a dazzling set of gold vessels and sumptuous table-linen. The wardrobe consisted of silks embellished with gold and the heaviest damask: it was accompanied

by the most costly armour with tooled arms and a harness that would
have filled with joy the heart of the finest horseman.

The pious King Manoel took care not to omit the things of the
spirit, and all that was needful for the celebration of high mass was
enclosed in coffers and entrusted to the care of Mateus. A venerable
gentleman called Duarte Galvão was detailed to escort the ambassador back to Ethiopia and to represent the Portuguese crown at the
court of Prester John. But Galvão had the misfortune to die on the
way, and of all those who accompanied Mateus, Padre Francisco
Álvares alone remained with the Abyssinian.

Unfortunately, they had not yet left Goa when Dom Lopo Soares
de Albergaria succeeded Afonso de Alburquerque (whom he
detested) at the end of 1515. The new Governor pretended to regard
his predecessor's protégé as a Moorish spy and treated him as such.
It was only at the beginning of 1520 that the unfortunate Mateus'
persecutor was replaced by Dom Diogo Lopes de Sequeira, and he
was able to depart with the faithful Francisco Álvares on one of the
ships sailing towards the Red Sea. On April 10 it appeared off
Massawa, the Eritrean port which received Muslim trade between
Egypt and India. There was enemy shipping in the port, and Jerónimo de Sousa pursued it until he came in sight of a village which
to his amazement consisted of houses built of stone apparently
bound with mortar like those of Portugal. A boat carrying three
men rowed out from the shore to the Portuguese brigantine. When
told that they were on a Christian ship, two of the men flung themselves at the captain's feet, repeating in transports of joy: 'Christians!
Christians! Jesus Christ! Son of Saint Mary!' They brought a letter
for the commander of the fleet from the captain at Arkiko, their
village, who had learned from the Muslims of Massawa that the
fleet belonged to the King of Portugal.

'One of these men,' notes the chronicler Fernão Lopes de Castanheda, 'begged permission to return ashore at once to advise the
captain of Arkiko that the people they had seen were Christians.
Of the two who remained on board one was an Abyssinian Christian
and the other a Muslim. They were taken before the Governor,
whose galley had already cast anchor. When he learned who they
were he welcomed them warmly and displayed his great joy at
reaching a Christian country. The Abyssinian then gave him the

letter with which he had been entrusted, together with a silver ring sent by the captain in token of peace. The Governor received the ring with pleasure and ordered the letter to be translated. It stated that the captain of Arkiko gave thanks to the Lord, since he had seen the fulfilment of ancient prophecies to the effect that one day Christians would appear at the isle of Massawa, an event which the Abyssinians had so long awaited and desired. Since the Portuguese Governor was lord of the sea, he begged him to give such commands as he desired ashore, for he, the captain of Arkiko, trusted him as a Christian, and for that reason had not evacuated the town. He awaited the Portuguese and begged the great captains of the fleet to send him a token of peace. Most of those present wept with joy as they heard the contents of this letter.

Dom Diogo ordered the two messengers to be rewarded with splendid clothes and presented them with a banner of white damask bearing the red cross of the Order of Christ to serve as the desired peace-token. As they left for the brigantine, bearing a letter to the headman of Arkiko, the whole fleet fired its cannon at once. Before the brigantine touched bottom, the Moor leapt into the water and swam ashore in order to be the first to inform the captain.

'As soon as the news circulated in Arkiko, there was such rejoicing that more than two thousand Christians and Moors gathered on the beach, and as the brigantine came in, they waded out and pulled it ashore with every sign of delight. Then the headman of the town appeared and reverently received the banner, warmly welcoming our men. He bade his people form a procession, and the banner was so carried to the town and hoisted above the houses. As the Governor had said in his letter that he wished to see the headman and also some monks from the monastery of Bissam, some twenty leagues away, the headman at once had them called and advised the Abyssinian Governor of the province who was his superior. The Governor's jurisdiction extended from the town of Arkiko as far as Suakim, sixty leagues away. The Governor was a vassal of Prester John and was continually at war with one of his neighbours, a Moorish king.'

While awaiting the arrival of this dignitary, Dom Diogo visited the isle of Massawa, where he proposed to build a fort. He had it surveyed and discovered that it measured twelve thousand fathoms in circumference. Its anchorage and harbour were excellent, and forty-nine cisterns, kept carefully locked, held drinking-water in case of emergency. Its population subsisted on its numerous cattle: gazelles abounded, and hares were so common that they could be killed with the foot. Dom Diogo concluded that this island would serve any purpose.

The Bahr Nagach, or Abyssinian Governor, appeared, with a following of two thousand warriors. He refused to enter the tent which Dom Diogo had erected on the shore and demanded that the interview should take place in the open. The two Governors finally sat facing one another on carpets, and many oaths were exchanged to the effect that Prester John would give full support to the Portuguese in their war against the Moors. Once the latter had been driven from Massawa and the Dahlak islands, Prester John would build a fort on each of the latter and the Portuguese would supply and garrison it. While presents were being exchanged, the fleet fired a salvo in honour of the Bahr Nagach, and one of the balls happened to fall in the midst of the Abyssinian warriors, it ricocheted among them; but miraculously there were no casualties. The Governor remained perfectly calm, and when Dom Diogo apologized profusely for the mishap, he replied that such occurrences were subject to God's will, and refused to take his departure until the representative of the King of Portugal had entered the boat and returned to his ship.

The Governor of India decided that the embassy he had promised to send to Prester John would be led by Dom Rodrigo de Lima, a gentleman of his household, who would take with him Jorge de Abreu as secretary and Fr Francisco Álvares as chaplain. Their little party mustered a dozen men, including Master John, who was barber, surgeon and apothecary, and was to escort the good Mateus back to the land of Prester John: he had now been absent ten years and was beginning to feel a little homesick.

As their fleet sailed off to Ormuz, having utterly destroyed the town of Dublak whose Muslim population had fled, Dom Rodrigo and his companions penetrated deep into the interior, marching towards the high mountains which form the natural defence of the Ethiopian empire. The rich presents sent by the Governor of India for Prester John (which included a hand-organ and a musician to play it) were conveyed on camel-back. Mateus, who asserted that he knew the way better than anyone else, rejected the guide offered them by the Bahr Nagach and led the caraven hither and thither across what Fr Álvares describes as a diabolical wilderness of mountains and forests, in which the camels, doubtless possessed by demons, constantly uttered fearsome cries. At last they came upon some aged starveling monks who they at first took for ghosts. They were from the monastery of St Michael, which provided a modest refuge for men and beasts, who were all in a woeful state. Master John purged and bled himself and then attended to the others, and especially Mateus, who was the most miserable of them all. He had scarcely recovered the use of his limbs, when he took it into his head to go on ahead to explore the route. The others soon found him not far away, dying by the roadside, and the priest had scarcely time to hear his confession before he expired.

The embassy resumed its journey on June 18. It soon reached the fantastic land of Tigré. Here the crest of every mountain was occupied by a hermit lying, dead or alive, on his rock-hewn cell. The women of Tigré, as the chaplain disapprovingly observed, were clad only in small primitive necklaces. 'In Portugal and Spain,' he sadly noted in his dairy, 'men wed for love of a pretty face, and the rest is hidden: in Abyssinia the bridegrooms risk no surprises.'

At long last, after four months of slow, difficult and dangerous progress, the embassy entered the land of Amhara, and learned on Monday, October 17, that it was within a league of the priest-King's court. The royal chamberlain himself brought the information, coming forward to visit Dom Rodrigo. After various comings and goings, the Portuguese were housed in tents at the foot of a hill: 'Dom Rodrigo had a good tent for himself and his suite, and those who had brought it informed him that it belonged to the Prester and that no one in his camp could boast another like it. The Prester did him this honour because he was the ambassador of a Christian king.'

'On the following Friday,' continued Castenheda, 'a monk came to him from the Prester with this message. Dom Rodrigo was to send the present to the Prester, and to proceed towards him with his suite and his baggage, for the Prester was anxious to see him. Dom Rodrigo and his companions, now surrounded with a great throng of onlookers, reached a series of arches erected in front of the tents in which the Prester was encamped. The arches were disposed in two rows, each consisting of more than twenty, and they were adorned alternately in white and purple cloth. They stood about a hundred paces apart, and had all been erected in honour of the ambassador. Before the Prester's white tent there stood a purple one, used only for festivities and great ceremonies. More than twenty thousand men were drawn up on either side of the arches, leaving a broad avenue between them. All these men had come to watch Dom Rodrigo and his suite advancing up the avenue, splendidly dressed and wearing gold insignia: the Abyssinians were astonished at the difference between the dress of the Portuguese and their own. Four horses stood at the entrance to the arches, two before each row. They were very richly harnessed, with covers of brocade like caparisons, and under the arches there were many more horses, all saddled, but less splendidly decked. As Dom Rodrigo advanced in the midst of his company, sixty richly attired men rushed forward to bring him a message from the Prester; they came running, for such was the custom. After delivering their message, they joined the procession.'

At the entry of the magnificent avenue there waited the four leading lords of the Prester's court, whom the Abyssinians saluted by touching the earth with their right hand: there were also four lions on leashes of chains. Dom Rodrigo and his company greeted the lords in the Abyssinian fashion. After a longish interval an old man appeared from the purple tent. This, they were told, was the royal confessor, and also a relative of the King: he enjoyed enormous influence, and was called Cabeata.

'What do you want and whence do you come?' he asked Dom Rodrigo.

'I come from India, and I am entrusted with an embassy in the name of my master, the King of Portugal,' answered the envoy.

Cabeata retired with this reply. He then returned and twice more asked the same question.

'What else am I to say?' exclaimed Dom Rodrigo, no longer disguising his impatience.

'Say what you will,' replied Cabeata stiffly. 'Whatever you say will be communicated.'

'Then I shall say no more. The mission with which I have been entrusted is to the King, your master, and to him alone.'

When Prester John had been informed of this, he sent word, still through Cabeata, that Dom Rodrigo should hand over the presents from the Governor of India. After conferring with his company the Portuguese complied with this request, and added four of the kegs of gunpowder he had brought on his own account.

'After Cabeata had shown the presents to the Prester, he had them placed under the arches and called for silence. Each exhibit was then described and the grand judge declared in a loud voice that they should all give thanks to Our Lord for this alliance between Christians: if any among the crowd were saddened by the alliance, they should weep, while those who rejoiced should sing. As soon as he had ceased to speak, the whole crowd shouted aloud, giving thanks to God. Dom Rodrigo was then dismissed, much displeased at not having been allowed to see the Prester. . . .'

The patience of the Portuguese nobleman was to be severely tested. On the evening of All Saints' Day, word was sent that the monarch had asked for him. Dom Rodrigo hastened towards the tents, which were surrounded by a wall.

In front of the tents there stood a large low house, covered with a roof of the peculiar long-lasting thatch they have in Abyssinia. It was supported by beams of cypress and the walls were crudely painted boards. At the door there were four sliding curtains, the two centre ones of brocade and the others of silk. In order to reach the entrance it was necessary to cross two yards surrounded by hedges. The first was full of guards who stopped Dom Rodrigo and his company from passing, and made them wait there a full hour, although the night was very cold and windy. In order to relieve their boredom the Portuguese fired two shots in the air. A messenger from the Prester at once came to ask why they had no more guns. 'Because we have not come to make war!' replied Dom Rodrigo. The majordomo and four lords of the court then approached and bade them enter. The majordomo came first and the other four in a line behind him, they in turn were followed by two men holding lighted candles. After crossing the first court, and then the second they halted from time to time to repeat in a very loud voice: 'Sire, that which you sent for, I bring you.' And from the bosom of the house came a loud reply: 'Enter!' Since this word came from the Emperor himself, all who heard it bowed their heads and touched the earth with their right hands. The ceremony was repeated several times, after which the majordomo, followed by the four lords, announced: 'Sire, the people who have come from Europe and whom you bade me bring, I have brought them.' And the voice from within again cried: 'Enter!' When this had also been repeated several times they all went in. Inside the house they saw a rich dais, before which stood 160 men, eighty on either side, all holding candles. The floor was covered wtih coloured mats. There everyone stopped and a page brought a message to Dom Rodrigo.

Prester John was astonished that all the presents mentioned in the King of Portugal's letter not had been received. Not caring to reveal the vicissitudes of Mateus (who was not there to contradict him), Dom Rodrigo replied through the page's interpreter that if the Governor of India's fleet had not brought the presents, this was because there had been no certainty of being able to land the precious chests at the port of Massawa. Consequently Dom Diogo had brought with him only the less important presents, but he would not fail to bring the others later. The nobleman must have blushed to utter this diplomatic lie, for he knew that the splendid gifts sent by King Manoel were rotting and rusting in a compound in Goa. 'All this was lost through Dom Lopo Soares,' says Gaspar Correa: 'All this was lost, and Dom Lopo Soares never repaid it!'

Dom Rodrigo's reply did not apparently have the good fortune to please the Prester, for he was once more dismissed. Forty-eight hours later, he was again summoned late at night. After he and his company had again submitted to the interminable ceremony with which they were now familiar, the ambassador was questioned at great length by the impassive Cabeata. The inquiries were idle ones, but he gave his answers with the best possible grace, standing before the curtains which concealed the august person of the Prester from view. Dom Rodrigo had shrewdly guessed that for some inexplicable reason the Abyssinians were attempting to exhaust his patience. He therefore displayed no surprise and no trace of annoyance when he was asked to order two of his men on the spot to fight a single combat with sword and buckler. The two men chosen for the demonstration were probably feeling the want of sleep, for Dom Rodrigo thinking their exhibition deficient in realism, himself replaced them, challenging his secretary, Jorge de Abreu, to a spirited duel. When it was over, he asked Cabeata to inform the Prester that as a Portuguese nobleman he would not have provided such an entertainment for any other Prince on earth, even if he had been offered 50,000 cruzados. Would not Cabeata urge the Prester to receive him so that he might speedily rejoin his waiting fleet?

His hopes were disappointed. As on the previous occasion, the invisible ruler ordered Cabeata to dismiss the visitors. Dom Rodrigo was summoned several times more at unconventional hours, but still failed to receive an audience. However, an improvement began to appear after Fr Alvares had been called for an interrogation on the rites and ceremonies of the Catholic Church. Cabeata requested him to put on his sacerdotal robes and explain the significance of each item.

'From that day Dom Rodrigo and his company were better treated. They were given a tent in which they might celebrate mass according to the Roman rite, for the Abyssinians celebrate theirs otherwise: and the Prester bade all the lords of his court attend, which they did very readily. The Prester and his followers all regarded Francisco Álvares as a holy man, and all begged him to pray to God on their behalf.'

Then at last the hour awaited by Christendom for four centuries struck. This occurred on the night of November 19, 1520.

'The Prester summoned Dom Rodrigo,' says Castanheda, and he and all the members of his company responded. They were kept waiting in the outer court for more than three hours, before entering the house with the usual ceremonies. This time, there was a much greater throng, with more armed men and more candles. The floor was strewn with rich carpets, the curtains were of brocade, and the dais covered with silk. Dom Rodrigo was admitted with only nine followers, the rest remaining without. As soon as he had gone in, two curtains were drawn at about two lances from the place where he stood, and he beheld the Prester.

Castanheda describes him as a man of middle height, aged twenty-three, his face—'the colour of a russet apple'—round but not fleshy and fringed with a youthful beard: his eyes were large and his nose hooked. Dom Rodrigo was impressed by his air of grave authority as he sat in his outer robe of brocade over another of silk, wearing on his head a high crown of two pieces, one gold and the other silver.

'Over his face he wore a piece of blue taffeta, like a veil, which covered his mouth and beard. From time to time a page would lift this veil so that his face was revealed: then it would be replaced and only half the face was seen. He bore in one hand a cross of chased silver, and sat on a royal stool on a dais six steps high covered with very rich materials. On his right stood a page with a silver cross in his hand, and on either side stood two others carrying bare swords. At the four corners of the dais, four pages held lighted candles.'

Dom Rodrigo saluted the Prester with a bow and touched the floor with his right hand. His royal interlocutor inquired through Cabeata if he was well and if he liked Abyssinia.

'My health is good,' replied the nobleman. 'I like this country because I am among Christians, and I am happy to come here as the first ambassador of the King of Portugal.'

Having spoken thus, he handed to Cabeata the letters from the Governor of India, written in the Abyssinian language. Prester John read them and thanked God for permitting him to see what his ancestors had never beheld. He expressed his joy on hearing that the Portuguese intended to build fortresses at Zeilah, Massawa and Suakim, whence the Mamelukes had been able to do his people much harm. He added that he was prepared to defray the whole cost of building them.

After the audience, Dom Rodrigo withdrew to his tent. He was delighted at having at last spoken to the Prester. It had taken him a whole month before being admitted to set eyes upon him: it was to take more than five years before he was able to leave the court of Lebna Dengel—such was the name of the emperor.

The young ruler was now consumed with a sudden passion for geography. He became much concerned on discovering that Portugal occupied only a small space on the map of Europe. Instead of dealing only with the King of Portugal, would it not be best to ask the King of France to build a fortress at Suakim and the King of Spain to raise one at Zeilah? It would be a heavy burden for the Portuguese to have to maintain Massawa. . . .

The very idea of setting up Spain at the mouth of the Red Sea would have made Prince Henry and King John turn in their graves.

Dom Rodrigo succeeded in getting out of the difficulty. He explained to the Prester that Portugal was so famous among the nations of the earth that it did not require to be drawn to the attention of those who consulted maps to discover the whereabouts of various kingdoms. Rome, Venice and Jerusalem were places universally renowned, yet they were only shown by a single dot, whilst the unexplored parts of the world required plenty of space to show mountains and wild beasts.

'The same is true of Ethiopia,' he added, not without a touch of malice. The area shown on the map before the Emperor's eyes greatly exceeded the real extent of his domains. Lebna Dengel thought carefully before taking his revenge: his retort was pointed: 'Sire, my brother,' he wrote to John III, who had now succeeded Manoel, 'I must declare to you that I cannot approve the conduct of the Kings of Europe. Though all Christians, instead of being of the same heart, they pass their time in making war on one another. If I had a Christian king as my neighbour, I should have no quarrels with him. . . .'

The ambassador at the court of Prester John had learned by a letter received in April 1523 from Dom Luis de Meneses, the commander of the Indies fleet, that King Manoel had died sixteen months earlier, and that his son Prince John, aged only nineteen, had succeeded to the throne. On learning of his monarch's death the new Governor-General of India, Dom Duarte de Meneses, had uttered a long wail of grief and had desperately beaten his face with the letter that brought the fatal news. Dom Rodrigo and his companions wept bitterly, and Lebna Dengel very civilly ordered his court to go into mourning for three days.

In this exotic court Master John had become very popular, having many times found occasion to display his medical skill. Prester John expressed the desire that he should remain in Abyssinia, and this was granted. The same applied to Lázaro de Andrade, whose skill as a painter was much admired by the king of kings. The two Portuguese thus swelled the foreign colony dwelling at the Abyssinian court. This included a dozen Genoese, a German, a Greek and three Spaniards who had escaped from Turkish prisons. But the Portuguese surpassed the rest in the estimation of their hosts, since they sang together so sweetly that the Abuna, or Patriarch of

Abyssinia, thought when he heard them that he was already in Paradise, sitting cosily amidst the choir of angels.

Like all his predecessors, the Abana came from Alexandria, where he had been trained in the Coptic faith. He was called Mark, after the evangelist from whom his church was said to descend. He was a small, bald, kindly old man who became deeply attached to Fr Francisco. Their first meeting was not without curiosity: the Portuguese priest sought to kiss the Patriarch's hand, while the latter refused to allow him to do so until he had kissed the foot of his brother in Christ. After a long struggle, they sat down quietly side by side. The worthy Mark confessed to Fr Álvares that he regarded the annual repetition of baptism required by the Abyssinian church as entirely contrary to the spirit of the Scriptures. Nor did he approve of polygamy, which his flock regularly indulged in. As those who married were spared from fasting for a month, some Copts used to take a new wife at the beginning of Lent, thus reducing its duration every year. Mark urged Francisco to settle down in Ethiopia, but the Portuguese priest refused. He hoped to behold the cliffs of Portugal topped with their white villages once more before he died.

Dom Duarte de Meneses had been succeeded as viceroy of India by the great Vasco da Gama, who had discovered the way thither; he died, however, four months later, and his place was taken by Henrique de Meneses: but the wastage of men in India was very great, and the new Governor had already expired while the ambassador sent by his remote predecessor was still awaiting a pretext to leave Ethiopia. When he finally succeeded in obtaining leave of the king of kings, Dom Rodrigo de Lima dallied at Massawa, awaiting the problematical arrival of the Portuguese fleet. Saga Zaab, the majordomo, who was sent to Portugal to represent Lebna Dengel at the court of John III, took their misfortune patiently.

'You will have a long wait for your ships!' the Moors of Massawa told Dom Rodrigo. 'There is no more Portuguese fleet on the Indian Ocean! No more Portuguese in India! Their vessels are all sunk and the Portuguese all killed.'

After six years at the court of Prester John, Dom Rodrigo's judgment had become numbed, and his followers were in no better case. Against their advice, he resigned himself to the idea of returning inland in search of the peripatetic court of the Abyssinian King. The poor priest, disappointed of his dreams, withdrew from his companions and wept his fill. Then, drying his tears, he reproached himself for them: had he not opposed God's will in shedding them? Evidently God intended that he should end his days in the company of his old friend the patriarch. And as the good priest had a lively imagination, he soon saw the future in smiling colours: he would begin by building a chapel and a presbytery; he would have cows and an ewe and breed lambs; he would cultivate his garden and exchange his vegetables for whatever he might need. The wool of his little flock would suffice to clothe him. . . . Full of new-found optimism, he unfolded his marvellous plans to his companions, and all but Dom Rodrigo were convinced. The nobleman remained faithful to his mission and maintained an ambassadorial aloofness; but the rest, like true Portuguese, were delighted at the chaplain's bucolic projects. They could, he pointed out, supplement all these things by hunting and fishing. . . .

In the midst of these schemes his servant, a certain Abetai, rushed in, wild-eyed, and announced that the Portuguese were on the sea! A man from the coast had seen them and had told the headman!

They vainly awaited for this man all that night and the following day. Finally he appeared and said he had heard the distant firing of cannon from the direction of Dahlak. Depression soon gave way to hope, and the priest went off at once to weep a little. Finally, after forty-eight more hours, the Indies fleet appeared before Massawa. The most astonishing thing was that no enemy had appeared for them to attack and their artillery had remained silent, both off Dahlak and everywhere else.

On July 24, 1527, accompanied by a few Arabs whom Dom Rodrigo had persuaded to visit the splendours of the court of Lisbon in order that they might bear witness to the might of Portugal among the coastal dwellers of the Red Sea, the little band at long last beheld the Tower of Belém which had been erected some ten years before to mark the entrance of the Tagus. This was not the last of Fr Álvares' surprises: the heat in his native country was so intense that two of the Arabs brought by Dom Rodrigo died of sun-stroke at Santarém, where the King was.

And what of Pero da Covilhã? The messenger who had been entrusted by John II with so important and delicate an undertaking was still alive. On hearing of the arrival of his compatriots at the court of Prester John he had hastened to welcome them. When they appeared, Pero, now well past sixty, shed many tears, and his joy was such that his Portuguese was mingled with phrases of Arabic, Amharic and barbaric dialects. When he recovered, his first thought was to ask the good priest to hear his confession. He explained that the secrecy inherent in the sacrament of penitence was not always rigorously observed in Abyssinia and he had preferred not to risk the possible indiscretions of the Coptic priests. He had been content to go to Mass and confide his sins privately to God. They were not few. Although he was married in Portugal, he had taken a wife in Ethiopia and this lady had presented him with a quiverful of children. Dom Rodrigo would have liked him to return to Portugal, but the old man demurred. Thirty-three years! It had been thirty-three years since the great King John II had bidden him farewell at Santarém in the presence of his cousin, the Duke of Beja! Now this was his country and he wanted to die here. If Dom Rodrigo would do him the honour of taking one of his sons, a stout lad of twenty-three, with, as the priest noted, a russet complexion. . . .

'He shall go and ask the King for the reward that King John promised me and I earned,' said the old man. 'And I will give him twenty ounces of gold-dust to share with the other son I may have at Covilhã. . . .'

Dom Rodrigo complied with his touching request, but the russet-faced boy died before the Indies fleet appeared off Massawa. The gold he carried was faithfully returned to their old squire, who ended his days where destiny had made a new life for him: he never knew whether his legal wife had borne him a son or a daughter.

❧ 8 ❧

The Great South-east Passage

HAVING entrusted Pero da Covilhã and Afonso de Paiva with the difficult mission of reaching Prester John by land, King John II had made active preparations for an expedition by sea to press forward the achievements of the intrepid Diogo Cão in the exploration of the Guinea coast and attempt to round the southernmost tip of the African continent and plant the cross of Christ on the shores of India: its *capitão-mór* or Captain-General was Bartolomeu Dias.

It was long thought, on the evidence of contemporary chroniclers, that Dias had sailed in August 1486 and that his return to Lisbon took place in December 1487 after 'sixteen months and seventeen days' absence'. It now seems sure, however, that João de Barros and Antonio Galvão were a year out in their statements, and that Dias' fleet sailed only at the beginning of August 1487, three months after Covilhã and Paiva had taken leave of their King and families whom they were never to see again. The point is an important one, for it fixes the discovery of the Cape of Good Hope, a milestone in the history of the ages, in 1488.

Some of the captains, fearing a shortage of supplies, turned back before accomplishing the task they had been set. It had been the King's will that they should not stop until they had reached their objective, and Dias had been provided with a supply-ship, commanded by his brother Pero, with João de Santiago as pilot and João Álvares as master. The flagship was the caravel São Cristóvão, on which Dias was assisted by Pero de Alenquer and one of the brothers Leitão. Another caravel, the São Pantaleão, commanded by João Infante, had Álvaro Martins as pilot and João Grego as master. Pero de Alenquer, Álvaro Martins and João de Santiago enjoyed an unequalled reputation. King John intended to run no unnecessary risks.

The three ships arrived safely at the point where Diogo Cão had raised his last *padrão* on African soil: this is now called Cape Cross. On December 4, they anchored off a shore which Dias called Terra de Santa Bárbara: on the 8th, they found a gulf, the Golfo de Santa Maria da Conceição (now Walvis Bay), and on the 21st another which they called São Tomé. On the 23rd they were at the Golfo de Santa Vitória, which our maps show as Hottentot Bay, and on the 26th they reached Golfo de São Estévão, Elizabeth Bay. On the last day of the year Dias explored a point which he baptized Terra de São Silvestre, and he greeted the new year at Serra dos Reis, the Mountains of the Kings, on January 6, 1488. He had drawn copiously on the calendar of saints, choosing the names of St Barbara, the Immaculate Conception, St Thomas, St Victoria, St Stephen and St Sylvester and commemorating Epiphany by bestowing the names of the Magi on a range of mountains: this procedure, among other merits, makes it possible easily to establish the date of each discovery. However, Dias abandoned his system in naming a certain inlet, 28 degrees south of the equator, Angra das Voltas, the 'Creek of Turns'. João de Barros says that this was because 'the ships turned round there under the stress of storm'. The tempest lasted five days.

'When they again set out the weather was still bad and they sailed for thirteen days under half-sail. As the ships were small and the sea rough and quite different from that of Guinea, the seamen thought it mortally dangerous, though the seas of Spain are also very rough in time of tempest.'

This is true, and the fishermen of Nazaré, to mention no others, prove it almost daily. The two caravels were each of about 150 tons by the modern system of reckoning, and were only half decked. It can readily be imagined that their crews, consisting of about thirty men apiece, were kept extremely busy. The ship commanded by Pero Dias was larger, but harder to handle and more vulnerable to the battering of the sea. Bartolomeu decided to find a sheltered spot for it along the coast, and to pick it up again on the return journey. From this long and dangerous experiment King John was to draw a lesson that stood Vasco da Gama in good stead: ships for the India route would have two masts with round sails, while the third, shorter and in the rear, was rigged with a lateen sail so that they could sail on a bowline. These ships were thus bigger and stronger.

'When the tempest at last abated,' Barros goes on, 'Bartolomeu Dias looked for land to the east, supposing that the coast still followed a north-south direction. But failing to sight it after sailing for several days, he tacked northwards and found a bay called "dos Vaqueiros", for there were many cowherds to be seen grazing their cattle in the fields.'

The ships continued to travel northwards, and the chroniclers tell us that 'their captains were well satisfied', as may well be

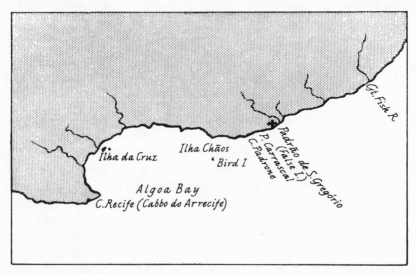

Fig. 14. Position of Padrão S. Gregorio

imagined! The continuation of land on the port side proved that Dias had passed the extreme tip of Africa without seeing it. This was the fabulous Agesimba mentioned by Ptolemy. Taking his quadrant in his hand, Dias measured the height of the sun at mid-day and found that he was 35 degrees from the equator. He decided to go ashore to interrogate the cowherds.

'Having no interpreters, our sailors could not converse with these people. The graziers were frightened by the sudden novelty and gathered their cattle and fled inland. Our men could learn nothing about them, except that they were blacks and had frizzy hair like those of Guinea.'

The Baia dos Vaqueiros, explored on February 3, seems to have been confused with Angra de São Brás, or St Blaise, whose feast falls on the same day. If so, they were at Mossel Bay, which appears on modern maps about two hundred miles to the east of Cape Town.

Continuing along the coast in a north-easterly direction Dias noted the position of a cape which he called Talhado, by reason of its indented appearance (today Cape Seal), Golfo dos Pastores (St Francis Bay), and Cabo do Arrecife (now Cape Recife), on which the important town of Port Elizabeth stands. Dias finally reached two groups of islands 'thirty-three and three-quarter degrees from the south side'; they were in a bay which he called Angra da Roca, which are known as Algoa Bay. He was in the Indian Ocean.

If the commander of the expedition gave full vent to his joy, his men on the contrary did not conceal their alarm. Consequently, after setting up the *padrão da cruz* which conferred the name of Cross Island on the one nearest the mainland, while the others became the *Ilheus Chãos* or Flat Islands (now Bird Islands), the crew expressed their desire to go no further.

'The men were weary and shaken by the great storms they had endured, and began to complain, saying that they had but little food and they ought to return, since they were far from the supply-ship and feared they would die before they reached the spot where it awaited them. . . .'

The old fears formerly inspired by Cape Não and Cape Bojador still slumbered in the hearts of these simple seafolk, and they were more revived by the spectacle of the unknown ocean with its constantly receding horizons. They had supposed that as soon as they had doubled the top of Africa India would be within reach. Now they had the impression that a new Dark Sea was opening under their feet and that if they sailed on they would be engulfed. In order not to anger the captain, they pleaded that their first duty was to try to discover the Great Cape they had unknowingly left behind them, and then to report to the King the surprising news that the coast suddenly had stretched out in a different direction.

'Bartolomeu Dias landed with the captains and officers and some of the senior seamen. He made them all swear to say what they thought would best profit the royal service: they all agreed, for these and other equally pressing motives, that it would be best to return.'

When his officers had expressed agreement with the men, who were by no means mutinous, but had performed their duties exemplarily under the most trying and terrifying circumstances, Dias could only comply. We must admire the coolness of a captain who, had he adopted a brutal or even arbitrary attitude and forced the crew to sail on, might have provoked a crisis and forever soiled his magnificent and bloodless feat: we may also remark on the royal wisdom of King John who, though only thirty-two years of age, warned Dias 'always to take account of the advice of the principal men sailing in his company'. Yet God knows how John burned to link his name with the discovery of the sea-way to India!

Bartolomeu Dias took the precaution of drawing up a document recording this decision and asked all who shared in it to attach their signatures. This they did. His own desire to proceed was such that he asked his officers and men 'to let him sail for a few days more along this new shore', doubtless hoping to make some discovery that would change their state of mind. Dias' proposal to postpone the return for three days has been loosely transferred by some writers to the mouth of Christopher Columbus. Although the Genoese is in no way responsible for this particular misappropriation, his general indebtedness to the Portuguese navigators remains unaffected.

Dias' men agreed to the postponement, but the three days that followed produced nothing more than the discovery of a river twenty-five leagues beyond the isle of the Cross at a latitude of thirty-two and two-thirds degrees. This reference illustrates the precision with which the coast was reconnoitred and the extent to which Dias controlled his own inclinations: in three days he had covered less than a degree of latitude, although the winds were favourable at that season. João Infante, the captain of the *São Pantaleão* had been the first to leap ashore, and the stream was therefore named Rio do Infante. Then Dias was obliged to turn back, for his men were beginning to complain.

'After passing the Ilhéu da Cruz he bade farewell to the *padrão* he had erected there with as much pain and regret as if a favourite son were leaving his house forever; for he thought of the dangers he and his companions had faced to reach that point and yet go no further, since God had not permitted him to attain their main object.'

The great headland which the storm had previously prevented him from discovery by driving him out to sea was now seen rising majestically before him. He raised the padrão dedicated to St Philip on it, and gave it the name of Cape of Storms. The sea began to swell, and his ships scudded before the hurricane that began to sweep round the inhospitable spot: Dias now began to search for the provision ship left on the way nine months earlier.

'Of the nine men aboard her when they left only three remained alive. One of them, called Fernão Colaço, was filled with such joy on seeing them that he expired at once from sickness and debility. The remaining six had been killed by the negroes of the region, whose greed had been aroused by the sight of the merchandise the Portuguese offered for barter. Dias took the plentiful supply of provisions that still remained on board the two caravels, and set fire to the provision-ship. He had insufficient men to work her, and she was now in poor condition. They then sailed towards the island of Príncipe, where they found Duarte Pacheco, a gentleman of the royal household: he had been prevented by ill-health from following the streams of the island and exploring their banks as he had been instructed. His ship had been wrecked after he had bartered goods with the negroes, and part of the crew had perished. Bartolomeu Dias took him and the remaining men on board.'

The *capitão-mór* went out of his way to cast anchor at the mouth of a river called *Resgate* or Ransom, from the slave-traffic carried on there. João de Barros mentions quite casually that the discoverer who had just opened the way to India called there 'in order not to return empty-handed'. He also put in at the fortress of St George at Mina, which he knew well, since he had helped to build it six years before. João Fogaça was captain of it, and Dias shipped some gold-dust. . . .

'With this wealth Bartolomeu Dias and his men returned to Portugal, arriving in the month of December 1487, after an absence of sixteen months and seventeen days. During his voyage Dias had discovered 350 leagues of coastline, or double as much as Diogo Cão had explored in two expeditions.'

This statement is incorrect. The point, now called Cape Cross, where Cão set up his last pillar is 1,450 miles from Cape Santa Catarina, which had formed the starting point for his first voyage of discovery. The distance covered by Dias is approximately the same. The parallel made by Barros long after Dias' death rests on false assumptions: it was not a happy comparison and Dias himself would certainly have repudiated it.

These captains who crossed unknown seas in search of India were all aware that they formed part of the long chain the first links of which had been forged by Prince Henry and those who had returned year by year from Cape Bojador, empty-handed and crest-fallen because their courage had faltered as they sought to pass what they thought to be the limit of the terrestrial universe. Yet one day a past filled with dark terrors had been linked with a future bright with great hopes. One of the Prince's squires, who too had at first retired defeated, had conquered his fears after his Prince had uttered the words he needed. Thereafter the way was open, and St Mary's roses symbolized the new hope of the future. If any deserve to be singled out, it must be the unknown crew of the *barcha* (the name of which has not been preserved) commanded by Gil Eanes: they surpass all the rest because on a day not recorded in the calendar of history a group of humble Portuguese seamen stifled their fears, choked back the appalling nausea that rose in their gullets and thrust out of their minds the thought of the loved ones they never expected to see again, silently praying to God and the Virgin Mary and prepared themselves to be the first to pass on into what seemed to them an unfathomable gulf peopled with monsters of the deep under a louring sky and in the teeth of a howling sou'wester driving forward mountainous waves that threatened at any moment to engulf them all.

As for the rest, one hesitates to attempt to draw up the muster, for it is incomplete from the very start. One would need to mention every name: captains, pilots, boatswains, seamen, carpenters, caulkers, sailmakers, and the women who waited day after day, month after month, in homes where only too often death put his mark upon the door. Nothing is more admirable in this long epic, unmatched in history, than the collective nature of a vast undertaking sustained by the efforts of a whole people uplifted by a single faith in God and the King, the living symbol of the nation. I know no grander crusade than this, and the figure of Prince Henry clad in his hair shirt and expiring on the rough bed of gravel which he had made his couch in his town of Sagres recalls that of the great King of France, St Louis, dying in the dust of a pagan land. Both were crusaders, Knights of Christ who never suffered their hands to snatch the smallest booty: each was generous, compassionate, patient, equitable, chaste, pious, devoted to Our Lady. Not far from Sagres stands a very ancient chapel devoted to Our Lady of Guadalupe in which the Prince spent long hours immersed in solitary prayer. The Lady to whose care he entrusted himself with child-like sincerity inspired him to build on the banks of the Tagus, where the river ends and the sea begins, another chapel for the use of seamen. It was consecrated to the Virgin of Bethlehem who would hear the prayers of all those about to set sail on the long quest. Like St Louis, Henry could not separate the service of God from that of the state: like Louis, he died with his dream still unachieved, and this is the infallible sign of true greatness.

When mountaineers launch their attack upon a peak, the most difficult task falls to the leader of the line. Any failure on his part threatens to drag all his companions into the abyss. He must try the snow that covers the crevasses, seek for the fissure in which the foot may find a hold, fix crampons in the rock on which he and his companions can hoist themselves to a higher level, and finally attain the summit. The captains sent out by Henry, King Afonso and King John explored the outline of the coast league by league, sounded the depth of the sea, studied the perils of the shore, became, each after the last, leaders of the line. Their mountain was called Africa. The summit they hoped to discover behind every horizon constantly receded, yet they never wearied in pursuing it. They pressed ever onward, at first cutting a cross on the bark of a tree, then erecting their pillars, stone shafts bearing above the royal arms the common sign of all who share in the faith of Christ. The last which Dias left so regretfully behind him was called simply 'the Holy Cross'. Erected at the very foot of the vast continent of Africa, its shadow fell across the ocean like a beacon for the ships of Gama on their way to plant another such on the still pagan shores of India.

❧ 9 ❧

I Leave You the Prince, My Son

IN his *Treatise of the Discoveries* António Galvão says of Bartolomeu Dias: 'And as Moses saw the Promised Land but never set foot in it, so he opened the way to India, but did not reach it.' The phrase might equally well be applied to Prince Henry or to his successor John II.

The King was overjoyed when he learned that his captain had found the south-east passage. There could now be no doubt that final success was only a question of time, and the King himself desired to hasten it as much as possible. He ordered the naval dockyards to procure at once all the timber that would be required for building a fleet of large ships, better equipped than Dias' two vessels to overcome the obstacles that had defeated him, and so without fail to carry the next padrão after the 'Holy Cross' to Calicut. He was so sure of victory that he perhaps resented the name Dias had bestowed on the great stone table which stands against the south pole, like an altar raised before the immensity of Africa. He substituted the name of 'Cape of Good Hope' for 'Cape of Storms'.

Whilst Dias' two caravels were sailing home to Europe, the agreement accepted nine years earlier under the Treaty of the Alcáçovas became due for execution. Prince Afonso had reached his fourteenth year; and the King rejoiced, for the marriage of his heir to the Infanta Isabella would end the ancient rivalry of his house with Castile and would one day bring the realms of Portugal, Aragon, Castile and Sicily under a single ruler. King John was already master of Ceuta, Alcácer Seghir, Arzila and Tangier, and he now proposed to found a town on the banks of the river Larache: this would be Graciosa, from which he felt that he could certainly impose himself on the kingdom of Fez, the centre of the powerful Moroccan empire.

After this, Ferdinand and Isabella could not fail to win Granada, whose capital was often believed to be surrounded by a thousand towers and to enclose a population greater than that of any of the great cities of Europe. Already possessing the west coast of Africa and now about to attack the east, whence they would pluck the prize of India like a ripe fruit, and with it the monopoly of the immense trade of the Orient and Far East, it might be expected that the United Kingdom of Portugal and Spain, once liberated from Islam, would become the greatest, richest and strongest in the world. Moreover, the Atlantic itself held out new and even more extraordinary perspectives; but the prudent John took care to keep them a close secret; he himself would neither be diverted from his first quest, nor assist others to pursue the important new trail. At the moment, the discovery of lands to the west would in no way match the double triumph he would achieve by destroying the Muslim ascendancy on the African shore of the Mediterranean and by having at his disposal the fantastic wealth of India. The wedding of Afonso and Isabella was to take place in the year of grace 1490, in Portugal.

'King John sent letters full of courtesy and joy to all the prelates and nobility of the realm announcing the betrothal of the Prince, his son,' says Garcia de Rèsende, the monarch's private secretary. 'He invited them all to the wedding festivities and bade them bring their retainers and bring beds and tables and whatever else seemed needful in order to offer a hospitable reception to the foreign visitors who were expected. The ladies were to bring their finest robes and richest trinkets.'

A caravel was sent to Italy with agents who were to purchase brocades, cloth of silver and of gold, silks, jewels and precious stones in Genoa, Florence and Venice. By the King's orders all the looms of these cities were to toil at once to satisfy the needs of the Portuguese court by the required time. King John seemed suddenly to have become insatiable, and nothing was fine enough to crown his son's wedding with the splendour he desired.

At this time the plague was again raging in Lisbon, where there were many victims. It was decided that the festivities should take place at Évora, the second town in the country, not far from the Spanish province of Extremadura. An 'infinite number' of workmen were employed to enlarge King John's palace there.

Rich tapestries, hangings, cloths, sheets of silver, cooks and musicians arrived from Germany, Flanders, England and Ireland. Castile sent goldsmiths skilled in decorating armour and in enamelling, as well as gilders and 'other artisans of all trades'. The royal treasurers reckoned the cost of the presents 'of coined gold, coral, jewels, chased silver plate, brocades, silks, horses and slaves', which the King proposed to offer to the guests of high rank. 'But all these things were done with such magnificent abundance and greatness that the expenses far exceeded what had been provided for. The King paid little attention, and settled all accounts amply and generously.'

The wax required to make the thousands of candles to light the palace was brought in enormous quantities from Barbary and Guinea: fresh fruit, dates, sugar, preserves, spices, honey, butter, rice, 'and other such things for dinners and suppers', flowed into Évora.

The guests responded with such alacrity that the King feared he would not find a large enough chamber in his palace for them all to sit down at dinner, despite the extensions already made. On his instructions 'a wooden house of most ingenious construction, consisting of a single hall of immense size' was built: it was 300 spans long, 75 in breadth and 72 in height; or approximately 216 feet by 54 by 52. Within, its walls were adorned with magnificent striped hangings 'which made a fine effect in contrast with the brocades and tapestries'. The great royal dais, approached by several steps, was opposite the main gate, 'very great with skilfully painted doors'. This splendid hall was further extended on either side by others crowded with court-poets, singers, and musicians on high platforms, while trumpeters and drummers occupied a raised box at the left of the main gate, and galleries for the courtiers and citizens taking part ran all the way round the building as far as the royal dais. No one was forgotten and in the upper gallery the King installed tables large enough to seat fourteen guests apiece. 'There were thirty very large and handsomely made gilded candelabra arranged in a cross and suspended from the roof by means of pulleys: each held four tapers and had under it a bowl to catch the drops of melted wax so that the people in the hall were not spattered. Thus during all the festivities there were always six score tapers burning in the candelabra, not counting those held by the serving-pages, who numbered 190, and the torches in the hall and in the kitchens. In all there were more than three hundred blazing tapers and torches, and the room was as bright as if lit by day-light.'

On Monday, November 22, 1490, the young Infanta, accompanied by the Cardinal, her suite and people dancing along the roadside left Badajoz, the first Spanish town the modern traveller enters after leaving the Portuguese frontier-post of Caia. At the same time, Dom Manoel, Duke of Viseu since the death of his brother, cousin-german to the King and brother to the Queen, left the fortified town of Elvas with a crowd of gentlemen to greet the young Princess. She received him, 'with great courtesy and friendship', on the soil of her native land which she was now about to leave. Crossing the frontier, she listened to an address delivered by the learned Dr Vasco Fernandes de Lucena on behalf of the King and people of Portugal, and she was delivered by the Cardinal to the Duke, with the customary ceremonies. 'Then several Spanish gentlemen took leave of her and returned to Spain, while others accompanied her to the town of Elvas, where she was grandly received and placed on a brocade-covered dais and so conducted, amidst great rejoicings, to the monastery of São Domingos where her chambers were richly adorned. There she received many presents and delicacies excellent to eat.'

It had been arranged that the Infanta should be presented to the King at Évora, but in his impatience to see her King John decided to go out to meet her and travelled to Estremós, accompanied by his son and some of the chief magnates of his kingdom.

'For this purpose,' says Rèsende, 'they all put on the finest and most splendid attire they possessed. Whoever observed them saw nothing but brocades, cloth of gold, linings of ermine and marten, and flashing jewels. 'They entered Estremós just as the Princess had arrived, and when she was informed of their presence and their desire to see her, her pleasure was so great that she lost all her appetite and rising from the table in great haste, she ran to her chamber to change her travelling dress for more magnificent garments. Her maids of honour followed her example, and orders were given to make the house worthy of the guests it was shortly to receive.

The King, the Prince and their company found her standing at the top of the great stair-case. She knelt before King John and kissed his hands, but he made her rise with great love, courtesy and joy. Having greeted her, he made way for his son. Dom Afonso knelt before her, and she knelt too, 'and so they embraced'.

The good folk of Portugal displayed their own love and joy after their own fashion. 'On the towers, the walls, and the highest houses of the small towns and villages through which the Infanta was to pass, there were many banners showing her colours and arms. Many shots were fired in the air, and there were entertainments and festivities by the roadside. The dancers were gaily dressed, and the streets decorated with hangings, branches and garlands of flowers.'

The wedding was not a whit less splendid than these preparations promised. The religious ceremony took place at Estremós where the Prince and Princess exchanged their vows before the Archbishop of Braga; three days later, they set off for Évora, in the midst of an immense throng of people shouting and singing for joy.

'At the bridge of Enxarama seventy gentlemen came forward to meet the procession, curvetting gracefully on the finest mounts. They advanced together in perfect order, wearing cloaks of brocade and cloth of gold, and cold chains and necklets. They were so handsome and splendid that the Castilians were dazzled, especially by their grace and fantasies. At the gate of Avis large triumphal arches had been raised, and fairies issued forth to greet the Princess, casting spells for her good fortune. A great representation of Paradise was placed there: all the orders of angels and celestial powers were depicted with incredible perfection and the music and singers were so harmonious that this Paradise was the most marvellous thing to see and hear. . . .'

The whole town was hung with silken hangings and tapestries. Valuable cloths were hung at the doors of the houses, which were decked with branches of laurel and orange-blossom. The sun was hidden behind the canopy of green, and incense was burnt everywhere. From that day onwards the festivities were carried on with unheard-of luxury. As to the royal banquet, it surpassed anything previously witnessed. Whenever a toast was drunk on King John's dais, or a new dish was presented, the trumpets sounded, sackbuts played and drums beat. In the middle of the feast a gentleman carrying the long pointed staff used by cowherds and dressed in a cowman's costume enriched with white velvet and brocade brought in a great gilded cart drawn by a pair of oxen, roasted whole with gilded horns and hoofs. 'The cart was filled with roasted sheep with gilded horns, and arranged on a low platform on hidden wheels so that the oxen seemed to be alive and walking.'

When everyone had done honour to this extraordinary dish, the gentleman cowboy led his team towards the great gate. It was flung wide before him, and what was left of the roast meats was distributed among the multitude outside, who greeted the King with vivas.

There were also peacocks fresh from the oven with plumes erect, and a thousand dishes of poultry, game, ragouts, fruit and garnishings. While the guests were dining, the King of Guinea appeared surrounded by his tribe, which included three terrifying giants 'who had the appearance of real giants forty spans high and dressed in gold garments'. This outlandish exhibition was followed by a Moorish dance performed by two hundred men 'painted black with their arms and legs shackled with gilded chains and an infinite number of bells'. The banquet was constantly interrupted by dances and pantomimes and only ended in the small hours. The days that followed were enlivened with jousting, tourneys and bull-baiting. When the last candles had guttered out the young Princess began to visit her future kingdom and was received with dazzling displays in every village she reached. This continued until the month of July 1491.

One afternoon King John decided to take a bathe in the Tagus, as he often did in the hot summer weather. He invited his son, who usually accompanied him, but the Prince was tired after the previous day's hunting. Before leaving the palace, the King went to make sure that Afonso was not ill and halted at the door of the Prince's apartments to ask after him. In order to reassure his father, the Prince appeared in person.

As he crossed the esplanade before the palace, King John could not help looking up at Isabella's window. He saw her sitting with her young husband at the balcony, and they both rose to return his greeting with a bow. The King then went off to the river, his heart full of happiness.

'Recalling that the King had come to ask after him and that he had stopped on the terrace to glance back at him, the Prince feared that his father might take the tiredness of which he had complained too seriously and thought that he should perhaps relieve his anxiety by going to meet him. He dressed quickly and had a mule made ready, but on reaching the terrace, he saw that the mule had disappeared, and had been replaced by a splendid black horse from his stables. It had been brought by the master of his horse, and the Prince at once mounted it, hoping to overtake the King. He rode off accompanied by several gentlemen of his household.'

Garcia de Rèsende emphasizes one mysterious fact. 'Although it was still the season of joy, display and festivity, the Prince was wearing a sleeveless jacket and jerkin of black cloth; his pourpoint was also of black satin, while the trappings of his horses were decorated with black silk cord and it was caparisoned with black velvet. . . . If we consider the difference between the gay and splendid attire the Prince had worn since his marriage and that which he donned to go in search of his father, and if we reflect on the strange chance that brought him a black horse so harnessed, we cannot fail to discern an evident sign of the great misfortune that was about to befall him.'

Prince Afonso soon overtook his father and accompanied him as far as the river. But he had no desire to bathe and while the King swam he amused himself by making his horse curvet. It was a sensitive and highly strung animal, and he challenged one of his gentlemen, Dom João de Meneses, to race with him. Meneses pointed out that night was already beginning to fall. Furthermore, the mule for which the Prince had asked had now been saddled and brought to him. Afonso started to mount it; but its surcingle broke, and he therefore returned to the black horse and again invited Meneses to run with him in such terms that the gentleman could scarcely refuse. He pricked the horse with both spurs and pressed it to a gallop.

'The Prince's horse fell at full stretch, throwing him and rolling over him so that he was crushed under its full weight. He lay unconscious and motionless, as if he were dead. The other gentlemen at once ran to the spot, and Dom João de Meneses was so affected by the calamity that he turned and rode off in despair, and was not seen again at court until several years later he received a royal summons to return. The gentlemen took the Prince in their arms and carried him to the first house they found by the wayside. It was a wretched hut belonging to a poor fisherman. . . .'

As soon as the news reached him, the King hastened to his son. His despair was beyond description. The Queen and Princess Isabella also appeared, beside themselves with grief. The Prince lay senseless as if he were already dead.

'The King summoned all his doctors and they ordered every remedy they knew to be applied. But King John was not content with mere earthly remedies, and addressed himself also to heaven, bidding messengers hasten to every monastery and pious foundation and cause the offering of prayers, processions and continual devotions: great vows were taken, and Dom Pedro da Silva, grand-commander of Avis, at once left on a pilgrimage to Jerusalem, followed by many others. . . .

'An innumerable throng surrounded the poor fisherman's hut. Nobles and peasants were in tears, and all prayed to God as fervently as if they were begging him to save their own lives. . . .

'They all formed a pious procession with the clergy and their relics and crucifixes. All went bare-footed and some stripped naked. In this guise they visited the monasteries and churches of the neighbourhood, in which they knelt and cried, weeping and clamouring: "Lord God! Mercy! Mercy!" It was a thing so terrifying to hear and see that all who watched or listened trembled with terror and fell into the deepest desolation. . . .'

At one o'clock in the morning the doctors informed King John that the Prince was dying. He told the Queen and Princess who had continued to caress and embrace the senseless body, never stirring from its side. 'And their grief was terrible.'

Then the King went to his son. He kissed him and gave him his last blessing. After this he took the Queen and Princess by the hand and led them from the hut. At the door he turned to the priests and said to them: 'I leave you the Prince, my son.' Then he strode off unable to utter another word.

The half-swooning Queen and Princess were borne on the backs of two mules to the country house of Vasco Palha, a gentleman of the neighbourhood. They had scarcely gone in when a messenger arrived with the news that the Prince had received extreme unction and breathed his last.

❧ IO ❧

The Succession to the Crown

KING JOHN never recovered from the fearful blow heaven had dealt him at the moment when he seemed to be approaching the peak of his power. 'Yet thou, O Lord God, hast willed this thing, and thou knowest wherefore: and since without thee we can understand nothing, may thy name be for ever blessed and glorified.'

Thus ends Garcia de Rèsende's account of the Prince's tragic death. This anguished and exquisite prayer is recorded by the King's confident and chronicler, who may well have heard him give vent to his grief in such noble and heart-rending words. The young Prince was then sixteen years and twenty days old: his marriage to Isabella had taken place seven months and twenty-two days before. Doubtless the King's nights were long haunted by the picture of the Prince and Princess chastely kneeling before one another to exchange their first embrace at Estremós. He himself, for all his strength and vitality, for all his confidence in his own destiny, the embodiment of that of his nation, was now a changed man. Something within him was broken; henceforward everything he tasted savoured of ashes. But just because his kingdom and his person were one, he buried his suffering in his innermost self and resumed his daily round like the great servant of the state he was. He was only to survive the dead Prince, in whom he had placed his highest hopes, by four years. But this short spell would suffice to consolidate his country's future in the most difficult circumstances.

His highest, but not his only, hopes. He had for a moment thought of a boy named Dom Jorge, scarcely adolescent, whom Rèsende depicts galloping by the side of the Queen and Princess Isabella in their frantic ride to the fisherman's hut.

King John's marriage to Dona Leonor had been the result of his father's tender regard for a young brother, Prince Ferdinand, Duke of Viseu. The wedding had taken place four months after the death of this Prince, on January 22, 1471, on the arrival of a papal dispensation. Leonor was a child of twelve, and John was fifteen. The only fruit of this precocious union was a son, newly born when the heir to the throne went off to join his father who was preparing to do battle with Ferdinand of Aragon before Toro in 1476.

John was presented to the daughter of a high official at court, Ana de Mendonça, who impressed him by her beauty. He was to meet her again only four years later, when she was dwelling in her parents' house not far from Coimbra, where the gentle and saintly Princess Joana had with patient obstinacy overcome her father's opposition and taken the veil. Here John and Ana passed a brief idyll, which was soon reported at court. The Duke of Braganza took up the cause of the deserted Princess; and with the authority of his fifty years soundly rated the fickle Prince. John curtly begged him to mind his own business and not meddle in the private affairs of others. It was said to be as a result of this incident that the Duke allowed his proud and violent nature to get the better of him and opened the treasonable exchanges with Ferdinand and Isabella that were one day to lead his steps to the scaffold in the main square of Évora.

As so often occurs in similar circumstances, Braganza's intervention produced exactly the opposite effect to that which he himself too confidently expected. On August 6, 1481, the fair Ana gave birth at Abrantes to a boy christened Jorge, whom John at once acknowledged as his son. He entrusted the infant to his sister Joana, who received it in her convent, though it is still not clear whether the mother was a party to this measure. The Prince's passion was probably an infatuation. On the 31st of the same month, two days after the death of King Afonso, John was acclaimed at Sintra and forsook his mistress for ever. The Queen soon after had the young Jorge brought to the palace and brought him up with maternal affection.

Why was the son of Ana Furtado de Mendonça, now approaching his tenth year, not legitimized and recognized as heir to the throne? The example of King John I, the victor of Aljubarrota and conqueror of Ceuta, showed what a bastard could achieve. . . . The King loved his cousin Dom Manoel, the youngest son of the Duke of Viseu, who on the death of Afonso became the heir-apparent, but he would have liked the crown to go to his own descendants. In this hope he attempted to persuade those about him, beginning with the Queen Leonor, who dividing her time between prayer and the indigent, was apparently willing to accept the change. But she was Dom Manoel's sister, and was not prepared to defraud him of his lawful rights in favour of the son of one who had outraged her wifely dignity. She found an ally in Cardinal Alpedrinha, an austere and rigid old man of more than eighty who had addressed a sharp and severe epistle to the King shortly after the death of Prince Afonso. 'Of all the sins of men,' he told the unfortunate monarch, 'that which God punishes most lavishly is idolatry. This was the sin of which Your Highness was guilty; for did you not say that you did not love your son, but rather adored him? To love one's son is natural; but to love him after this fashion is against divine law. . . . Your Highness had placed all your faith in a creature of flesh and blood, who though issued from his father's body, was yet in truth no more than a heap of excrement and corruption. . . .' The ordeal that God had inflicted on the King was intended to show him the path of truth which he should follow by submissively accepting God's infinitely merciful will.

In April 1492 Dom Jorge was installed with great ceremony as Master of the Orders of Avis and Santiago. A German, who, following the fashion of the day, called himself Hieronimus Monetarius (his name being Muntzer or Munzer or even Munzmeister), who had the opportunity to meet the young Prince two years later, has depicted him as a diligent and studious boy who knew Horace and Virgil, had learnt the rules of versification and recited poetry. It was already understood that the throne of Portugal would pass to Dom Manoel.

The bonds which united the King to the still recent past, lately so full of extraordinary promises, were finally broken when King John complied with the request of the rulers of Spain and escorted the unfortunate Isabella back to the frontier. Rèsende tells that they parted 'with many tears and few words'. When the Princess' litter, draped with black hangings, disappeared down the road to Badajoz, King John spurred his horse and galloped away, leaving all his company behind.

The Treaty of Tordesillas

KING JOHN had recently ascended the throne when, in about 1482, a German of about fifty called Martin Behaim appeared in Lisbon. The Portuguese soon adapted his name to their own ears, and he became Martim de Boémia or Martinho Boémio. He was a native of Nuremberg, and had been attracted by the extraordinary fame of the House of Mina, cherishing the idea of setting up what would now be called an import-export house on the banks of the Tagus. He was also bitten by the urge to travel overseas, and hoped to be able to take part in one of the profitable expeditions which stirred the interest and envy of all Europe.

The newcomer introduced himself as having studied mathematics and astrology under the famous Regiomontanus, alias Johann Muller. Some claim that King John knighted him and introduced him to his holy of holies, the junta of experts which had given such precise instructions to Pero da Covilhã. This is exceedingly doubtful, and the originator of the legend was probably none other than Behaim himself, following the well-worn principle that if one wants a thing done one must do it oneself.

By 1488 he was married to Dona Joana de Macedo, herself the daughter of a Portuguese mother of noble rank and a Flemish father, Johst Hurter, known in Lisbon as Joz d'Utra, or Josse de Hurtere. He was quite a figure, for the King had granted him the captaincy of the islands of Fayal and Pico in the Azores: the people of Pico derived an enviable prosperity from vines brought from Crete to yield Malmsey wine.

Two years later, Martin felt the desire to breathe his native air; and when in 1493 he returned to Portugal he had made good use of his time. He had left behind in Nuremberg a globe of his own manufacture measuring one foot eight inches in diameter, and constituting, according to unimpeachable (especially if they are German) writers, an invaluable indication of the geographical knowledge of the time.

As we know, John, like his father Afonso, took the greatest care to keep secret the maps drawn up by his junta on the basis of the information brought back by his captains. The best proof that Behaim was never a member of the junta is the fact that the outline of West Africa, as shown on his globe, is grossly inaccurate, despite the fact that Bartolomeu Dias had returned from his expedition more than a year before Regiomontanus' pupil revisited Nuremberg. The Cape Verde Islands, discovered some thirty years earlier, are shown out of their proper place, while a number of islands which never existed except in Behaim's imagination are strewn about the Atlantic ocean. Their creator had, however, a secret motive in allowing his inventive faculty to place them on his globe.

While he was staying in Nuremberg, one of his countrymen was composing his *Liber chronicarum*, a compilation of chronicles of the time. Schedel's book did much to enhance Behaim's reputation, for among other compliments, it stated that King John was so impressed by his knowledge that he gave him a prominent place in Cão's expedition: '. . . In about 1483 the King of Portugal, John II, a man of great courage, sent certain galleys, supplied with everything that was needful, to sail southwards beyond the Pillars of Hercules in the direction of Ethiopia. He appointed as their captains Diogo Cão and Martin Behaim the German, of Nuremberg, a member of a good family. . . .' Unfortunately among many inaccuracies (and the reference to the 'galleys' is quite a considerable one), the *Liber* refers to a camel which Cão and Behaim are supposed to have brought back, having rather surprisingly found it on the banks of the Congo or the coast of Mina. It is no less strange that Martin's name does not appear on the rocks of Yellala, on which not only Cão's name is legible, but also those of Pero Anes, Pero da Costa, Álvaro Pires, Pero Escolar, João de Santiago, Diogo Pinheiro, Gonçalo (or João) Álvares and Antão. It seems a little surprising that 'Captain' Martin Behaim or Boémio should have been omitted, unless it indicates an unexpected streak of modesty scarcely warranted in the circumstances. There is every reason to suppose that

Behaim was in close collaboration with the writer of the *Liber chronicarum*, at least in so far as the recording of his imaginary deeds is concerned.

At Nuremberg Martin made the acquaintance of Munzmeister or Hieronimus Monetarius, who on July 14, 1493, using the authority of the Emperor Maximilian, wrote to the King of Portugal at some length in order to advise him to link Lisbon with the rich land of Cathay by sailing due west from the Portuguese coast. According to Monetarius, the voyage would be extremely simple, since the distance between the westernmost edge of Europe and the eastern shore of Asia was relatively short. This statement fits in with the conception of the universe as shown on Behaim's famous globe, in which the breadth of the Atlantic Ocean is shown as much less than that of the Old World.

The King, Munzmeister amiably concluded, would be wise to appoint Martin Behaim to command the expedition: his knowledge of the subject would assure its success. This flattering recommendation was so far from displeasing the person in question that he himself undertook to deliver the letter to its destination. The reference to Maximilian was ingenious, for King John held the Emperor in high regard, since he was the son of John's aunt Leonor by her marriage to the Emperor Frederick III. But Behaim was apparently unaware that the King of Portugal and his company of experts had long since ceased to use the word Cathay for the 'Kingdom of the Great Purity' or Ta Tsing Kouëh: they called it simply China.

Two or three months before Monetarius wrote to King John a letter bearing the signature of the man known to the Spanish court as Cristóbal Colón was published in Rome. The writer stated that he had crossed the Atlantic and reached the eastern fringe of India.

Cristóvão, as the Portuguese called him (though they usually referred to him as 'the Genoese adventurer'), was not unknown to Martin; far from it. His arrival in Portugal in 1476 has been much romanticized: a French fleet was supposed to have sunk the ship in which he was travelling, and he first set foot on Luistanian soil not far from Cape St Vincent, wounded, bleeding and clinging to a spar. The truth seems to have been more prosaic: his ship had sailed from Genoa for England and Flanders and it calmly cast anchor before Lisbon, after successfully eluding its pursuers.

After a short absence, during which he stated that he visited northern Europe, Columbus, who claimed to be the son of a humble Genoese wool-carder of noble stock, returned to Portugal in 1477, and in the following year astonished everyone by marrying the daughter of Bartolomeu Perestrelo. This was an authentic gentleman who had been made captain-donatory of the small island of Porto Santo, not far from Madeira. He had discovered it long before in company with Tristão Vaz Teixeira, and Prince Henry had had it settled and cultivated at the same time as Madeira. The Spaniard Bartolomé de las Casas, who went with his father on Columbus' second voyage and later became a Dominican and was Bishop of Chiapa in Mexico, tells us that Columbus received from his mother-in-law all the maps and papers that had belonged to her late husband. The Genoese presumably told Las Casas that the study of these papers had convinced him that a ship sailing due west out of Lisbon would reach land beyond the Atlantic, on the coast of an island which could only be Cipangu or Cipango (in Chinese Zi-pen or Ji-pen, that is the Japan of our own times, known to its inhabitants as Nippon).

Columbus drew up a plan for such an expedition and succeeded in having it brought to the attention of King John, who was sufficiently curious to grant the Genoese an audience, doubtless in order to discover whether Columbus had any precise information about the existence of land to the west, despite the secrecy that surrounded the information already amassed by the Portuguese navigators. The interview left King John the impression that Columbus was a verbose and presumptuous visionary. In order to satisfy himself he did however ask his junta of experts to examine the plan: but their opinion was that Columbus' scheme was a futile hotchpotch composed partly of the rumours that proliferated round the House of Mina and partly of reminiscences of the tales of Marco Polo.

According to the admirers of Columbus, he thought that the treasures of the Indies should be devoted to financing a new crusade to recover the Holy Sepulchre. The claims the Genoese made in the presence of King John hardly bear out this assertion. Apart from three caravels, fully equipped and laden with merchandise for barter with the people of Cipango, Columbus asked the King to knight him, appoint him admiral and grant him the title of viceroy of whatever lands he might discover, and also to award him a tenth of the revenues they might bring to the crown.

When he learned that this astounding offer had been rejected, Columbus thought it safest to set the frontier between himself and his creditors, who were now becoming threatening. In the last days of 1484, or at the beginning of 1485, he found asylum in the Franciscan monastery of Santa María de la Rábida, near the small Andalusian port of Palos, not far from the Portuguese Algarve. There he met Fr Juan Pérez de Marchena, until recently confessor to Queen Isabella, and a friend of Fr Hernando de Talavera, who had succeeded him in this office.

Three years earlier, on November 12, 1481, when the Portuguese cortes met at Évora, the third estate had urged King John, then recently proclaimed King, to show less indulgence than his late father towards the many foreigners who pullulated in Lisbon. 'Sire,' they said, 'the Florentines and Genoese have never done anything but rob this kingdom of gold and silver coin, and divulge the secrets of Mina and the islands. If they remain long in the country, they will become a scourge that will devour the land.' Presumably Columbus, before taking French leave, carefully concealed the papers he had received from his too trustful stepmother, which might well justify a charge of espionage against him. It seems equally probable, to judge by the variability of his plans, that the notes and sketches of the good Perestrelo consisted only of vague indications destitute of any real value.

The King was better informed than anyone else about the possibilities offered by sailing to the west, and the decision to exploit them rested with him alone. The calculations of the mathematicians of his junta were sufficiently exact to make it plain that the distance from Lisbon to Cipango was at least five times greater than Columbus' estimate, which Martin Behaim was to take up on his own account six or seven years later; and John realized that the lands shown to exist by the reports of his captains could not form part of Asia. Such lands were of no immediate interest to him, and he refused to squander the resources of the House of Mina in exploring them. On the contrary he intended to devote them wholly to the current series of voyages down the west coast of Africa, for he was intent on the discovery of the south-east passage which would link

Lisbon with the coast of India. This route first adopted by Prince Henry had two advantages over the western sea-passage. It was self-balancing, as people would say today, for the profits the royal treasury drew from the House of Mina sufficed to cover the expenditure required for each new jump southward. It also provided ships with the opportunity to obtain supplies, or at least fresh water, and they had the advantage of the protection of the fort at Arguim, the Castle of St George, and the way stations in the Cape Verde Islands, St Tomé and Príncipe. It may seem surprising that the careful King John should not have thought it necessary to set up other calling-points on the coastline now discovered by Cão, even though the new territories were unable to support the expense of maintaining them. There is only one answer to this objection. In King John's mind the way along the African coast from the equator onwards was of no immediate interest except insofar as it lay on the route to the tip of the continent. Once this extremity was reached the coastal route would no longer be used for sailing to India, for reasons we shall presently discuss.

In the very year in which King Afonso V entrusted his son with the supervision of the 'parts of Guinea', he also awarded on January 28, 1474, to a high official of his court, Fernão Teles de Meneses, such uninhabited islands as he might discover or cause to be discovered, provided that they were at a distance from the African coast. The King also permitted Fernão Teles to buy the Floreiras (now the islands of Flores and Corvo) far to the west of the principal group of the Azores. They had been drawn to the attention of Prince Henry by his squire Diogo de Teive in 1452. The present concession explicitly stated that the King renounced all his claims over the islands.

By a further document dated Zamora, November 10, 1475, Afonso (then at war with Spain) granted the same beneficiary the island of the Sete Cidades or Seven Cities, which the Florentine astronomer Paolo del Pozzo Toscanelli called Antilia, and placed on the east coast of Asia. Influenced by Marco Polo's hypothesis, Toscanelli greatly exaggerated the prolongation of Asia to the east, and Columbus, whose own plans were based on the astronomer's reckonings, was to commit the same error. Neither now, nor in the course of his four expeditions spread out over ten years, did he suspect the existence of a continent between the Atlantic islands and Asia.

The concession of 1474 applied only to uninhabited islands, while the second document dated a year later referred to occupied islands. Why should this distinction have been drawn unless a discovery had been made in the meantime?

On March 3, 1486, some two years after rejecting Columbus' offer, King John granted a new concession referring to the same island of the Seven Cities to Fernão d'Ulmo, captain of Terceira in the Azores. Meneses was thus excluded: unless indeed he had merely lent his name and withdrew of his own accord. Fernão d'Ulmo undertakes to organize the expedition at his own expense, it being, however, stipulated that if the conquest of the island is beyond his resources, the King shall send him ships and fighting-men to act under his orders. In the event of success Fernão d'Ulmo will be rewarded with such titles and honours as the King shall think fit: we are far from the exaggerated demands of Columbus, who has been represented as a paragon of disinterestedness!

La Rábida is sufficiently near to Lisbon for the Genoese, who always had his ear to the ground, to have heard of the contract. He was evidently kept in the picture; for in May of the same year Don Pedro González de Mendoza, Grand Chancellor of Castile, introduced him to Ferdinand and Isabella at Córdoba, and in repeating the offer that had been rejected by King John, Columbus supported his arguments with an allusion to the mission recently confided by the King of Portugal to Fernão d'Ulmo, whom he calls Fernaldomos: his Portuguese was evidently garbled.

Columbus was required to unfold his schemes before a committee of Salamancan theologians, who were as unconvinced as the junta at Lisbon, though not for mathematical reasons. They fell back on the authority of St Augustine, who declared that it was absurd to believe in the existence of antipodes, which would imply that men could walk head downwards. When the learned members of the famous university had listened to Don Cristóbal they had no hesitation in giving vent to their distrust and scorn for his views. The unhappy Columbus made his way back to La Rábida, no better off than before. What he did not know was that in the concession received by Fernão d'Ulmo, the Seven Cities were defined as '*terra firma por*

Costa', implying that King John was no longer unaware that it was in fact a continent. Who but Fernão d'Ulmo himself could have informed him of this?

King John realized that Columbus would probably sooner or later be received by Ferdinand and Isabella; they were in the habit of offering a welcome to any seamen who came from Portugal. It is quite possible even that he should cause the Genoese to be informed of the contract with Fernão d'Ulmo, at least in an abbreviated form: for the clause by which the beneficiary would in case of need receive ships and armed men was well calculated to discourage his Spanish rivals. Chastened by recent experiences on the Mina coast, Ferdinand and Isabella would hesitate to undertake such a hazardous venture. Meanwhile, John was devoting all his energies to the preparation of the expedition under Bartolomeu Dias, which was to result in the discovery of the south-east passage. He required a respite before profiting by the information he had received about the lands to the west. It appears to me that the concession granted to Fernão d'Ulmo (who was generally known to be quite incapable of equipping the two caravels required for the undertaking from his own resources) was simply a device to parry a possible attempt by his rivals. As soon as he knew that Ferdinand and Isabella had dismissed the Genoese, John dropped the whole business.

As to Fernão d'Ulmo, he made an agreement with a rich resident in Madeira, a certain João de Estreito. This contains three note-worthy clauses: the expedition would take place in 1487; it would include a 'German gentleman'; and Fernão d'Ulmo would command it for the first forty days, after which he would transfer his authority to Estreito. This last clause shows that the captain of Terceira thought that forty days would suffice for his caravels to reach the *'terra firma por Costa'* (it would take Columbus only thirty days more to get from Palos to the island of Guanahuani, his San Salvador, in the slow old Santa María). The 'German gentleman' in question is probably Martin Behaim, who was a neighbour of Fernão d'Ulmo's partner at Fayal. The plan came to nothing, and there is no indication that King John was in the least perturbed by its failure.

For the unfortunate Columbus everything had turned out amiss. Clutching at every straw, he sent his brother Bartolommeo to approach Henry VII of England; at the same time he wrote despairingly to

King John asking the monarch's permission for him to re-enter Portugal. His letter, which probably reflected his natural apprehension at the welcome he might expect from his creditors, has disappeared; but the royal reply, dated March 20, 1488, has survived. 'Given what you tell us,' says King John, 'and for other reasons wherefore your skill and talent may be useful to us, we earnestly desire that you should come hither: and as regards the securing of your own interests, everything shall be done to satisfy you.' The King of Portugal carried his amiability even to the point of pressing the Genoese to hasten his return.

Buffon remarked: 'When the marvellous is only the false which we desire to believe, it grows and develops the more heads it passes through.' This phenomena explains why Columbus' adherents are legion. They never fail to quote King John's letter as an unequivocal proof of the monarch's regard for their hero and of his regret at not having accepted Columbus' offer. But they have never succeeded in distinguishing any new factor which came into play between 1485 and 1488 and may be supposed to have caused King John to modify his first severe judgment—a judgment that was fully confirmed by the examination of the experts. On the contrary, the 'for other reasons' in the royal letter seems to imply that the far-sighted monarch preferred to have safely at hand an unpredictable individual whose persistence might lead Ferdinand and Isabella to embark on an undertaking which he, King John, intended to preserve for himself in his own good time, knowing what its result would be. In the journal of his third voyage, undertaken three years after the death of King John, Columbus, now Admiral, himself hints that the Portuguese King knew of the existence of land to the west: '. . . The Admiral again declares that he is sailing to the south, since he hopes to find lands and islands there. . . . He desires to verify the intention (the assertion) of King John of Portugal to the effect that there is a continent to the south. . . .'

Columbus states that he was present at the return of Bartolomeu Dias, which would imply that he had in fact taken advantage of the royal safe-conduct. But there is no record of his return to Portugal. It is moreover difficult to believe that if the Genoese had re-entered the kingdom John would not have given instructions to prevent his returning to Spain. His letter to Columbus involved a risk: the recipient might well use it to bolster up his credit with Ferdinand and Isabella; and we may suppose that he in fact did so.

The years that followed were those of the marriage of Afonso and Isabella, soon followed by the sad death of the young Prince. As he escorted the Princess back to Badajoz, King John suspected that the struggle with Castile and Aragon might burst out with renewed violence after the brief lull. He had certainly read the *Chronicle of Guinea* written by Gomes Eanes de Azurara on the instructions of his father, King Afonso. When he learned that on January 2, 1492, the future 'Catholic Monarchs' had conquered Granada, whose sultan, Boabdil, had trembled under his mother's fearful reproach: 'Weep! Weep like a woman for the throne you did not defend like a man!' the warning of the great King John I must have re-echoed in his memory: '. . . I am sure that the Castilians hate us, and much more so after the defeats we have inflicted upon them. The conquest of Ceuta may then well be followed by that of Granada, and at this I could not rejoice, for the increase of their domain would render us weaker to defend our own soil, and them stronger to seek revenge for their past reverses.'

Eighty years had passed since the victor of Aljubarrota had thus addressed his sons, but his warning had not lost its force. There had indeed been the treaty of the Alcáçovas, confirmed by that of Toledo; but King John was shrewd enough to know that dead treaties infect the relations of their signatories and that if they have not been denounced, they, like every other living thing, demand a struggle in defence of their existence. The Plan of the Indies required peace between the two countries. It was therefore necessary to compromise with Ferdinand and Isabella, and the only place in which territory could be given up to them without serious loss was to the west: in due course steps could be taken to limit the extent of the damage.

Eight months after the fall of Granada, on Friday, August 3, 1492, a little before daybreak, the *Santa María*, *Pinta* and *Niña* set sail from Palos on a voyage that was to become immortal. One fact will suffice to illustrate the credit Columbus enjoyed among the Spanish seamen, who knew him well, since he had dwelt among them for eight years. On the night of May 24, when the royal notary had read a letter from Ferdinand and Isabella enjoining the town of Palos under pain of a fine of ten thousand maravedis to place at Colu mbus' disposal ships with their crews paid for four months in adv ance, every vessel in the port put out to sea, and it was necessary to seize the *Pinta* by force. Owing to the urgent pleading of the good monks of La Rábida the brothers Pinzón, the shipowners of the p lace, at length lent their old *Gallega*, which became the glorious *Santa María*, and an undecked barque, the *Niña*. Only after long ch affering did Ferdinand and Isabella accept, on April 14, the exorbita nt conditions that King John had rejected. Columbus' demands now included assurances for his descendants: he would be gover nor and viceroy of the lands he discovered and would receive a tenth of the profits to be derived from them. He would also become Ad miral of the Ocean Sea. His Portuguese creditors would have been quite surprised to learn that he had undertaken to pay an eighth of the cost of the expedition from his own purse.The future admiral took care to have an Arabic interpreter on board, confidently declaring that this was the language spoken in the outlying parts of Asia he expected to reach. The rest is well known.

In the first days of March 1493, instead of going at once to report his exploit to Queen Isabella, who had supported him through thick and thin, the Genoese cast anchor in the port of Lisbon and somewhat haughtily made known his wish to be received by the King. John was at the moment resting at his palace of Val do Paraiso (the Vale of Paradise) near Santarém. On being informed, he granted an audience to the man who had left his kingdom so surreptiously and now returned to it as if in triumph.

The scene is described by Garcia de Rèsende. Columbus had lost none of his volubility, and gave a flowery description of the island he had mistaken for Japan. According to him, it contained so much gold that the natives put it to the most trivial uses. Spices, perfumes and precious stones were to be seen on all sides, and there were innumerable slaves. If only the King of Portugal had listened to him, Columbus, when there was still time!

Columbus had vainly searched Cuba and Haiti for the cities imagined by Marco Polo; but he found no houses with walls of ivory or alabaster, or roofed with tiles of gold, but only wretched huts of leaves and branches inhabited by almost naked savages. This did not disturb him: intoxicated by his own eloquence, he even went so far as to criticize the methods of the King who listened impassively to his vapouring. He went so far that one of the gentlemen present asked John in a whisper to permit him to challenge the impudent Genoese to a dual. With a wave of his hand the King bade the courtiers, now quivering with exasperation and fidgeting with the hilts of their swords, to remain calm. When the captain had finished, he gently inquired: if he had understood aright, the islands to which Columbus referred could not be far beyond the Azores: could the Admiral give an assurance that they were not in Portuguese waters? For his part, John would see to it by immediately despatching a fleet under the command of Dom Francisco de Almeida, in whom he had full confidence.

On John's instructions Columbus was escorted aboard with all the consideration due to his new rank, and even honoured with a present and supplied with clothes to cover the nakedness of the savages he had brought back. Having attended to him, early in April John sent Rui de Sande on a mission to Ferdinand and Isabella: he was to request the Catholic monarchs to forbid their subjects to fish south of Cape Bojador until such time as an agreement should have been reached on a line of demarcation, rendered necessary by their captain's discovery. The King of Portugal thought that such a line might run from east to west at the latitude of the Canaries, everything to its south being reserved to Portugal.

A glance at a map will show that such a line would pass through the middle of modern Florida, thus extinguishing Columbus' discovery. The Genoese had naturally carefully avoided supplying King John with precise information about the island he had mistaken for Cipango and baptised Hispaniola—the modern Haiti and Dominican Republic. It may be deduced that the King of Portugal already knew what he was about.

It has been stated that the natives of Haiti informed Columbus on his first voyage that 'white men with beards' had already landed on their island. Moreover, the Admiral's son, in chapter IX of his *Historia della Vita e dei Fatti di Cristoforo Colombo*, published at Venice in 1571, indicates that a pilot 'Pietro di Velasco', a native of Palos, had supplied the Genoese, during his stay at the monastery of Santa María de la Rábida, with information he had gathered while serving under the orders of Diogo de Teive, one of Prince Henry's squires. Leaving the island of Fayal in the Azores, Teive's ship had run a hundred and fifty leagues south-west and on its return had followed the flight of birds and so discovered the Floreiras. In the same year, the squire had set off again, this time to the north-west. He had reached a westerly region where, despite strong winds, the sea remained calm, and deducing that land was near, he was preparing to explore it when an oncoming storm forced him to turn back.

Columbus' death was at once followed by a lawsuit, which was fought in Seville and is known from the court-records preserved in the Archive of the Indies there. The crown of Castile and the successors of Maria Alonso Pinzón, the owner of the *Pinta*, contested the rights of the Admiral's heirs with the object of limiting the extent of the concessions awarded to the Genoese in the time of Queen Isabella. The case continued until 1564, or for over half a century.

The alcalde of Palos, Alonso Vélez, accompanied by his fellow-townsmen Alonso Gallego and Fernando Valiente, bore witness that he had known one Pero Vásquez de la Frontera, a seaman who had retired to Palos after participating in the voyages of discovery undertaken on behalf of Prince Henry. According to these three, Pero gave Columbus and the Pinzón family much information about the existence of land to the west and encouraged them to try the venture.

There is every reason to suppose that Pero Vásquez, a Portuguese subject who had crossed the frontier for reasons best known to himself, after serving under the orders of Diogo de Teive, was identical with Ferdinand Columbus' 'Pietro di Velasco'. Like his father, Ferdinand had the habit of latinizing proper names which he then translated into Italian.

Teive's expedition to the north-west goes back to the year 1452. It seems very unlikely that Prince Henry should not have taken the trouble to check the information his squire had obtained, and it appears certain that John was aware of this when in 1474 he gained access to his great-uncle's records as superintendent of the 'parts of Guinea'. It would be astonishing if so enterprising a Prince (and one so jealous of the rights of the crown) should have neglected to find out more about this 'westerly region where, despite very strong winds, the sea remained calm'.

Finally, when in 1500 the physician and geographer Master John, who accompanied Pedro Álvares Cabral, wrote to King Manoel to describe the land called Santa Cruz, which would later take a new name from the Brazil-wood so plentifully found there, he referred to a map in the possession of Pero Vaz Bisagudo, a pilot then in Portugal. 'Your Majesty,' he says, 'may see from this map where this land is to be found: *it is an ancient map: and Your Majesty will also find Mina on it.*'

I have italicized the last phrases: following the sturdy good sense attributed to M. de la Palice it seems clear that if the land that Cabral called Santa Cruz appeared on this ancient map it must have been known at least some years earlier.

King Manoel informed the Catholic monarchs of the 'discovery' newly made by Cabral in a letter dated July 29, 1501: its veiled irony doubtless did not escape the recipients. 'The land discovered by Cabral is very convenient and necessary for sailing to India, and for that reason our Lord miraculously willed that it should be found.'

In sailing to the west, Cabral was following the very precise instructions laid down by Vasco da Gama, whose fleet had also described a great westward curve in order to take advantage of the prevailing winds. These drove it much more rapidly towards the Cape of Good Hope than if it had hugged the African shore from the Cape Verde Islands and so run into the dead calms which constantly impede coastal navigation. If it is true that the pilots were, as the chronicler João de Barros writes, ignorant of the existence of this coast, which they described as a great island 'situated at a distance of 450 leagues from Guinea, to the west, and at ten degrees of altitude towards the antarctic pole', it is none the less certain that the area had been explored in 1498 by that very Duarte Pacheco Pereira whom Bartolomeu Dias had found ten years earlier sick with fever on the island of Príncipe. Duarte Pacheco was a remarkable man, at once geographer, navigator, soldier and historian, and his extraordinary conduct in the Indies (the true Indies) earned him the well-deserved epithet of 'the Portuguese Achilles'. In his *Esmeraldo de situ orbis* he has described the voyage he secretly performed that year under the King's instructions: 'From the other side of the Ocean Sea, to the west,' he says, 'there is a land with the same inclination to the sun as that of the negroes of Guinea, though the people who live there have brown skins so light that they seem white.'

We thus see why the land called Santa Cruz by Cabral appeared on a map described by Master John as 'ancient'. Its discovery seems to fall between the establishment of the castle of St George on the Guinea coast in 1482 and Pacheco's expedition sent 'beyond the greatness of the Ocean Sea' by King Manoel in 1498 to check the information received not only by himself but by his predecessor. The discussions that preceded the Treaty of Tordesillas leave no doubt that King John was aware of the existence, at least in the southern hemisphere, of the continent which would one day be called America, before Columbus undertook his famous voyage. Why should the King have maintained secrecy about the discovery and thus allowed the credit for it to go to the Genoese? This question is accounted for by the future course of events.

The Catholic monarchs had beaten their Portuguese rival by a narrow margin in the diplomatic field. When Rui de Sande arrived in Barcelona, a Spanish ambassador was delivering in Lisbon an official intimation that Columbus had discovered an island, or perhaps a continent, 'in the direction of the Indies'. However, King John's mission had one concrete result: Ferdinand and Isabella sent a new envoy to Portugal with a request that the departure of Dom Francisco's fleet should be delayed until negotiations between the two courts had been concluded. The King of Portugal acceded to this request, which coincided with his own interests, and dispatched representatives who received extremely detailed instructions.

Immediately after Columbus' return, the rulers of Spain had secretly asked Pope Alexander VI to issue a bull confirming their possession of the lands that had been discovered. Roderigo Lenzuoli Borgia could refuse Ferdinand nothing: he owed him his election to the papacy and the Aragonese bishoprics which Ferdinand had bestowed on his sons Cesare and Pedro, as well as the duchy of Gandía which had been given to the latter in April 1493. Alexander decreed that all lands discovered or to be discovered in the west towards the Indies should become the property of the Catholic monarchs. However, knowing King John's jealousy and not wishing to give him umbrage by revealing the alacrity with which he had satisfied Ferdinand, he carefully postdated the bull to May 3. He also specified that his award should apply only to lands not already in the possession of any Christian Prince.

Taking into consideration the treaty of the Alcáçovas, this reservation did not satisfy Ferdinand and Isabella. At their request, a new bull, signed in June, but antedated to May 4, was substituted for the first. This granted Spain all lands and continents discovered or to be discovered, not only to the west but also to the south, whether in the direction of the Indies or elsewhere, beyond a demarcation line running north and south a hundred leagues west of the Azores and Cape Verde Islands. The Catholic Monarchs were thus fully protected and duly informed the Portuguese representatives of the steps taken by the Sovereign Pontiff.

The Portuguese, adhering to the instructions they had received from King John, persisted in demanding that the line of demarcation should run east and west at the latitude of the Canaries. They expected to meet with a refusal, but this was strengthened when one of them most inopportunely admitted that there were rich territories opposite the African coast. Ferdinand and Isabella alluded to this unfortunate revelation in writing to Christopher Columbus on September 5, 1493: '. . . certain persons assert that what lies between the cape the Portuguese call Good Hope . . . as far as the line you say should appear in the Pope's bull may include islands and even a continent'. They therefore urged the Admiral to do all he could to accelerate the preparations for his second expedition.

They also made a new approach to Alexander VI, which resulted in a further compliance by the Pope. In a bull dated September 26, he declared that the possession of newly discovered lands must be effective in order to be valid in his eyes: all guarantees previously issued by Rome in favour of the Portuguese court were annulled, though without reference to Portugal by name, and the way to the Indies by the south-east passage was opened to Spain.

King John was left with only one means of defending the results of the efforts his countrymen had made over the past three-quarters of a century. This was war. But before having recourse to so extreme a solution, he delivered a sharp protest in Rome: what value did the Pope attach to the assurances that had been solemnly entered into, the spiritual jurisdiction conferred by Calixtus III on the Order of Christ in respect of all territories discovered by Portuguese navigators beyond Cape Não and still to be discovered 'as far as the Indies'.

John's firmness forced Ferdinand and Isabella to give way, and they proposed a compromise. After lengthy discussions this was embodied in the Treaty of Tordesillas, which provided for a line of demarcation as proposed by Alexander III, but placed it not a hundred, but 370 leagues west of the Cape Verde Islands.

It is obvious that to the mind of the Portuguese King this difference of 270 leagues was sufficient to safeguard his rights to a discovery which he had proposed to keep secret until his ships had finally touched the shores of India, following the route opened by Bartolomeu Dias. As we have seen, Cabral's pilots estimated six years later that the land of Santa Cruz lay 450 leagues from the coast of Guinea. King Manoel then officially announced the discovery because it could no longer be kept secret. The numbers of seamen and soldiers who sailed in Cabral's fleet of twelve ships were too great for there to be any chance of silencing them all.

'The land discovered by Cabral is very convenient and necessary for sailing to India,' wrote King Manoel; and these few words suffice to explain why King John refused from 1482 until 1493 to publish the discovery of what he knew to be a continent from information brought him by one of his captains whose name may never be known.

The south-east passage was one thing, and the rapidity of communications with India was another. The prevailing winds that blew across the vast lake separating the South-American continent from the African coast below the equator are so disposed that Vasco da Gama was to sail outwards from the Serra Leoa on a south-westerly course which brought his ships almost to the Brazilian coast: Cabral was subsequently instructed to follow the same route. In King's John time the possession of the terra-firma discovered in the west before Columbus' voyage was of no more than strategic interest: if his Spanish competitors had possessed a base for intercepting his fleet, the security of the sea-way to India would have been compromised. Moreover, the King would not consider building a fortress on that coast as a sort of counterpart to the castle af Mina without running the risk of warning his rivals, whose official or unofficial spies were constantly on the watch on the shores of the Tagus. Finally, as we have seen, prudence decided him not to disperse his efforts, but to concentrate them on the opening of the sea-route to Calicut.

Moreover, King John had no illusions as to the immediate profit to be expected from a savage land whose existence between Africa and Asia had been unsuspected before his own time. Seven years after his death, the Florentine Amerigo Vespucci was to declare scornfully that all he had found there was monkeys, parrots, cannibals and wild animals (among which he inadvertently included a lion, a worthy counterpart to the camel discovered by Martin Behaim on the banks of the Congo). Vespucci, however, noted that there was cassia-wood to be had, as well as a wood called 'brazil', which produced a red dye like embers (Ptg. *brasa*). But of precious metals or marketable goods, not a trace.

When Vespucci offered his services to King Manoel for the expedition which is believed to be that of 1501 (like Behaim, Vespucci indulged generously in imaginary exploits), his main object was to acquire information about the possibility of exploiting the land whose discovery had so recently been made public. But the astute Florentine did not return empty-handed. Through his daily intercourse with Portuguese officers and seamen, he had succeeded in penetrating the secrets which, under royal instructions, they were required to bury in their hearts when they returned to Portugal. Vespucci stealthily copied the precious *Regimento do Estolabio e do Quadrante*, or *Rule for the use of the Astrolabe and Quadrant*, ardently coveted by Spain and by all other foreign seamen in Portugal. The illicit possession of this invaluable document enabled its purloiner to establish the school of pilotage at Seville after delivering it to the Catholic Monarchs. Evidently the former agent of the Médici did not hand it over for nothing. By a strange irony, fate mischievously bestowed the name of America on the vast continent stretching from Cape Horn to the neighbourhood of the North Pole which had been taken for the Indies by the Genoese who had not been its first discoverer.

If the Treaty of Tordesillas had shifted the line of demarcation from one hundred to 370 leagues west of the Cape Verde Islands, the nature of these leagues had still not been settled. The matter was one of some importance, since the Portuguese league was the equivalent of 6,173 metres, while the Castilian league was only 4,177. It may be thought that the oversight was deliberate on the part of both signatories, for the treaty safeguarded the future and avoided the risk of a conflict which both Spain and Portugal equally feared. From the Portuguese point of view the 370 leagues were approximately 1,200 modern sea-miles, and the demarcation line would therefore fall almost along the 50 degrees of latitude west of Greenwich: evidently King John knew what he was about. He had plenty of reasons for distrust, and he therefore demanded that once the definition of the line had been ratified by Rome, no decision taken unilaterally by the Soveriegn Pontiff should bind either of the two contracting parties. In this way, the Pope was reduced to the role of a witness.

Quite involuntarily, Columbus made himself the ally of the King of Portugal. Despite the pressing instructions of Ferdinand and Isabella, his second voyage did not take him beyond the Lesser Antilles which lie a good ten degrees north of the equator (it is true that the reckonings made by Columbus included more than one error affecting the ten degrees, and the Admiral perhaps genuinely thought he had crossed the Line). After a short tour of Dominique, Marie-Galante, Guadeloupe, Désirade, the Saints and Puerto Rico, he again cast anchor off Haiti, the name of which, even when heard from the lips of a native, bears only the slightest resemblance to Cipangu. The Portuguese captains had often lacked interpreters, but their native shrewdness always enabled them to tell chalk from cheese. But the Admiral did not boggle at such trifles: if Ferdinand and Isabella moved heaven and earth to ensure that the demarcation line which was to fix the limits of Portuguese influence in the Atlantic should stand at a hundred leagues west of the Azores this was because Columbus had assured them with extraordinary self-confidence that beyond this distance everything was different—sky, stars and ocean. This strange, incorrigible dreamer whom psychiatrists would classify as a mythomaniac sent his archers to look for Prester John on the coast of Jamaica and thought the earth was shaped like a pear or a woman's breast with the nipple nearer the celestial vault than any other part of the world and so forming the Paradise described by Moses as Eden. This delightful region, washed by a splendid river, must, he thought, lie to the south of the province of Mangi, in the land of Cathay. The river was later identified as the Orinoco and the land it watered as Venezuela. Columbus had unknowingly lighted upon one of its fifty mouths.

As he was setting sail on his second voyage, the German Martin Behaim delivered to King John the letter in which Monetarius introduced him in such flattering terms. On the brink of a struggle with the Spanish court, the Portuguese King forgot his cares for an instant when Behaim offered to link Lisbon direct to the land of Cathay by setting his course straight for the setting sun. But his own affairs were too serious and too immediate for him to pay much attention to such fairy-tales; and the German was politely dismissed.

Monetarius came to Portugal in person in the following year. The King readily granted him an audience and listened carefully: the visitor (who probably now realized the gaffe he had made through Behaim's presumptuousness) noted that 'he asked that proofs should be produced of the assertions that were made'. In response to the King's invitation he visited the House of Mina and came away marvelling: he was even more astonished by the King's extreme unpretentiousness.

In order to explain the premature death of this great monarch, some writers have insinuated that he was removed by poisoning. But the malady that King John felt in his heart was not the work of any paid assassin: he could not tear his thoughts from the picture of his beloved son from whom he had expected so much and whom a purposeless accident had stretched lifeless on the pallet of one whom God had picked out among the humblest of his subjects. Since the death of the Prince, the King, once so full of force and vitality and so enthusiastic for work or pleasure, frequently swooned like a woman. He had renounced the idea that his son by Ana Fustado should wear the crown after him, and had accepted the succession of the Duke of Viseu who, on the death of Prince Afonso, replaced his murdered elder brother as heir to the throne. Tormented in body and soul (frequent attacks of uraemia caused him terrible pain), he nevertheless persisted in his labours until he was assured that the achievements of three generations of Kings spread over a period of seventy years would survive. At last, the time came for him to take his long rest.

'The King suffered greatly,' says Garcia de Rèsende. 'The Bishop of Tangier came to his bedside to hold forth on those pious subjects which are so profitable in such circumstances. When he spoke of the Bible, King John stopped him, saying: "Bishop, do not speak to me of the Old Testament".'

The Bishop of the Algarve was there, as was also the Bishop of Coimbra. Although he was generous and charitable, his reputation was not that of a good priest: it was said that he had never celebrated the holy office of the Mass with his own hands and paid little attention to the performance of any other religious duty. 'Bishop, the King told him, 'for your sake I bear a heavy burden with me. For the love you bear me and for God's service, promise me that you will change your course of life.' The Bishop promised, and the King took his hand as if it were a pledge.

He was asked to attach his rubric to a document containing a settlement he had decided to make in favour of Dom Jorge's mother. He dropped the quill from his fingers, and wept copiously; and when those who were present sought to comfort him, he replied: 'Do not console me, for I have been such a poor creature that I bit whenever I was baited.' Still weeping, he signed the donation, and those about him called him Your Highness, he murmured: 'Do not call me Highness for I am nothing more than a vessel of clay and worms.'

'Then Francisco da Cunha, from Terceira in the Azores, came to him and begged him for love of the five wounds of Jesus Christ to grant him a favour, for, though a gentleman, he was very poor. The King ordered a letter to be written at once granting him a pension of thirty milreis, and he signed it, bidding Francisco take the money there was in the house, since he could give him no other. When he had gone, the King said: "I can tell you now that, all my life, if I have been asked for anything in the name of the five wounds of our Saviour, I have never refused it to anyone." '

He asked them to go and look at the tide. When they told him where it stood, he said: 'In two hours hence, it will be over.' And it was so.

In his mortal agony, amidst long and deathly gasps, he said: 'I have such a bitter taste in my mouth that I can scarcely bear it.' Then the Bishop of Coimbra replied: 'Sire, think of the vinegar and gall that were offered to our Lord Jesus Christ when he was on the Cross and the taste will no longer be bitter.'

'Ah, Bishop,' replied the King, 'how grateful I am to you for telling me that! It was the only moment of his Passion that I had forgotten.'

His body trembled and stiffened so suddenly that all those about him thought that his death had come. The Bishop of Tangier closed his eyes and mouth, but the King revived and whispered: 'Bishop, the hour is not yet come.'

'Then, uttering many holy words, he bade those who were present to weep no more lest they distress him. He repeatedly kissed the face of Our Lord and the Cross, and with his eyes fixed upon it and a candle in his hand, he continued to pray, repeating verse after verse after the Bishops, with a clear understanding and all his senses intact. Then at last, with the name of Jesus on his lips, he said with great devotion: "Agnus Dei qui tollis peccata mundi, miserere me", and his soul left his flesh as the sun was about to set on Sunday, October 25th, in the year of Grace, 1495. He was forty-five years and six months old, had been married to Dona Leonor, his wife, for twenty-five years and had reigned fourteen years and two months. And having been very virtuous all his life, he finished likewise, in a manner greatly to be envied.'

The Treaty of Tordesillas, which gave Portugal her golden age, had been signed a year and four months earlier.

The Vigil

IN the chapel built in the lifetime of Prince Henry in honour of Our Lady of Bethlehem at the point where the Tagus narrows before its waters merge with the ocean, a man is praying. Around him all is darkness and silence.

Vasco da Gama has been appointed by King Manoel to crown the enterprise begun by the recluse of Sagres and pursued by two Kings. On the morrow, Saturday, July 8, 1497, his ships are to set sail for India. They are lying at anchor, almost within hailing distance, in mid-stream before the strand of the Restelo, named after an instrument used in carding flax and hemp. The chapel dedicated to Our Lady stands just above the beach.

There are four ships, the *nau capitana* or flagship, *St Gabriel*, in which Gama is accompanied by the famous Pero de Alenquer, the pilot of Bartolomeu Dias' caravel, and a brother of Dias, Diogo, who sails as 'secretary' or assistant to the captain; the *nau St Raphael*, commanded by Paulo da Gama, Vasco's brother, with João de Coimbra as pilot and João de Sá as secretary; and the *nau Bérrio*, commanded by Nicolau Coelho assisted by Álvaro de Braga, with Pero Escolar as pilot. In addition there is a supply ship laden with provisions for the other three vessels and destined to be burnt when its cargo has been used; it is commanded by a servant of Vasco de Gama called Gonçalo Nunes.

The *St Gabriel*, *St Raphael* and *Bérrio* are built of pine and cork-oak. The timber had been cut by João de Bragança on the instructions of King John, and was stored at the House of Mina in 1494, when its treasurer Fernão Lourenço was placed in charge of the building-programme. The construction of the *St Gabriel* and *St Raphael* was supervised by Bartolomeu Dias in person. The *Rutter of the voyage of Vasco da Gama* describes the *St Gabriel* as being of 120 tons, the *St Raphael* of 100 tons and the *Bérrio* of fifty. The provision ship was heavier and faster, and reached some 200 tons. According to João de Barros the crews, seamen and soldiers combined, numbered 170 souls, but Gaspar Correa raises the figure to 320.

Vasco da Gama was born some time after the middle of the century, and was now in his prime and well able to withstand the hardships and trials of the expedition. In appointing him King Manoel is generally believed to have confirmed a choice already made by King John. He was the youngest of the four sons of the late Estévão da Gama, *alcaide-mór*, or Governor, of the port of Sines, halfway between the mouth of the Tagus and Cape St Vincent: the bells of this town had been recovered at Ceuta by Prince Henry and had been used to celebrate its capture by the Christians in 1415. Vasco's family was noted for its devotion to the crown. He himself was still unmarried, and this had influenced King Manoel's choice: for the achievement of the task that lay ahead, it was best that the *capitão-mór* should have no domestic preoccupations.

Vasco is aware of his own strength and intelligence: he is firmly resolved to face every danger and he knows from experience that his will is stout and unyielding. As he probes his conscience before the altar lit with tall candles in honour of the presence of Christ's body, he is forced to confess that his natural spirit sometimes impels him to fall into the sin of pride: he is quick-tempered and inclined to violence.

The young captain in his thirties is required not merely to bring the ships under his orders to port in India and to return them safe and sound to Lisbon, and therefore to command the full confidence of all who sail in them; but he is also appointed as ambassador of the King of Portugal to Prester John and the ruler of Calicut. He must strive to establish peaceful relations with this oriental potentate, described in Pero da Covilhã's report to King John as the 'Samorim'. The Moors have for centuries enjoyed a complete monopoly of the Indian coast, and it seems certain that they will oppose the intrusion of the Portuguese with all the means at their disposal. For his part, King Manoel is determined that the intrusion shall be followed by the execution of the infidels and the destruction of their power. It will be necessary to watch every move, and Vasco da Gama will therefore have to curb his natural impulsiveness.

He has carefully locked away the letters of credence addressed by the King to the Samorim and to Prester John, and also Dom Manoel's confidential instructions. The King has not only given his orders privately to his captains, but has also addressed them publicly in order to emphasize with all due solemnity the importance of the undertaking, the more so since most of the members of his council have tried to dissuade him from it, just as, fifteen years earlier, they had pusillanimously advised King John that it was unwise and inopportune to build a fortress on the Mina coast. King Manoel therefore summoned his captains to court at the castle of Montemór and told them:

'Ever since I received with God's grace the sceptre of this kingdom of Portugal, it has been my most constant care, first to govern these realms in peace and justice, and secondly to increase the patrimony of the Portuguese crown the better to reward the good services of you all. I have considered which, of all the undertakings that have occurred to my mind, would be the most glorious and profitable to this end. In Europe we have with God's aid forced the Muslims at the point of our lances and spears to quit our soil and return to Africa, and in Africa we have conquered by main force the ports and chief towns of the kingdom of Fez. It therefore seems to me that no enterprise is more fitting to my purpose and to the profit of the kingdom than the discovery of India and the lands of the Orient.'

India . . .! For three-quarters of a century the magic word had haunted men's minds. As it passed the royal lips the whole throng started. Every Portuguese heart blazed with pride and desire, while the ambassadors thought of the accounts they would send to their masters. King Manoel continued:

'I hope that with God's aid this undertaking will permit us to proclaim and propogate the faith of Our Lord Jesus Christ in India, and that this will bring us God's divine reward and that we shall find renown and praise among men. But I hope too that we shall conquer new estates and kingdoms and so enlarge our own land by the force of our arms, as it itself has been little by little conquered and pieced together by the valour of my ancestors and yours. Since in our new discovery of Ethiopia our crown has already gained new titles and new profits, what may it not expect from a continuation of its enterprises in the midst of that oriental opulence celebrated by the writers of old, and whose commerce has given such power to Venice, Genoa, Florence and other great towns in Italy?'

The chronicler does not tell us of the reactions of the Venetians, Genoese and Florentines who were listening to this speech. The King continued:

'It seems to me then that we should be guilty of ingratitude towards God if we were to scorn what he now offers us, and that I should offend the memory of the glorious Princes whose discoveries are my heritage, and that of your ancestors who have contributed to our glory, if we were to dismiss this expedition from our thoughts. Having considered in my heart that Vasco da Gama has discharged every task with which he has been entrusted to his own honour and mine also, I have chosen him as a loyal vassal and a brave knight to carry out this difficult mission. May he and all those who go with him win honour and glory: I have chosen them because I have faith in their loyalty, mindful of the services they have already performed. I bid them obey their captain in all things.'

Turning towards the *capitão-mór*, King Manoel declared:

'I recommend them all to you, Vasco da Gama, as I have recommended you to them. And I pray God to give you all as your constant companions peace and concord that are such powerful allies against all sorts of danger and able to lighten the heaviest cares.'

Then Gama advanced towards the throne. Kneeling, he kissed the King's hand, and was at once imitated by all his chief followers. Then amidst a general stillness, he returned to King Manoel and knelt again at his feet while an official of the royal household unfurled before him a silk standard bearing the cross of the Knights of the Order of Christ, of which the King was commander and administrator.

'I, Vasco da Gama,' he said, 'who now go to discover the lands and seas of the orient in obedience to thy commands, most high and mighty King, do swear by the sign of this Cross on which I place my hand that in God's service and thine own I shall always bear this standard unfurled, and never folded, before Moors or Gentiles or what peoples soever I shall chance to meet. And I swear also, that through all perils, whether by water or by fire or steel I shall always preserve this Cross and defend it to the death. And I swear likewise that I shall serve thee with loyalty, vigilance, courage and faith in this enterprise of discovery with which thou has entrusted me, in obedience to thy will and commands, and shall so do until the day when, if God pleases, I shall again appear in thy presence.'

Dom Manoel then took the standard and delivered it to Gama with his own hands. He then entrusted him with his letters of credence and his written instructions, together with a copy of all the information King John had obtained about those distant lands. The *capitão-mór* then took leave of the Prince and set off with the officers of his fleet for Lisbon.

At Belém they were all kneeling at his side: Paulo da Gama, his brother, with Nicolau Coelho and Gonçalo Nunes, his other captains and their pilots, Pero de Alenquer, João de Coimbra, Pero Escolar, Afonso Gonçalves; and likewise the 'secretaries' Diogo Dias, João de Sá and Álvaro de Braga. Bartolomeu Dias was also there, for his caravel was to leave with the fleet on its way to the castle of St George. Their eyes were fixed on the standard hanging before the altar to receive the protection of the Holy Virgin Mary and her divine son. As they prayed, they laid their pride, their fears and their hopes at the feet of her whose name means in Hebrew 'Star of the Sea'.

The glass in the windows lightened, and the flames of the candles grew yellow. A religious of the Order of Christ, one of those brought by King Henry from the convent at Tomar to be ever ready to administer the sacraments to departing sailors, mounted the altar and celebrated the divine sacrifice. Gama and all his captains, officers and pilots took Communion. They all understood that henceforth all formed part of one body.

That July 8, 1497, was a feast consecrated to the Virgin. As the *capitão-mór* and his companions left the chapel, they paused for a moment, dazzled by the sight of the immense throng which even at that early hour covered the strand. There were the wives, children, families and friends of all those who were about to depart. There came, too, men, women and children, all anxious to do honour to the seamen and soldiers and their leaders. The four ships waited motionless in the stream, their sails still lifeless, their rigging gay with brightly coloured flags fluttering in the sun. Their crews were lined in silence on the decks.

From all the neighbouring parishes and the near-by convents and monasteries, priests and religious had gathered in great numbers to join those of the Order of Christ and add their prayers to those just uttered before the altar of Our Lady of Belém. The force of these prayers was such that it held the great crowd assembled on the beach bound as by an invisible net that held it motionless and expectant. Then suddenly its thousands upon thousands of mouths breathed a single sigh as a tall silver cross, followed by the monks, appeared in the door of the sanctuary. Behind them, the *capitão-mór* advanced alone, holding a lighted candle like those placed in the hands of dying men. His captains and the chief men of his fleet followed a few paces behind, each also holding a candle. As the Cross came forward, those on either side fell to their knees, then rose to join the procession. The priests chanted the litany of the saints:

> Kyrie, eleison!
> Christe, eleison!
> Kyrie, eleison!
> Christe, audi nos!
> Christe, exaudi nos!

'Miserere nobis!' cried the throng, responding to the invocations. 'Miserere, Santa Maria! Miserere, Sancte Gabriel! Miserere, Sancte Raphael!'

'So,' says João de Barros, 'they advanced to the small boats that were to carry Vasco da Gama and his men to their ships. Now there was a great silence, and everyone knelt while the vicar of the hermitage recited aloud the general confession. He then gave Absolution to those who were about to leave, according to the bulls granted long before by the Holy See to Prince Henry in favour of all those who might die in the course of these discoveries and conquests. Then many tears were shed. . . .'

For long after the Restelo was known as the Beach of Tears. When the sails were unfurled and the seamen cried, according to custom: 'Fare well! Fare well!' all who were present wept copiously.

In his *Lusiads* Luis de Camões has described the despair of mothers, wives and sisters. 'Oh, my son, you were all I had: you were my only consolation, the tender support of my declining years and my failing strength, now ebbing with the bitter tears of my despair. Oh, my beloved son, why do you abandon your sorrowful and grieving mother? Why do you go so far away on the cruel ocean that will be your shroud, where the fishes will devour your poor body?'

The poet tells us that these plaints were mingled with the imprecations of an old man, addressed to the seamen: 'You who go so far in search of foes to fight, why do you not turn against the enemy that rages at your gates? In your eagerness to win fame and the titles it brings you, Lord of India, Persia, Arabia, Ethiopia, you go to face unknown perils, and your ancient kingdom is depopulated, weakened and ruined. . . . May heaven curse the man who first launched timber on the sea and first unfurled a sail!'

❦ 13 ❦

Adamastor

PRESSED on by favourable winds, the five ships sighted the Canaries on July 15. On the following day, they stood off the Terra Alta, a foreland on the African coast not far from Cape Não, first discovered some eighty years earlier by Gonçalo Velho. A thick fog then suddenly descended on the face of the sea, and in it each ship lost sight of its nearest neighbour and the fleet was dispersed. A similar fog is described by Admiral Jurien de la Gravière.

It was only on the 23rd that the watch on board the *St Raphael* discerned three sails on the horizon, and Paulo da Gama recognized the *Bérrio*, Bartolomeu Dias' caravel and Gonçalo Nunes' supply-ship. Three days later the whole fleet was reunited at its arranged meeting place, the island of Santiago in the Cape Verdes.

This happy event was celebrated with music and with round upon round of cannon-fire. After taking on fresh water and provisions and making the necessary adjustments and repairs, Gama ordered his fleet to sea again on August 3. Off the Gulf of Guinea, Dias saluted the *capitão-mór* and parted from the rest of the ships to follow the course for Mina, while Gama began to sail out on the vast arc which would take him far to the south-west and bring him to within sight of the Cape of Good Hope, according to the calculations of the royal Junta. After sailing for eighty-three days without sight of land, his crew saw a great quantity of weed floating on the surface of the sea. Three days later, on November 7, Vasco cast anchor in a bay he called St Helena, a name it still retains.

On the following day he went ashore to take his bearings, for the ships were tossing and rolling and he could not be sure of his reckoning on board. By taking the line of the sun and measuring the elevation of the star, he calculated that he was only thirty leagues

short of the cape discovered by Dias. The Portuguese sea-league was
then 6,173 metres and subsequent events showed that Gama's error
was no more than two leagues: such a result was a real feat of
navigation and a proof of seamanship.

On the 7th Gama had sent Nicolau Coelho in search of a river

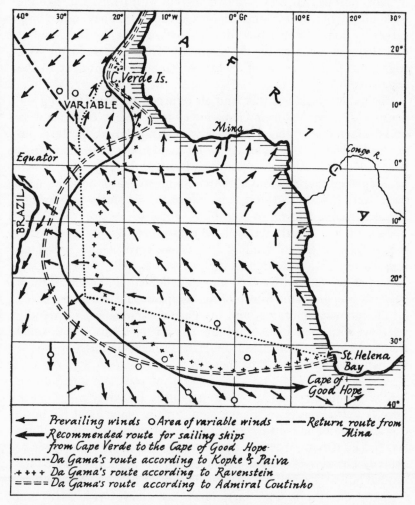

Fig. 15. Vasco da Gama's route from the island of Santiago to St Helena
Bay (according to Admiral Gago Coutinho's map)

mouth. He found a 'stream of sweet fresh water' which he called Santiago. He brought back fire-wood for cooking food and supplies of meat from 'sea-wolves as big as horses'.

While Gama was carrying out his calculations, his captains and some of the crew walked 'in little groups in each direction', Damião de Gois tells us that they saw two negroes with frizzy hair, like the men of Guinea, but rather lighter in colour. They were busy gathering honey, which they did by smoking out the hive, and at first they did not perceive the strangers. Then they suddenly took fright and fled, but one of them was caught and brought to the *capitão-mór*.

'He was very glad at this, and all returned on board, taking the negro with them. Vasco da Gama hoped to be able to converse with him through one of the interpreters who was on board, but he could not find anyone in the whole fleet who could understand the negro's language, and it was only possible to talk with him by signs. When he discovered that they did not intend him any harm, he showed no more fear, and ate and drank heartily with two ship's-boys whom Vasco da Gama told off to keep him company.'

The sun had already set, and the negro spent the night on board the *St Gabriel*. Before sending him ashore again, Gama presented him with brightly-coloured clothes, as well as bells, pieces of glass and other trinkets, with which he was delighted. The sight of these presents brought some fifteen of his companions down to the beach on the following morning, and the Portuguese established friendly relations with the natives until one day one of Gama's men called Fernão Veloso (or Ferdinand the Hairy) sought permission to visit the native village to see how they lived.

'The negroes had found a sea-lion on the way, and killed it and held a banquet in honour of the stranger. But during the meal, Fernão Veloso regretted his decision, for the manners of his hosts displeased him, and their cooking no less. He got up and made his way backward towards the place where the ships were lying at anchor. The natives were disappointed by his departure, since they wanted him to stay and be feasted at leisure, and they went with him, bringing out the young warriors of the village with darts and assegais ending in points of horn or bone, capable of wounding just as cruelly as if they were of tempered steel. This alarmed Veloso, and as soon as he was in sight of the ships, he began to shout for help. As he was a great braggart, very inclined to boast of his own doings, no one was in a great hurry to respond, especially as they saw that the negroes surrounding him were doing him no harm. Vasco da Gama was informed of the incident while he was at table; he decided to go ashore, and ordered his captains to accompany him with some of their men.'

The incident now took an unpleasant turn. When the negroes saw the rowing-boats putting out from the ships, they took fright and scattered. But scarcely had Gama landed when he found himself suddenly surrounded by hostile natives. In the ensuing skirmish the *capitão-mór* and three of his men were wounded.

Camões describes how the boastful Veloso was greeted by the jibes of his comrades as he went aboard.

'You came down that hill faster than you went up, Fernão!' shouted one of them.

The braggart was not put out.

'So I did,' he retorted, 'there were so many of those dogs there that I thought you would need a hand, and put my best foot forward.'

On November 10, Gama sailed on, taking advantage of a fresh south-west trade-wind. Forty-eight hours later, he sighted the Cape of Good Hope.

There the poet of the *Lusiads* described the appearance of a monstrous giant:

> . . . a form appeared, high in the air, filled with prevailing might.
> The face was heavy, with a squalid beard.
> Misshaped he was, but of enormous height.
> Hollow the eyes, and bad and to be feared
> The gesture, and the colour earthen-white,
> And, thick with clay, the lank hair twisted hangs.
> And the mouth was black and full of yellow fangs.
>
> And the voice seemed to thunder from the sea,
> As he spoke thickly with a ghostly sound.
> Our hair stood up on end, our flesh went cold,
> Only to hear the monster, and behold.[1]

[1] The Lusiads, V. 39, 40: Leonard Bacon's translation.

Camões' monstrous Adamastor thus represents the spirit of the place, which in the mind of Dias and his men, was still the Cape of Storms. As if to justify its reputation, a tempest now rose, and the ancient legends that had once instilled fear in Prince Henry's sailors filled the hearts of Gama's men. The men began to complain: they had been deceived, there was no passage to the east, behind that shore lay the end of the world and the beginning of nothingness.

Fleeing before the storm, Gama sailed out to sea, leaving the cape behind and assuring his frightened crew that it would soon be passed.

'He did not sleep or rest,' writes Gaspar Corrae. 'Sustaining his men by his own words and example, he was always by their side as they worked, and obeyed the boatswain's whistle like the least of them, repeating that none had any right to complain of weariness, for they had all known the difficulties of the voyage when they left. If their hope and their trust in God were strong enough, the Cape would soon be rounded. . . .'

The storm brought the ships together again. In the fog that lay over the surface of the sea, the short daylight hours were no more than a dull lightening that soon gave way once more to darkness. Under the stress of the wind, the masts creaked and groaned with all sails set, while the sea unleashed such fury that the ships seemed liable at every instant to break under the weight of the enormous waves.

'Sick with fear and weariness, and starving for lack of food, for it was impossible to prepare anything, the men shouted that they must return to Portugal, for they were not among those sinners who put an end to their own lives. On the other ships the clamour was even louder than on the *St Gabriel*, but the captains refused to alter their course and said that they would obey Gama in everything. He himself devoted his every effort to pacifying his crew. Alternatively mild and stern, he sometimes gave way to anger, and silenced the men with harsh words. In his heart he forgave them, for he understood that the poor wretches feared that they were going to their doom. The hulks were letting water on all sides, and the labour of the pumps was exhausting. The length of the nights and the darkness of the air added to their despair, and they were frequently numbed with icy showers. They had no more hope of saving their souls as they muttered pitiful pleas to heaven, beseeching God to save their souls.'

There was no question of taking bearings in this wild sea and constant darkness, and when the *capitão-mór* supposed that he had left the Cape of Good Hope behind, he altered course 'swearing that, if the Cape had not yet been passed, he would turn back towards the high seas, and would continue to repeat the process until he had succeeded, and that no will on earth should be strong enough to break his own.'

The storm at last abated. The *St Raphael*, *Bérrio* and Nunes' supply-ship followed the *St Gabriel's* stern lantern, and signalled to one another with lights. They all thanked God for having delivered them from the jaws of death. On the 24th they saw on the west mountains so high that their peaks seemed to touch the sky. They fell on their knees, weeping tears of joy and the crews recited the *Salve Regina*. At mid-day on November 25 the shore could be seen. The sea was filled with such a multitude of fish that they could be speared, and the men flung themselves on their food with such voracity that a number of them were taken seriously ill. The ships cast anchor in the bay Dias had called Baia dos Vaqueiros and Angra de São Brás. Here Gama had the supply-ship destroyed since it was no longer needed.

The black herdsmen were this time less timid, and even exchanged a good number of their cattle for bells and pieces of glass. The crews thus enjoyed excellent meat, though the animals were draught-oxen and carried on their necks 'yokes like Castilian yokes made of wood'. Sheep, 'very large and fat', were obtained in the same way, but the men took care not to go too close to the 'very great elephants' that were seen wandering across the veldt. Gaspar Corrêa tells us that Gama's seamen discovered on a near-by island more than 'three thousand sea-lions, so fierce that they attacked men like bulls'. Gama had on board a dozen convicts who had been sentenced to death and had obtained reprieves by volunteering to perform the most dangerous tasks on the expedition. Two of them were now sent by the *capitão-mór* to study the habits of the natives, with orders to remain with them until the fleet should return from India. The ships put to sea again on the feast of the Immaculate Conception, on December 8, 1497.

'As soon as they were at sea, they continued to follow the coast with great patience, fearing its reefs and sand banks. They entered the mouths of other rivers and bays, but they found no men. They were faced with many difficulties and great hardships in entering and leaving the rivers, and grew desperate because they no longer knew where they were. Since they saw nothing but a desert of rocks with no living soul on shore and no ship on the sea, they resolved to leave the estuaries and pursue their voyage along the coast, putting on all sail during the day and keeping as close in shore as they dared in the hope of discerning signs of human life. At night, they sailed out to sea under half-sail. The breeze on which they had come gradually died down, and the new wind forced them out of sight of shore, for they were afraid a cross-wind might take them by surprise. The sea began to swell, and a storm rose. . . .'

The sea grew so rough that Gama could no longer think of approaching the shore for fear of being cast on the rocks. Moreover the ships suffered severely from the constant buffeting they received. Pero de Alenquer and his boatswain Gonçalo Álvares went to speak with the *capitão-mór*. In the opinion of this most skilled of all the pilots, the *naus* could not long withstand this treatment. The flagship was making water on all sides, and the men were already exhausted and too few to man the pumps. The state of affairs on the *St Raphael* and *Bérrio* was probably no better. To avoid disaster it was necessary to seek shelter in the mouth of the large river they had already entered. The wind was favourable, and Pero was sure that he could safely negotiate the bar.

But the mouth of the great river lay behind them, and Gama understood their meaning. He sharply replied that he had made God a promise, in his heart of hearts, that he would not turn back a single cubit. He told the two men that the first who proposed to turn back would be thrown overboard on his orders.

They bowed their heads and withdrew without pressing the point. While the violence of the storm grew hourly greater, the fleet sailed on. The squalls of wind were followed by sudden calms, which were even more dangerous to the ships, which were deprived of the help of their sails and tossed like corks on the monstrous waves with every beam creaking. The men feared momentarily to be flung into the ocean and cried in terror to heaven, begging the *capitão-mór* to return. But, says Corrêa, Vasco da Gama answered their clamour with 'stormy and harsh words'.

'He had already told them that he would not return by a single cubits' length, even if death itself appeared a hundred times before their eyes, for he had promised Our Lord this. He, Vasco da Gama, would not allow them to lose all they had gained thus far through weakness or lack of faith. He ordered them to remember that the Cape had been rounded, and that they would soon reach the land of India they had come to discover.'

'If you have faith in God,' he cried, 'the storm will soon die down.'

As if heaven had heard him, there followed a calm, and the ships could come within shouting distance. But that was even worse.

'You captains,' cried the men, 'you are only one on each ship, but we are many! You may despise death, but we don't want to die! You will have to account to God for each one of us, and for the lives of our wives and children at home!'

In order that his captains should know his intentions, Vasco da Gama shouted to them: 'By the life of King Manoel, my sovereign, I should not turn back even if the three ships under my charge were suddenly laden with gold, until I have reached harbour in the land I am to report to the King. Understand that I should not attempt to sail towards the shore even if I were sure of finding shelter. I want my men to prove that they have a true faith in the mercy of Our Lord Jesus Christ! If they have no such faith, I can hardly believe that they are true Portuguese.'

He had not finished speaking when there was a great crash of thunder, followed by a long gust of wind. The sky grew as black as ink, and the day seemed to turn to night. The sea opened and its waves reared so high that the decks of the ships could scarcely be seen except when they were carried on the wave-crests and were thrown so high that they seemed to be touching the sky.

The men were determined to rebel against their captains and sail for home, saying that they could throw themselves at the King's feet and beg his mercy. They said too that if the King condemned them they would rather die in their own country among those they loved than be eaten by the fishes of this accursed sea. Perhaps the King would not have them all hanged together, and some might flee to Castile and await a pardon there. . . .

'They were so filled with such thoughts,' Corrêa says, 'that they forgot the mortal peril that threatened them on every side.'

Among the crew of the *Bérrio* were two brothers, one of whom had been brought up by the same foster-mother as the son of Nicolau Coelho. The other forewarned him of the plot that was being prepared: in order to achieve their ends, the men had decided to seize the captain and put him in irons. Coelho was warned and took steps to defend himself, determined to die rather than suffer arrest. As a gust of wind brought the ships together, he hailed the *St Gabriel* and asked to speak to the *capitão-mór*. In the hearing of his whole crew, he urged Gama to change his course and seek shelter in shore.

'Even if we do not desire it,' he said, 'we must think of our men who are clamouring for it. We cannot continue to flout their will, or they will end by clapping us in irons and do whatever they think fit in the interests of their own safety. If we ignore their demands, we shall have to face the worst! For my part, I am determined to give them their way, for I won't burden my conscience with the consequences if I refuse.'

Gama was sure of Nicolau's loyalty and courage, and realized that he had chosen this method of warning him of the danger that hung over them all, simply because it was impossible to inform him privately. He remembered how Bartolomeu Dias had acted in a similar case, though the circumstances on that occasion were far less dramatic, and he therefore had all the men summoned to appear before him.

'I am as afraid of death as you are,' he told them, 'and I am not so hard of heart as not to be touched by your tears. We shall go and seek shelter then as you wish. But I shall have to justify my conduct to the King, and you must each sign the paper I shall draw up.'

'Heaven's mercy is on us! It has touched the captain's heart!' cried one of the seamen. His companions raised their hands to heaven, and declared their willingness to sign.

'I shall not require every man to sign,' replied Gama. 'Which of you know most of seamanship?'

The pilot and the boatswain at once picked out three men. Then, says Corrêa, Vasco da Gama withdrew to his cabin and ordered his servants to stand at the door, taking his secretary, Diogo Dias, and the three seamen inside with him. When the documents had been drawn up and signed, he took the men into a closet under his cabin,

together with the secretary, and gave orders for the pilot and boatswain to be called, telling them that they too must come down to read
and sign what had been written. As they entered Gama's cabin, he
had them seized and put in irons by his faithful servants. When they
were all at his mercy, he had the pilot and boatswain locked away
in the hold, and brought out the three seamen loaded with irons.
He then gathered the whole crew, and ordered the prisoners to hand
over all the instruments in their possession, threatening to hang
them if they disobeyed. They were stricken with terror, and delivered all the nautical equipment they had. Vasco da Gama seized it
all and threw it overboard in full sight of the whole crew.

'Consider, men!' he told them, 'You have no longer any pilot, or
boatswain, or anyone who can show you your course, for the men
who promised to sail you back to Portugal are now locked away.
I know you have plotted in secret to betray your captains and return
to Portugal. But as you have seen, all the instruments are at the
bottom of the sea. As for myself, I need no pilot, no boatswain, no
one who knows how to navigate. God alone will be my pilot and my
boatswain. He will lead us and save us by his divine mercy, if we are
worthy of it. If we are not, let his will be done! I have recommended
you to him. From today on let no one ask me to put in to shore! I tell
you that if I do not find what I have come for, I shall never go back
to face the King.'

Eminent historians have refused to admit the existence of the
mutiny described by Gaspar Corrêa, thinking it incredible that
Gama should deliberately have destroyed the instruments necessary
for the execution of his mission. Moreover, the *Rutter*, or log of the
journey, contains no reference to this attempted mutiny, or even to
any expression of hostility on the part of the crews.

'Who proves too much proves nothing,' says the proverb. We
might reply that it seems surprising, given the conditions in which
these men were living at sea and the spirit of the times, the back-
ground of terrifying legends, the hardships undergone and the
natural fears of the men in the face of an unknown world, that there
should be no record of any sign of trouble or any act of indiscipline
on board the *St Gabriel*, *St Raphael* or *Bérrio*. 'Success without
danger is triumph without glory': where would be the men of the
courage of Gama's men if they had not had to overcome fear? There

is no denying that Dias was forced to give way to his crews, whose fears as they entered an unknown sea without any immediate danger to his ships, the *St Christopher* and *St Pantaleão*, were far less justifiable than the terror produced in Gama's men by the fearful hurricane they had just experienced. We agree that he would never have left himself without astrolabe or quadrant, but Gaspar Corrêa does not say that he threw overboard the instruments with which he took his bearings in St Helen's Bay; and he was later to display to the 'pilot of Malindi' the great wooden astrolabe, and others of metal which he used for reckoning the height of the sun. Corrêa, who never omits a detail, would not have failed to tell us if these instruments had been stolen from him: those thrown overboard in this theatrical gesture were evidently not his own.

If one goes so far as to assume that no astrolabe or quadrant was left on board the *St Gabriel*, and that (against all probability) neither Paulo da Gama and Nicolau Coelho possessed a single set of these indispensable instruments, Gama might still have had the equipment used by Gonçalo Nunes before the destruction of the supply-ship, from which everything of future use was salvaged.

Gaspar Corrêa was a soldier, and a man of such honesty and loyalty that the great Afonso de Albuquerque, who was a good judge of men, made him his secretary. His intellectual honesty appears in every line, and it seems improbable that one who writes' . . . as to the events I have not myself witnessed, I have sought with great care to ascertain the truth by asking those who have themselves been witnesses, men who formed part of the crew of Vasco da Gama and others . . . ' and who also used the daily notes set down by a priest João Figueira, who was on board the *St Gabriel*, should have concocted an episode which he must have regarded as in some ways likely to strike an unpleasant note in the epic he was recounting.

We may say finally that the details of the narrative would suffice by their tone to persuade us of their truth, especially when they show Vasco da Gama's strange obstinacy in humiliating the pilot and boatswain. Evidently the *capitão-mór* had over-riding reasons for his treatment of them, and to these we shall return. But if we examine closely his portrait in the Lisbon Geographical Society or even the milder picture made twenty-five years later when he became Viceroy of India, we shall scarcely be surprised at it. In his eye, in the deep line between his brows, in his thin-lipped and determined mouth, and in his whole expression with its air of strong-willed pride, we can discern a man who may be capable of mercy (and will show forgiveness in order to gratify his King) but who never forgets an injury and must always struggle with his own nature to overcome his vindictiveness.

There was in fact no actual mutiny, though the discontent of the men might have produced one if Gama had not acted as he did at the critical moment, and in a manner which commands praise, even in his device to strike the imagination of the seamen by convincing his hearers that the *St Gabriel* was thereafter deprived of all means of navigation. The circumstances were quite different from those which had forced Dias to come to terms with his officers: the *capitão-mór* was certain of the absolute devotion of his brother and Nicolau Coelho.

Moreover Dias might well consider that the essential part of the mission confided to him by King John had been accomplished when he had discovered the south-east passage, while Gama, if he had given way to prayers or threats, would have had to bear the responsibility for a great failure. The solemnities amidst which the expedition had taken its departure would have redounded to the discredit of the King and the whole country, and the repercussions of a defeat would have reached the very shores of India itself. King Manoel would not have been able to attempt another undertaking of the kind for several years, and others would not have failed to seize the opportunity to snatch from Portugal the fruit of hardships and sacrifices borne for over a century. Gama was right in asserting: 'If I do not find what I have come for, I shall never go back to face the King.' It would have been impossible for his ships to cast anchor in the Tagus where, five years earlier, the Genoese Christopher Columbus had proudly strutted on returning from his first voyage, unless they brought with them the news of the discovery of India. When he thanked King Manoel for having picked him for the command, Vasco da Gama was fully aware of the terrible dilemma he had placed himself in by accepting and which had presented itself to him with terrible simplicity as he performed his vigil at Our Lady of Belém: either he would bring back the trophy of India for his King, or he would remain forever at sea, until his ships were, one after another, engulfed in eternity.

❧ 14 ❧

Mozambique

WHEN as he faced his crew, he saw the three prisoners fall to their knees, Gama knew that he had won and that India lay already within his grasp.

All the crew of the *St Gabriel* followed the example of their captive companions. Kneeling on the deck, they clamoured for the captain's forgiveness. The three men confessed that they had planned to seize him, and to take refuge off a lee shore until the weather should improve. They admitted naïvely that they had not meant to kill their captain, but only to take him captive to the King in order to prove that he had opposed their demands. They had arranged that the seamen on the other ships should follow their example, and confessed that they had behaved like traitors and deserved death. But, they said in the simplicity of their hearts, since God had willed that their treachery should be discovered before it bore fruit, they begged the *capitão-mór's* pardon, and begged him not to leave the pilot and boatswain in the hold where they would surely perish.

Gama had the two men brought before him and gave orders that they should be taken to their quarters still in irons. He told them that he did this solely because the entreaties of the crew had moved him to pity, for he had no need of their nautical skill and even forbade them to intervene in the navigation: all they were permitted to do was to give orders for the setting of the sails and the general working of the ship.

Coming up to the *Bérrio*, Gama informed Coelho of what had happened on his ship, and also told his brother Paulo on the *St Raphael*. This sufficed to induce the crew of each ship to swear before its respective captain that they would follow the flagship wherever it went. Sure of himself and of his authority as leader, Gama did not wait for a reply. He was already far ahead, and his *St Gabriel* was leading the way for the other two ships.

He was well aware that Pero de Alenquer and Gonçalo Anes were telling no more than the truth when they painted so black a picture of the state of the ship. It was leaking dangerously, and the exhausted crew were kept toiling night and day at the pumps. Many of the water casks had been smashed or washed overboard in the storm, and the half-spoiled supplies had to be cooked in sea-water. Since all their vegetables were gone, and their biscuit was rotten, this did their health no good. Gama was well aware of all this, and had resolved to put in to shore as soon as the wind and sea abated. But he intended to make the decision of his own free will, at the day and time he desired: otherwise he would have seemed to give way to the urgings of his men, and his authority would have vanished.

God heard the moving prayers of these poor wretches, who in their utter exhaustion humbly besought him to let them behold the land once more before they died. The wind dropped: they crowded all sail, and soon some islands came into view. They were the same that Dias had seen at the end of his voyage ten years before. Because of the strong currents which drove the ships first forward and then back, the crew did not see the pillar of the Holy Cross barely five leagues away from them. On Christmas Day they discovered a coast which they called Natal, but they did not land. At Epiphany they found a river which they gave the name of Rio dos Reis, but some said it was the 'Copper River', for the *capitão-mór* bartered some of his goods for a quantity of metal there. They also obtained some ivory, and above all, fresh water and fruit. The natives proved friendly, and Gama bestowed on this coast the name of Terra de Boa Gente, 'the Land of Good Folk'.

The *Bérrio* had gone forward to explore; and the *St Gabriel* sailed on and in the night passed the Cape later called Corrientes, the Cape of Currents, where there now stands the Portuguese town of Inhambane. Beyond it lies a broad bay, but Gama did not dare to enter it lest the currents should prevent him from coming out. 'Because of this fear he sailed far out to sea, and passed clear of Sofala, a town very famous in those parts for the great quantity of gold which the Moors obtain by trafficking with the negroes there', according to João de Barros. 'Gama learned of this only later.'

It will be recalled that in the letter to King John entrusted to the care of the Jew José of Lamego, Pero de Covilhã had reported that it was easy to approach the coast of India from the port of Sofala. According to Gaspar Corrêa, the King of the place allowed no one to appear before him unless they brought a present, even if it were no more than a lemon. The *capitão-mór* did not make the acquaintance of this insistent monarch until his second voyage, when he had been newly appointed Admiral of the Indian Sea. Fifty leagues further on, Gama saw boats with sails made of plaited palm-leaves entering a great river, and he followed them with his fleet. This was the Cuama or Zambeze which enters the Mozambique Channel through four principal mouths. Nicolau Coelho had reached it in the *Bérrio* the day before, January 24, 1498.

'What the Portuguese discovered on its shores restored their hopes. Of this indeed they were sorely in need, for they were weary and depressed after sailing for so long and finding nothing but negroes as savage as those of Guinea. Among the people here, most of whom had frizzy hair, there were also mulattoes, doubtless the children of Arabs and negroes. Some of these understood Arabic, when one of our seamen spoke to them in that language, but none of us could understand the language they spoke among one another.'

The presence of these half-breeds revived Gama's expectations. It seemed highly probable that these negroes, like the Jaloffs who intermarried with the Azenegues in West Africa, were in touch with the Moors. They almost all wore loin-cloths of blue cotton, but some had loin-cloths and turbans of silk, or pointed caps of camlet, a textile of hair or wool mingled with silk. Delighted by these tokens and by the statements of the natives that they had seen other white people sailing in ships like his own towards the east, Gama called this the river of Bons Sinais, or Good Signs. He now felt secure among people who readily supplied food in exchange for the wares he had brought.

But here, too, the first cases of scurvy occurred. The victims suffered from greatly swollen feet and hands, and their gums grew so painful that they could not touch food. Many of the unfortunate soldiers and sailors succumbed to the disease: they had indeed many excuses for their attempt at mutiny against their leaders.

Paulo da Gama displayed great kindness towards the sick, he often visited them and gave them medicines he had brought for his own use. He also begged his brother to set Pero de Alenquer and Gonçalo Anes free; and Gama agreed to do so, though he warned them that they would have to appear in chains before the King on their return to Lisbon, so that King Manoel should realize the difficulties he had had to overcome. This action does not show the commander's character in a very agreeable light, but there is nothing to suggest that those concerned were at all shocked by it. 'All were agreed,' Corrêa briefly remarks.

In order to avoid any unpleasant surprise, Gama and his captains decided that, in spite of the friendly attitude of the natives, it would be best to scrape the sides of the ships and carry out the necessary repairs at sea.

'They unloaded the flagship and placed its contents in Paulo da Gama's ship. Then they moved all the heavy ballast under the *St Gabriel's* deck to one side and thus made her lean over at an angle. By fastening hawsers to the top of the main tree, they contrived to bring her so far over that her keel was bared. Planks were hung down her side, and everyone set to work scraping shellfish and seaweed from the side or pulling rotten tow out of the seams and replacing it with fresh and sealing it with pitch melted over a brazier in a rowing boat. The captains stayed with the men day and night, and supplied them with food and drink. They were all in such good heart and worked with such a will that in a day and a night that side of the ship was done.'

When the whole task was completed, Gama had a hole dug in the rock at the mouth of the river. Of the pillars he had brought, he decided to erect the one named after St Raphael at this spot. Two shields were cut in the stone, one bearing the royal arms and the other the inscription: 'Under the dominion of Portugal, land of Christians'. Two convicts remained with the same mission as those left at the Baia dos Vaqueiros, and they soon saw the sails of the fleet disappear below the horizon.

'Vasco da Gama was content with the way in which all the seamen had worked, as well as the boatswains and pilots, especially his own, although he had put them in irons, and he assembled them all on deck as they left. In a speech, he bade them never again allow their hearts to give way to fear or weakness so as not to fall back into the error from which he had saved them. Treachery, he told them, was a thing so repugnant in the sight of God that it always held the threat of a miserable end. He understood that their error came from mere weakness, and for that reason he pardoned them. . . .'

Since God had been willing to save them from such grave dangers, he said, they must all be prepared to entrust themselves to his divine mercy, being sure that he would lead them to their due end, for which they would receive great rewards from the King, and likewise great honour when they returned to their own country. He, Gama, would report to the King the good services they had rendered and the great hardships they had courageously borne. What a wonderful day that would be for them all!

The men were stirred by his speech and wept for joy. They cried: 'Amen, amen so be it the will of Our Lord Jesus Christ!'

One might have expected, as they did, that the *capitão-mór* had renounced his grim intention of bringing his pilot and boatswain before King Manoel in chains, but this was not so. Gama's character was firm to the point of obstinacy.

Soon after the three ships had left the mouth of the river where they had spent a full month and were continuing their way with the help of a fresh wind, the watch saw a sail coming in from the open sea, and everyone rejoiced. Since the fleet had lost sight of Bartolomeu Dias' caravel, this was the first time that such a thing had happened. Officers and men thanked God devoutly for having guided them to this spot, but they were shortly after disappointed to find that the unknown ship had tacked and disappeared in the closing darkness.

During the following days they saw one of the large ships with sails made of closely woven palm-leaves which came and went on the Rio dos Bons Sinais and were known to the natives as sembuks. When they saw the Portuguese ships, the crew put out in an almadia, a kind of long canoe and rowed furiously for the shore. A Portuguese boat was sent after them, but as it came up the Kaffirs leapt into the water and could not be caught. However, Gama's seamen seized a Moor, who, being unable to swim, had been forced to stay on board.

'He was,' says Corrêa, 'dressed in a shift of white silk with a cord at the waist and a sort of striped cloak: on his head he wore a round cap made of pieces of many-coloured silk sewn together with cloth of gold. He also wore gold rings in his ears. Our men took him into their rowing-boat and then visited the sembuk, but found nothing on board.'

Gama was delighted by this capture and hoped to obtain useful information from it, but no one on the *St Gabriel* could understand the Moor. Even a slave who could speak some Arabic and had been brought from the African coast to serve as an interpreter met with no success. However, by dint of words and signs, the Moor signified that a little further on there were people who talked that language. The *capitão-mór* had him supplied with wine, sugared cakes and olives, and the man ate, but refused to drink. He seemed astonished and amazed at everything he saw, and was delighted when Gama far from treating him as a prisoner, presented him with a blanket. After many attempts, they understood him to mean that his name was Davane, and showed him many samples of spices. He made it clear by means of signs that they could quite easily fill the holds of the three ships with such things. Gama thought that the man was a trader and that he was already anxious to repay the friendly reception they had given him by working for them.

On March 2 they cast anchor near some islets about a league from the shore. There sembuks put out to greet them, carrying men who played the trumpet and other musical instruments and sang. Some of these were dressed in striped cotton robes like those of the Moors of North Africa and wore turbans of fine cloth with silk edging embroidered with cloth of gold. They carried in their belts a kind of broad short Moorish sword, and had leather bucklers strapped on their left arms. Their intentions seemed peaceful, and this they proved by approaching the three ships and greeting the Portuguese in Arabic as they came aboard.

But Gama remained on his guard. Taking care not to reveal his mistrust, he plied his visitors with fruit, and questioned them closely through the interpreter as they ate. He also learned that the town that lay before them was called Mozambique, and that its shaikh was a vassal of the King of Kilwa, the capital of which stood on another island, further away to the north, on the coast of Zanzibar. He also learned that this kingdom of Kilwa drove a great trade in gold and merchandise with India and the places of the Arabian sea. But the

Moors pointed to the south and said that there was most gold at
Sofala! Gama thus understood that he had passed the place without
seeing it.

The Portuguese examined the sembuks more closely and saw that
they were made of boards joined by wooden pegs and a palm-fibre
which the natives called '*cairo*'. To the touch the sails seemed like
mats, for the palm-leaves were cut into strips and very closely
woven. The *capitão-mór* was surprised to discover that the seamen
steered by means of needle, quadrant and chart.

They told him that the town of Mozambique had a very good
port, but that the land on which it was built was marshy and flat,
and that it was therefore very unhealthy. The natives were negroes,
but Moors from various countries controlled everything. The houses
were all built of adobe and covered with thatch, except the mosque
and the shaikh's palace, which had flat, terraced roofs.

After their meal the Moors went off with great demonstrations of
joy, for they were convinced that the captains and crews of the three
ships, though they did not speak the same language, shared their
own faith. Gama took care not to undeceive them. He loaded them
with presents, and sent a gift for their shaikh.

The latter also supposed from the account brought him by his
men that the visitors were of his own religion. He immediately had
food brought to the ships and ordered the inhabitants of Mozambique to supply them with whatever they might need at the fairest
price. Not to be outdone, Gama entrusted the shaikh's emissary with
some robes, blankets and valuables as a present for his master.
The name of the latter was Caçoeija.

'Having thus established friendly relations,' says Damião de Gois,
'the shaikh went out to visit Vasco da Gama in the midst of a great
concourse of ships and people, all well dressed, and carrying bows
and arrows and other arms they use. Their robes were of striped
cotton, and some of silk in various colours. They played the pipe,
trumpet, small ivory bugles, and other instruments, which all
together made a deafening din. In this wise they approached the
St Gabriel.'

Caçoeija was a handsome man in the prime of life, tall, spare and
well proportioned. He was dressed after the Turkish fashion in a
caftan of very fine cotton with a second robe of Mecca velvet worn

over it and left unbuttoned. At his waist he carried a Moorish sword with a solid gold pommel inlaid with many precious stones. His round shield was similarly decorated. On his feet he wore fine velvet slippers.

Gama received his guest on deck, and went forward to greet him between a double row of men carefully chosen from among the healthiest, best-looking and best dressed in the crew: the sick and the ragged were instructed not to let themselves be seen. He greeted the shaikh nobly and had wine and fruit served for him.

'They ate and drank and became very gay. During the meal Caçoeija asked Gama among other things if he and his men were Turks or Moors, whence they came, and if they had brought the books of their law, which he would like to see, as well as their arms. Gama replied that he would show him the books of the Law later, and that as to their arms, he could easily see what the men had—cuirasses, lances, swords, arquebusses and crossbows. He ordered the soldiers to fire several salvos with their arquebusses, and also had the cannon fired. Caçoeija and his companions joyfully applauded. Meanwhile, Gama took every opportunity to ask through his interpreter for information about India and the way from Mozambique to the town of Calicut. Having obtained some useful suggestions, he begged Caçoeija to supply pilots for the journey, and this the shaikh promised to do.'

Among the natives who came daily to the ships to sell provisions, there happened to be three men who differed in appearance and stature from the rest, and they fell to their knees before a painting of the Archangel Gabriel, the patron of the ship. It was learned that they were Abyssinians from the land of Prester John, and Gama had them brought before him, but he could not glean much information from them, since they had difficulty in understanding the Arabic spoken by his interpreter. Moreover, they had been brought from their own country as children and had forgotten even much of what they knew of it from hearsay. Nevertheless, although they had been brought up in the Muslim religion, they had preserved a great devotion for the Archangel Gabriel, whom they remembered was greatly honoured in Abyssinia.

Gama could get no further. When the Moors saw the joy with which he received these men who still preserved traces of their

Christian faith, they suddenly displayed great haste to leave the ship, and dragged the Abyssinians with them: it was not possible to see the latter again.

The *capitão-mór* feared that this incident would arouse the shaikh's suspicions, and therefore pressed him to supply the promised pilots. Two Moors appeared, and from their replies seemed to be good seamen. They accepted the salary Gama offered, consisting of a sum of silver, and Gama added for each of them a hooded cloak of fine, bright scarlet cloth. They insisted on being paid in advance, saying that they would not leave without providing for their families while they were away. The *capitão-mór* complied with their request, but he took care to insist that they should not in any circumstances both go ashore together.

Forty-eight hours later, as two of the ships' boats went to the beach where the natives left daily supplies of wood and water for the ships, seven boatloads of armed men surrounded them. A hail of arrows fell around the Portuguese, who replied with their arquebusses and crossbows, and forced their assailants to seek safety in flight.

Having only one of the two pilots available, since the other had been in Mozambique at the moment of the attack, Gama took his ships out of the port and on Sunday, March 11, dropped anchor off a remote island, where he erected the pillar of St George. The crews then listened to Mass, and after it they again set sail.

After constantly struggling for four days against the currents, the ships were becalmed five leagues short of Cape Mozambique. The Moorish pilot advised Gama not to persist: it would be better to wait for the new moon off the island they had just left. There was a good anchorage there, and a good supply of fresh water from which they could replenish the casks. The *capitão-mór* resigned himself to following this advice.

It was a trap: scarcely had Paulo da Gama landed from the *St Raphael* with his water-party than Moors appeared on all sides. Since the departure of the fleet they had built a palisade round the spring and lain in wait for the Christians on their return: this had been prearranged in some unknown manner with their comrade, the pilot. In order to disperse them, Gama had to bombard them with his cannon. His first impulse was to hang the pilot from the yard-arm, but he then decided to have the man lashed to the mast and flogged: his services were too valuable to be dispensed with until they had reached the coast of India.

The following night, another Moor was brought before him, together with a boy of about twelve. The man had been surprised as he was climbing aboard the flagship with his son. When questioned, he said that he wanted to return to Mecca and knew the art of navigation. Expecting to obtain useful information about the Arabian sea from him, Gama gave him a ready welcome. He also learned that there was a pilot among the prisoners Paulo da Gama had brought in from his skirmish. The ships were now well supplied, and as the wind had changed, they set sail on April 1.

₿ 15 ₿

The Good King of Melindi

GAMA'S intention had been to put in at Kilwa, but the pilot he had had flogged (who seems to have borne no malice) declared that the breeze was too light to make headway against the currents. He sailed so far out to sea that no land was sighted until April 7, when they cast anchor off Mombasa. This was a handsome town with houses made of stone bound with mortar and whitewashed. It was embowered in the midst of a rich vegetation, and the air had a delightfully fresh and healthy tang. Those on board the *St Gabriel*, *St Raphael* and *Bérrio* thought they were back in Portugal again.

The Moorish pilots said that in Mombasa they had met Christians, who lived in their own villages. Gama rejoiced and decided to entrust the sick who could not be cared for on ship-board to these good people of his own religion.

Scarcely had the sails been furled when a large dug-out holding about a hundred men left the shore and soon approached the flagship. Its occupants were dressed in the Turkish style and armed with cutlasses and defended with round shields. Four of them, who seemed to be the chiefs, prepared to come aboard the *St Gabriel* accompanied by some of their followers, all so armed. But Gama stopped them, and had them told that he would only receive them if they came alone and unarmed. The Moors accepted this requirement with apparent good grace, saying that it was a wise precaution which should never be disregarded in foreign lands. They said that the King of Mombasa was expecting the arrival of the three ships and desired to visit their commander.

After eating and drinking, the four men took their departure, showing great joy at the welcome they had been given. The next day was Palm Sunday; and a boat sent by the King brought fruit

182

and sheep to the *St Gabriel*, and Gama was begged to enter the port and told that he would find all the spices and merchandise of India there without having to undertake the long sea-journey, which was one of the most difficult in all the east. The royal messengers added in confidence that they were Christians and that the captain might place full trust in the pilots that their King would supply.

They left the *St Gabriel* laden with presents and accompanied by two men chosen by lot from among the convicts, Damião Rodrigues and João Machado. They were required officially to visit the town and inform the King that the ships would enter the port on the following day. It was secretly understood that Machado should arrange to remain ashore until the fleet returned from India, for the purpose of collecting information.

The same evening Rodrigues brought back a most encouraging report. He had been most warmly welcomed by the King and had been allowed to walk with Machado freely through the town. It was a large and handsome city built on a rock overlooking the sea. At the entrance to the port there was a tower which was well guarded and supplied with artillery. Rodrigues had shown samples of pepper, nutmeg, cinnamon, ginger, cloves, amber and ivory. The King of Mombasa had begged him to inform the captain of the fleet that he had an abundant supply of all these things and would be happy to provide all that was demanded.

Gama was very glad to hear this news, and at break of day he gave orders for the ships to be brought in. Guided by the King's pilots, they sailed towards the bar, but a very violent current caught the flagship and turned it on to a sand-bank, where it would have become grounded but for Gama's presence of mind in having the anchor immediately dropped. The *St Gabriel's* mishap obliged the other two ships to follow suit in order to avoid a general collision. Amidst the confusion that ensued on the three ships, a group of Moors who had come aboard before they sailed bringing supplies and had tied their boats alongside now leaped into their dugouts and made for the harbour at all speed. As one of them passed under the flagship the pilots from Mombasa leapt into the sea and were picked up by their comrades, ignoring Gama's shouts that they were to return on board.

The whole episode smacked strongly of treachery. In order to clear his mind of doubts, the *capitão-mór* ordered that the two men who had been taken on the isle of St George should be tortured. These wretches confessed that the pilots had fled in a panic because they thought Gama had discovered their design to deliver his ships to the King of Mombasa, who intended to murder all the Portuguese.

'Vasco da Gama and everyone in the fleet gave thanks to God on their delivery from so great a peril,' says Damião de Gois. 'Fearing lest the Moors should come and cut their cables under cover of night, they kept an unusually strict watch, and this permitted them to escape the dangers that threatened: during the two nights they spent there, groups of Moors armed with cutlasses and axes appeared on several occasions. . . .'

During the disorder that reigned on the *St Gabriel* when she was in danger of grounding and the *St Raphael* and *Bérrio* threatened to crash against her hull, the convict Damião Rodrigues had slipped into the water unobserved. He was an excellent swimmer and reached the shore safe and sound. He knew the strand because he had visited it on the previous evening with his friend João Machado. These two had been accused of killing a man and flung into prison in Lisbon, and both had benefited by the royal pardon and had been taken on board the *St Gabriel*. Their adventures together had made them inseparable, and Damião Rodrigues, disconsolate at having left his companion behind, had seized the first opportunity to rejoin him.

Three years later the fleet commanded by Pedro Álvares Cabral anchored before Mombasa, to the great alarm of the King, who imagined that Vasco da Gama had returned in person to visit his treachery on him, and therefore came forth to beg the Portuguese to spare him. He threw the whole responsibility for the incident on his advisers, and declared that they had paid heavily for their misdeeds. The captain might do whatever he wished with his person and estates. 'You have only to command,' he told Cabral, 'and I shall obey.' Cabral dismissed him with a present of a great scarlet cloak lined with blue satin and embroidered with gold frogging, and a red silk hat gaily adorned with a white panache. Wearing the hat and robe, the King 'announced throughout the town that all the inhabitants were to serve the Portuguese, and that any who harmed them or gave them offence would be beheaded'. Apart from

the plume and the colour of his hat, we often meet in the uncertain
times we live in persons who seem to have chosen the King of
Mombasa as their model.

He now led the Portuguese to the other end of the town and
showed them a tomb with a cross standing at its head. Under the
symbol of Christ there was a board bearing an inscription cut with
a point of a knife: 'Here lies Damião Rodrigues who was left in this
country by Vasco da Gama. He was condemned to death and sailed
as a seaman on the *St Gabriel*.' Cabral at once asked the King to give
him the piece of ground whereon this cross had been raised, and
had it walled in and consecrated. The 'field of St Gabriel' was thereafter to receive the bodies of many Portuguese seamen and soldiers,
and a church was in course of time built on this holy ground.

João Machado was 'a man of much education and a great talker,
very brave and acquainted with the art of war'. He became the King
of Mombasa's favourite, but he had the wandering urge, and after
having passed into the service of the King of Kilwa, and later that
of the King of Melindi, he won the favour of the King of Cambaya
on the other shore of the Indian Ocean. Ten years later Albuquerque
found him comfortably installed with Ismail Adil Khan, the son of
Sabayo, King of Bijapur, and lord of Goa.

Vasco da Gama's fleet had sailed on April 13, on Good Friday.
The man who wished to return to Mecca with his son promised to
show the *capitão-mór* the way to the port of Melindi, where he
would be sure to find good pilots for Calicut.

As they sailed along the coast of the territory which is now Kenya,
the Portuguese sighted two sembuks. One of them escaped by
entering the mouth of a river, but the other was captured with its
crew of eighty, commanded by an old man with his 'very young and
beautiful wife' attended by four serving-girls. It had a cargo of ivory,
and a coffer filled with jewels and precious stones was also found in
it; but Gama forbade anyone to touch these. He put six of his seamen
and a few of the prisoners to help them on the sembuk, and divided
the rest of the captives into three groups, one for each of his ships.
On Resurrection Saturday, he reached Melindi.

When they saw Melindi, the Portuguese fancied, as they had at
Mombasa, that they were beholding a corner of their own country.
The town was large, with white-washed houses, and reminded them

of Alcochete on the Tagus. It was surrounded by a fine strong wall which securely protected it from invasion by sea.

'When our ships anchored before the port, they saw many ships, all beflagged, within, while standards were fluttering on the walls as if to celebrate a festival. The reason for this was that news had reached Melindi of the appearance of strangers on the coast and of their experiences at Mozambique and Mombasa, and the King had called his chief soothsayer to ask his advice. This was to the effect that he should remain at peace with the Portuguese if he wished to avoid the misfortunes that would befall those who received them ill or attempted treachery against them. The soothsayer added that the Portuguese were destined to become the masters of the whole of India, and that friendship now shown to them would last forever. The King had great confidence in this man, and carefully stored these words in his heart.'

The sun was about to set as the *St Gabriel*, *St Raphael* and *Bérrio* cast anchor. Next morning Vasco da Gama saw a dugout approaching carrying a splendidly dressed passenger. This was the King's ambassador, who was brought before him and asked what the strangers wanted. He added, on his master's behalf, that the people of Melindi would sell them honestly and willingly whatever they required. Gama replied that he had many needs, and the first of these was permission to enter the port.

The messenger returned to the dugout and did not reappear that day. As evening was about to fall, Gama accepted the offer of the old man whom he had captured on the sembuk, that he should go ashore and seek the King's reply. The Moor went ashore in one of the *St Gabriel's* boats and faithfully performed his mission, informing the King that he and all his company had been captured, but that they had suffered no harm and lost none of their property. He also told how the people of Mozambique and Mombasa had behaved treacherously towards the strangers who were guilty of no offence.

The King was reassured and advised Gama that he might enter the port as soon as he wished, sending him a boat laden with supplies, followed by another carrying a pilot. Gama asked the trader Davane to go and seek the King's permission for the fleet to send a man ashore to buy the articles most urgently needed on board. The King put a host of questions to Davane, who could only reply that the Portuguese had behaved generously towards the people of Mozambique, but that the shaikh had coveted their cargo and plotted to seize it by treachery. Confronted by Davane, the captain of the sembuk threw himself at the King's feet and said: 'Sire, if you will, beg these Christians not to hold me prisoner any longer and to release my wife and my men, they will readily grant your request, for they have not touched any of my property and have done no one any harm. They seem to be men who do not take what does not belong to them.'

The King sent the honest old man back aboard the *St Gabriel* with Davane and an emissary who told Gama that his master would not reply to any of his questions until his great desire to meet the captain had been satisfied. This message was accompanied by a further gift of supplies.

After taking counsel with his brother, Gama assembled all his captives and ordered the old Moor to check that none of the cargo was missing from his sembuk. Speaking from the top of the flagship he asked the old man in the presence of the King's emissary if his wives or servants had been harmed in any way or if his goods had been touched.

'You have touched nothing,' replied the old man, 'and you have treated me well, and my wife and servants and men.'

Gama then dismissed the emissary with a present of a scarlet cap and a silk veil embroidered with gold thread, and he released the Mozambique pilot from his bonds. The royal emissary was still standing in the poop of the sembuk, and Gama asked him to tell his master that the Moor had come to no harm because he had at once lowered his sails at the first bidding. If his people had tried to resist, or had not obeyed the King of Portugal's flag, fluttering at the masthead, he, Vasco da Gama, would have burnt their ship and sent them all to the bottom, as he would punish all he met at sea if they did not promptly obey his orders or if they attempted to offer resistance.

'Since the King of Melindi has received me well without even knowing him,' he ended, 'tell him that I offer him all these people, their sembuk, and all it contains to do with as he wills.'

'May God in heaven prosper you and all those who are with you as you deserve!' cried the old Moor and his companions. 'And may you return to your own country safe and sound!'

'Amen! Amen!' replied the crew. 'Lord God, give us a good voyage and save us by thy divine mercy!'

The *capitão-mór* thought that the desire that he should return safe and sound to Portugal was perhaps a discreet way of wishing to see the back of him. He prudently had the King of Melindi informed that his master, the King of Portugal, had forbidden him to set foot ashore anywhere until he delivered the letters he carried to the Princes of India. In order to take the edge off this reply, he sent with it a piece of scarlet stuff, another of crimson satin, and a 'fine large Flemish mirror with gilded and painted leaves'. The King of Melindi had the good taste to express his appreciation.

'Moreover,' says Gaspar Corrêa, 'in order to please the King, Vasco da Gama sent to him Nicolau Coelho, a handsome and gallant gentleman in whose wisdom and ability he had full confidence. He put on fine clothes and got into the boat with the Moor Davane and the negro who served as interpreters. Gama had given him full instructions about all he was to do and say. He landed before the palace, and the royal guards had to force a way for him with many blows owing to the thickness of the crowd that had gathered on the foreshore. The King rejoiced greatly to see so handsome and richly clad a captain, and even more at the respectful bow with which Coelho saluted him. He invited the Portuguese to sit on the rich carpet on which his throne was placed, a stool inlaid with gold and ivory still visible under its silk covering. Using Davane and the negro as interpreters, the King interrogated Coelho at length about the voyage, the Portuguese method of navigation and the affairs of Portugal and the Portuguese.

'The King of Portugal has the same name as God,' said Coelho, 'for he is called Emmanuel. He is the greatest lord on earth among the Christians, and can send thousands of unconquerable knights against those who refuse him obedience. His military might is no less at sea, for he has two hundred ships constantly ready for the fray. His wealth is so great, and he possesses so many towns, villages and estates, that every moon two hundred thousand gold cruzados enter his treasury over and above what he spends. In his desire to discover new lands, the King my master has sent a hundred ships to sea for this purpose, and has bidden their captains bring back whatever merchandise they find, and especially pepper and other spices. They have orders under pain of death to do no harm to anyone without provocation and never to go ashore without permission of the governor of the place.'

Gama's instructions, faithfully mirrored in Coelho's speech, show that the *capitão-mór* was fully aware of the infinite use of what we call propaganda. But the King of Melindi was astonished: he could only see three of the hundred ships of the King of Portugal; what had happened to the rest?

'The ships you see before the port of Melindi,' replied Coelho with assurance, 'have become separated from the rest of the fleet by a terrible storm that struck us two years since. We were lost amidst unknown seas and did not know what course we were following. Finding ourselves at the mercy of the tempest and overwhelmed by our toils and hardships, in which more than half our crew were lost, we were forced to destroy two of our ships; yet we were determined still to wander across the face of the sea until we should have discovered the land we were ordered to look for and were able to bring news of it to our lord the King. If God does not permit us to find this land or to rejoin the rest of our fleet, we shall continue to sail on, putting into land at hazard on our way and setting sail again until the last of us is dead.'

The royal audience lasted until after sunset. Night had already fallen when Coelho asked the King's permission to return to his captain, and he was taken back to the *St Gabriel* in the King's own richly decorated barge, bearing a gift of two pieces of the finest cotton, two of brightly coloured silk interwoven with gold thread, and a gold ring set with a large blue stone.

In order to complete his conquest of the King's good will, Vasco da Gama sent one of the convicts ashore accompanied by the Moor Davane with orders to buy the supplies they needed at double the usual price, paying for them in silver pieces. There were ships from India in the port and their crews asked to visit the *St Gabriel*. When they saw a painting of the Virgin Mary at the foot of the Cross with the body of her son in her arms, they prostrated themselves and uttered words among which the Portuguese thought they heard the name of Christ. It was more probably that of Krishna, the eighth incarnation of the god Vishnu, but the men on the flagship were convinced that these good people were Christians and descendants of those converted long ago by the Apostle St Thomas.

Urged on by his soothsayer, the King of Melindi still insisted on a personal interview with the *capitão-mór*, though his dignity—and perhaps also a lingering shadow of distrust—forbade him to go aboard the *St Gabriel*. On the advice of his brother Paulo, Gama sent to tell him that although he had been forbidden by his King to go ashore, he would nevertheless go half-way in a rowing boat and another boat carrying the captain of the *St Raphael* would follow. The King was not told that the crew, under their silk and velvet cloaks, would be fully armed, and that stores of other arms would be hidden under the decorations of the boats and under the awning erected for the captain-general.

On the appointed day, amidst the cheers of the seamen, the fanfare of trumpets and the ruffle of drums, Vasco and Paulo da Gama left the ships. 'As this occurred on the third octave of Easter, a day of great rejoicing in our country,' writes João de Barros, 'all our men were extremely joyful.' But Gama, when he had covered half the distance from the ship to the shore, realized that the royal party had not appeared. On his instructions the rowers lifted their oars in token that they would go no further. The royal palanquin was then seen on shore. It was borne by four men and surrounded by a crowd of superbly dressed lords, while a great throng marched in front and behind, in decent order and to the accompaniment of much music. The King took his place in his barge with the principal personages of his retinue, while other lords embarked in escorting boats. Out of courtesy towards Gama, they carefully left clear the side of the royal barge from which the Portuguese embassy would approach.

'The King,' said Damião de Gois, 'sat on a great high-backed chair made of shining metal: its seat was covered with a velvet cushion and there was another cushion as a foot-rest. He was dressed in a caftan of crimson damask lined with green satin, and wore a rich turban on his head. To protect him from the full force of the sun, a servant carried a great shade of crimson satin on a gilded stick. By the King's side there sat an old man holding his short Moorish broadsword, richly garnished with gold and bluish silver. In the barge the minstrels played trumpets and ivory-horns, in such good tune that the sound might have issued from less barbarous instruments.'

Gama responded to their music in a martial fashion, with the arquebusses on his boats, the thunder of his artillery and the cheers of the crews. The people of Melindi were alarmed by these noises and made as if to return to the shore, but Vasco da Gama called for silence and approached the royal barge. The King's greeting was that of a man whose heart conceals no evil intentions. According to João de Barros, their interview was as cordial and trusting as if they had always known one another.

'The King of Portugal possesses so many cannon and so many ships larger and stronger than these that he could if he desired cover the whole Indian sea with them. If the King of Melindi shows himself a good and loyal friend to the Portuguese, these ships will come to defend him against his enemies.'

The people that Gama and his men had taken for Christians were 'Gentiles from the Kingdom of Cambaya', called banians, 'so devout in the sect of Pythagoras that they do not even kill the vermin on their bodies and eat no living thing'. They returned on board the *St Gabriel* to offer the image of the Virgin grains of pepper and cloves, and worshipping her with great devotion. A man who came with them on the King's orders introduced himself as a Moor from the land of Gujerat, on the Gulf of Cambaya. The inhabitants of Melindi said that he was a 'mulimo' and 'kanaka', pronouncing in their own fasihon the Arabic word 'muallim' or pilot and the Sanskrit 'ganika', astrologer (astrology and astronomy then being the same science). His name was Ahmad ibn Majid, and he belonged to a family of great Indian navigators from the uplands of Arabia known as the Nadj or Nedjed. The Portuguese found it easiest to call him 'Malemo Cana', or simpler 'canaca'.

He was extremely intelligent and well-informed, and he took great pleasure in conversing with Gama. Gama was not a little surprised and delighted when he produced a great chart which showed the whole of the western coast of the vast Hindu peninsula. 'This chart,' says João de Barros, 'was made in the Moorish fashion, that is to say with meridians and parallels very close and without the way of the winds; for as the curve of the meridians and parallels was very small, the whole coast could be accurately shown by reference to two rhumbs, North-South and East-West, with no need for the multiplication of indications of wind-directions which we have on our maps, and use for drawing new ones.'

Gama proudly produced the great wooden astrolabe and others of metal which he used to measure the height of the sun. But Malemo Cana was not in the least surprised by them, and said that some pilots in the Red Sea used triangular instruments of brass by which they took the height of the sun and the star which they used as their guide. But the navigators of Cambaya and the whole of India, though they set their course by certain stars, including not only the north and south pole stars but certain others which crossed the sky from east to west, relied on only one instrument which he showed Gama: he himself used no other. It consisted of three pieces of wood and Gama had no difficulty in recognizing the Jacob's staff used by Portuguese seamen. The captain-general was delighted when Malemo Cana agreed to serve as his pilot.

The King of Melindi behaved as a good and faithful ally and did all he could to assist his guests. Gama and his brother Paulo often conversed with him, and on his advice, they put off their departure, though Gama was anxious to go and was consumed with impatience to see the shores of India appear over the bows of the *St Gabriel*.

'Keep your heads among the people you will meet,' the good King advised him. 'You will find that some of them are cunning and presumptuous, but do not let them see your reactions. Do them no harm unless to repay harm, so that all your actions may find approval among them. Pay a fair price for what you buy lest you draw down on your heads their hatred of foreign merchants. Never go ashore in the land of the King of Calicut unless you have good hostages aboard, for his people are treacherous. May God protect you and your men!'

On the King's orders, the carpenters at Melindi had built large tanks for the ships, designed to carry a great supply of fresh water. 'They were made of boards closely fitted together with palm fibre,' says Gaspar Corrêa, 'and they were coated with bitumen so that they were more watertight than casks. They were placed in the hold near the mainmast; each held thirty barrels of water and there were four in each ship.'

When the work was done, Gama told the King:

'The dangers of land and sea threaten our lives on this voyage, and we depend on God, whose will we do not know. It may be that death will prevent us from returning hither. We shall therefore leave a sign behind which shall remain always with you so that you and your descendants may remember us, and this sign shall be in the form of the name of our King written on a stone. We leave these in all lands whose inhabitants become friends of our King, and he has bidden us do this in token of their loyalty.'

The good King (who had long ceased to be surprised that Gama should have forgotten the supposed instructions that he was not to set foot on shore) was so glad at this that he asked that the stone should be set up at the very entrance to his palace. Gama refused this friendly suggestion and said that it should stand where any ship approaching from Melindi could see it, and he chose a slope over-looking the harbour to raise the pillar of the Holy Spirit, one of the three he still had on board. It was consecrated by three priests to the accompaniment of fanfares of trumpets and salvoes of artillery. Then Mass was solemnly celebrated in a tent on one side, in which an altar had been erected bearing the famous picture of Our Lady. All the Portuguese from the captain to the humblest cabin-boy received Communion, and the people of Melindi watched this, to them, strange spectacle with admiration.

Before setting sail, Gama presented the convict who had made his purchases in Melindi to the King, saying that he desired to leave him behind, so that if God willed that he himself should not return from his voyages, the man might tell other Portuguese who would come in the future, of the help the King of Melindi had given him. The captain also gave the King a written and signed report of all these matters.

Gama turned to the convict and told him:

'I am leaving you here because the King of Melindi is our friend. You are in no danger in his kingdom, and I bid you to take careful note of all you see about you here and to learn all you can about this country. If you lead a good and useful life here, and return to Portugal thereafter, I, Vasco da Gama, promise to make you a knight of King Manoel's household, and I shall do as much for all who do this duty to the King in this difficult and dangerous service. I shall leave you this promise in writing together with the money you will need.'

Next morning at daybreak the ships were decked with flags, and at full daylight they hoisted their sails, and while the trumpets rang out aloud, the men knelt on the deck, thanking God for having cared for them so well at Melindi.

⟫ 16 ⟪

Calicut

'THERE can be no mistake: yonder lies Calicut! The land for which you have prayed lies before you, and if you do not desire to make a fresh discovery, this is the goal of your long voyage.'

The poet of the *Lusiads* puts these words into the mouth of the 'pilot of Melindi'. But Gaspar Corrêa, who used the daily diary of one of the priests on board, João Figueira, used other terms: 'According to the pilot, this was said to be a mountain on the Indian coast, in the Kingdom of Cananor, called Mount Deli.'

The fleet had left the hospitable port of Melindi on the morning of April 24, 1498, on its attempt to cross the great 'gulf of Arabia'. On May 18 a bluish line, the range of the western Ghats, appeared above the horizon. According to Camões, Gama's heart was so full of joy that he could not control his feelings; he fell to his knees, and lifting his hands to heaven, gave thanks to God for this crowning blessing. It may well be that the poet was right, though the chronicler merely notes soberly that the *capitão-mór* obeyed the custom of rewarding the pilots when land was sighted at the end of a long voyage and presented each of them with a quantity of money and a garment of red cloth.

As the ships approached the coast, its details could now be picked out. 'When they saw a large town with many houses covered with thatch, the pilots said that this was Cananor. There were a great many small boats at sea occupied in fishing, and many of them came close to the ships to inspect them. The Portuguese later discovered that the fishermen had been astonished to behold ships of a kind never before seen in those parts and to find white men on board them and had gone ashore to spread the news.'

On this coast of the 'land of pepper', known to the Hindus as

195

Malayalam and to the Arabs as Bilad al-Filfud, and described on maps as Malabar, soothsayers played an important role, as they still do in our own days. Corrêa calls them 'Canayates'.

'In Cananor,' he says, 'there was of old a very diabolical sorcerer who had won the confidence of all the people. Whatever he said was written down, and his writings were preserved as great prophecies. They said that one day all India would be ruled by white people from a distant country, and that their King would do great harm to those who were not his friends.'

The fishermen who had watched the approach of the *St Gabriel*, *St Raphael* and *Bérrio*, floating under their great white sails bearing the cross of the Order of Christ in red, were taken before the King of Cananor. When he had heard them he called his soothsayers and bade them tell him what were these ships and whence they came. 'After invoking their devils', the sorcerers replied that the ships belonged to a great King and came from a great distance, and that India would be subjected by war and peace to people who came with them, in accordance with the ancient writings.

'Sire, we tell you the truth! These men are not numerous enough to conquer kingdoms from their three ships, but those who come after them will be more powerful on this ocean than those who now sail upon it. For this reason, the peoples of the earth must obey them. And if they come back in such great strength, what will be the fate of your kingdom if you do not receive them in peace?'

Soon after it was learnt that the three ships had cast anchor before Calicut, barely a dozen leagues from his domains, and the King of Cananor sent trusty informers to the port to see what would happen and bring him their report.

Calicut was then the most important town on the whole of the Malabar coast, and one of the richest in the whole of India. The rajah who ruled it was called the '*Samorim*', or 'Lord of the sea'. He forbade his people to build their houses of durable materials, and the use of stone and mortar was restricted to his own palace, which stood outside the city, and to the temples. These were 'very large and covered with very fine sculptures made of the material of the walls, and very richly decorated within, with images of angels, devils, men and women, and other things', says Damião de Gois, who draws an attractive picture of the town, standing above the reefs of a rocky shore.

'It is very large, in extent rather than in the number of its buildings, for the houses are spaced out at intervals and surrounded by many gardens. . . . These are a sort of cottage with roofs of palm-leaves, for the laws of the country do not permit them to be otherwise. The town has a very cheerful appearance. Gardens, orchards and nurseries are scattered here and there, and it has many norias and pools of water, and is shaded with groves of palms and arecas which make it fresh and pleasant. . . .'

Like their comrades in Cananor, Cranganor, Cochin, Coulan and Travancore, the Moors of Calicut held a dominant position in the Samorim's kingdom. Gois says that some of them owned as many as fifty or sixty ships. Sailing with the monsoons, they ranged as far afield as Aden and Jedda on the Red Sea, where their cargoes from the orient were transhipped on to smaller vessels designed to navigate the land-locked sea, and so reached Suez. There the bales of goods were loaded on the backs of camels, and carried in caravans to Cairo. From Cairo they went in heavy barges down the Nile to Rosetta, whence another caravan departed for Alexandria. Here the merchants of the companies of Venice, Florence, Genoa, Amalfi, Pisa and other places impatiently awaited their arrival. There were also ships which sailed up the Gulf of Oman as far as Ormuz at the entry to the Persian Gulf. The merchandise was landed and conveyed to Bisrah, whence it crossed Mesopotamia and the Syrian desert, and was so conveyed to Tripoli, another distribution-centre, or else was sent by caravan towards Persia, Turkey and Turkistan. When the monsoon changed, the ships returned to India, laden with European goods which the brokers of the Calicut Moors had acquired. These Moors brought the Samorim his principal wealth, for they paid him large revenues in return for his protection. The wealth amassed by these ingenious traders was so great that Damião de Gois says that 'the Portuguese were astonished by it'.

Receiving his wealth from the Moors, the Samorim's power rested on the noble sect of the *naïrs*, or warriors. They appeared with their torsos bare and their bodies wrapped in silks or cottons from the waist down: they were never without their swords, their round shields, and a bow and quiverful of arrows: some even had an arquebus. They were extremely agile and athletic and showed great skill in the use of their weapons, which they handled constantly from childhood. However, the Samorim did not allow them to bear arms until he had knighted them.

Every trading Moor had a *naïr* attached to his person, by the Samorim's orders, under an arrangement which recalls the 'protection' formerly forced on American traders by gangsters. The merchant paid his *naïr* handsomely for promising to defend him, and the *naïr* also only allowed him to deal with traders who were willing to grant him a substantial cut. Moreover, the *naïr* also drew his pay every month from the King of Calicut's treasury, which in turn laid heavy taxes on the merchants: the whole system was thus completely watertight.

The *naïrs* were very conscious of their privileges. They did not marry and had to do only with women of their own caste. The children belonged to the mother, not the father. If one of these supercilious warriors was found with a woman who was not a *naïr*, his companions would mercilessly strike her down with their swords and kill her.

Obviously the lower classes drew no benefits whatever from this trade, which was carried on over their heads and enriched the Samorim, the *naïrs* and the Moors. They were regarded as untouchable, and obliged by law never to appear in the streets without shouting aloud, so that any *naïr* who happened to be abroad could avoid the slightest risk of defiling himself by their vile proximity. If any unfortunate untouchable failed to carry out this obligation, and a *naïr* crossed his path, he would be ruthlessly slaughtered.

The Moors had astutely turned this state of affairs to their own advantage, as Gaspar Corrêa notes.

'They began by telling the kings and lords of the parts of India where they did their business that the task of carrying their goods was extremely difficult for lack of labour, since the low-caste Hindus could not approach the rest for fear of being slain by the *naïrs*. They therefore asked that the poor should be allowed to embrace Islam if they wished, so that they should no longer be subject to Hindu law, threatening that if this were not done, they would no longer be able to carry on their trade in India. At the same time they offered large sums of money to the Samorim's officials, who were thus corrupted and influenced their master in order to assist them to gain their ends. The wretched outcasts who lived in the fields and bush and had no food but herbs and land-crabs preferred to become Muslims and live where they pleased, walk freely along the high-ways, earn their bread and eat when they were hungry, and the Muslim traders gave them loin cloths and clothes. So many were converted to Islam that the whole Malabar coast was filled with them, especially the town of Calicut, which became for the Moors the most important emporium for pepper and other spices for transport to Mecca and Turkey, and thence to the lands of Christen-dom. . . .'

The Moors were not slow in realizing the danger to their interests presented by the appearance of the Portuguese ships. For their trade it was a matter of life and death to prevent the intruders from establishing themselves on the Indian coast. The arrival of these ships meant that the hated Christians had found a direct sea-way, with which it would be impossible to compete, since the long route hitherto used exclusively for the distribution of oriental goods necessitated many transhipments, all of them extremely costly. Furthermore, the slow progress of the caravans across the desert by routes which were permanently fixed by the sites of the oases rendered them extremely vulnerable to the attacks of bandits.

The traders of Calicut lost not a moment, but taking counsel together they agreed unanimously to do all within their power to strangle this rude Christian interruption at birth. They sent mes-sengers to their co-religionists the whole length of the Malabar coast urging them to drive off the intruders who had dared to break into the traditional system and threatened to compromise a monopoly much too precious to be lost.

While a conspiracy against him was thus brewing, Gama at once sent Malemo Cana ashore with one of the convicts who were still left. They were to inform the Samorim that the captain-general of the fleet had a message from the King of Portugal to deliver by his own hand. It was May 20, 1498.

⁜ 17 ⁜

The Apostate of Seville

THE Samorim was in his palace five leagues from Calicut. Ibn Majid decided to go on there without first informing Gama. Consequently the latter began to fear that the pilot's prolonged absence implied a trap. He had, as we know, received from King Manoel copies of the information collected by King John with reference to India. He therefore knew that the greatest circumspection was required in approaching the Samorim, and that he would have to struggle against the influence exerted at court by the Moors. Even if he had not known it, his recent experiences at Mozambique and Mombasa would have taught him to take every possible precaution, and the warnings of the good King of Melindi were still fresh in his memory. Finally, the inexplicable disappearance of the pilot was designed to strengthen the feeling of mistrust to which his own venturesome but calculating nature already inclined him. It therefore seems improbable that he should have at once accepted the invitation of the Samorim as João de Barros and Damião de Gois state, instead of first ensuring his own security by bringing hostages aboard: at Melindi, whose King had given many proofs of friendship, he had taken the most elaborate precautions before venturing to quit his ship. The version of events given by Gaspar Corrêa seems to conform much more closely to reality, and this is the account we shall follow, including nevertheless elements from the others where they add new details without conflicting with it in essentials.

After an absence of two days, ibn Majid returned safe and sound with his companion and bringing with them a person who was introduced to Gama as a pilot in the Samorim's service. He informed the captain-general that he was delighted at his arrival in Calicut, and that as soon as the ships had been anchored in the place he would indicate, which was safer than their present anchorage, Gama would be informed of the date of his reception by the Samorim.

The man directed the ships to a roadstead called Capocate, which Gama observed was situated more than two leagues' distance from Calicut, or about seven modern sea-miles. This was a considerable way, and it suggested that the monarch had in mind the idea of getting the Portuguese away from the town.

Gama was far from showing disquiet, but instead took care to express in the pilot's presence his gratitude to the Samorim for having had the goodness to take such care for the safety of his ships. The man was rewarded with a present and left the ship. Two whole days passed without any news from the shore; it was only a few cables length away, yet it seemed to have shrunk into inaccessibility.

Gama was now beginning to have sufficient experience of the customs of the east to realize that patience is the first of all virtues and the surest of weapons. He understood that the King of Calicut intended to test his patience, and to assert his own prestige by forcing the strangers to wait. He therefore avoided any gesture that might have betrayed his impatience, and on the contrary expressed satisfaction at the respite, which, true to his custom, he employed in studying the custom of the Samorim's kingdom.

It was not until May 24 or 25 that Davane went ashore in a boat with a convict. This was a 'New Christian' or marrano, a converted Jew called João Martins who spoke fluently not only Portuguese, but Hebrew, Arabic and Spanish. He was carefully coached by Gama before leaving the *St Gabriel*.

Leaving Martins in the town, Davane went to ask the Samorim's permission to buy provisions. He told the King that it was the captain-general's desire not to exchange any goods until after he had executed the mission with which his King had entrusted him.

The Moors had not failed to learn of the appearance of the boat, and they went down to the shore and clustered round Martins, plying him with a host of questions. The convict was on his guard and 'did not answer them as they would have wished'. Meanwhile, Davane returned with the permission he had sought, and the two men went off to make their purchases.

The Moors did not give in, but decided to prevent the Portuguese from returning on board that night. They demanded that the Gozil, or royal official entrusted with questions of justice, should take steps to secure this. The Gozil had his own reasons for not refusing the merchants anything, and he complied with their demands by summoning the two strangers to appear before him after sunset.

Davane and Martins were on their way to obey this behest when they came across a person who from his dress appeared to be a Moor. Martins was therefore astonished when he was addressed in Spanish with the words: 'God save you, brother!'

Martins was delighted to hear a Peninsular language spoken in a place as remote from his own country, and he replied courteously in Portuguese: 'God save you!'

The Moor joined them and persuaded them with great insistence to sup with him. During the meal, he adroitly attempted to interrogate Martins in the course of their conversation, but the Portuguese faithfully observed Gama's instructions and revealed nothing. Then, with the air of one suddenly resolved to burn his boats, his host said:

'My name is Alonso Pérez, and I was born at Seville. The Moors captured me when I was very young and I was taken from prison to prison until I became the slave of one of their lords, who set me free on his deathbed. When I was free, I was in great danger, for the Moors hated me because I was a Catholic. In order to save my life, I assumed a Moorish name and pretended to adhere to their ways. But God knows that in my heart of hearts I am still a Christian.'

He ended his confession by expressing his joy at being able to talk to Martins in Spanish. Having consulted with Davane, Martins proposed to take him on board the *St Gabriel* on the following day and to present him to the captain-general. This suggestion appeared to fill his heart with joy.

According to João de Barros, the man was a real Moor called Monçaida, a merchant's factor and a friend of the pilot Malemo Cana, who, again according to Barros, had gone ashore with Martins. He had been born in the kingdom of Tunis, and had met Portuguese at Oran, where King John's ships went to buy striped cloth for sale to the natives of Mina. 'This man was already attracted to the Christian faith,' says Barros, and he acquired 'such devotion to Vasco da Gama that he would not leave him, but accompanied him back to Portugal and died a Christian.'

However, the version recorded by Gaspar Corrêa seems much

more plausible, and therefore preferable to Barros' account. It is extremely improbable that a Moor should feel 'attracted to the Christian faith' by the inclination of his own heart; and every missionary will agree that no one is more difficult to convert to Christianity than a Muslim. The merchants of Calicut had moreover every reason to use the services of a Pérez who might take advantage of his original nationality and his supposed fidelity to the Christian faith to overcome Martins' mistrust and insinuate himself into his confidence, just as Gama had sent the Moor Davane to accompany Martins. The question seems to be decided by the certificate to which we shall refer, and it is highly probable that Pérez, who himself admitted that he passed under a Muslim name, and Monçaida are one and the same.

The captain-general received the Spaniard warmly and interrogated him closely about his adventures. When it was time to dine, he set him to eat with João Martins, while he himself sat at table with his brother Paulo, not far away. After this Gama took Paulo into his cabin and invited Pérez-Monçaida to join them. 'Inspired by God,' Gaspar Corrêa assures us (and we have no difficulty in believing him) the man suddenly confessed:

'My lords, captain-general and captain, I beg you to hear my confession. When I came on board this ship, I carried treachery in my bosom. But as soon as I entered this cabin, God suddenly bade my heart reveal the truth.'

Gama impassively ordered Pérez to explain himself.

'The Moors,' he said, 'are afraid and angry at your arrival in Calicut, for they understand that it means their ruin unless they can encompass yours. They have resolved to pay the Samorim's officers money so that they will turn his heart against you and set traps for you. They have already sent word to the Moors of all the other kingdoms to devote their wealth and influence to force you to leave India.'

Gama stood as if turned to stone. Pérez took his courage in both hands, and poured out his confession.

'The Moors know that I was born in a Christian land, and they think that it is easier for me than for anyone else to win your confidence and bring about your ruin. They have offered me a great reward if I tell you many lies and win your friendship and so learn from you the secrets they desire to know. It was to this end that I invited your men to share my hospitality in the hope that they would bring me to you. But when I entered this cabin, I was filled with the fear of God which bid me be sincere with you and serve you as best I can. Now that I have told you the truth, tell me what I am to do, and you shall see whether I am true or false. But how shall I expect you to place your trust in me, a Moor among Moors?'

'What you have just done,' replied Gama, 'is a virtuous thing, and worthy of a good Christian. You may rest assured that we shall not forget it. It you serve us with the same loyalty as you have just shown, you shall have no cause to regret it. As captain-general of this fleet, I will engage to reward your services fittingly.'

Gama put more questions to him, and after consulting with his brother Paulo he told the Spaniard how he was to act and sent him back on shore. Pérez went at once to the Moors who had devised the plot in which he was to play a leading part and spoke to them somewhat as follows:

'The ships that have appeared are part of a mighty fleet sent out by the famous King of Portugal. A great storm has separated these from the rest of the ships. The Moorish factor and the pilots from Melindi have confirmed everything the captain-general has told me, and he has spoken frankly to me, believing me to be a Christian. His object is to conclude a treaty of peace and friendship with the Samorim and to barter his goods for what he can find at Calicut. He seeks especially pepper and other spices. He has given me five ells of fine green cloth, and dismissed me as if he had no more need of me, though he has asked me to go with him and act as his interpreter when he pays his visit to the Samorim. I told him that no one could appear before the King of Calicut unless he were summoned. Thereupon he sent me away.'

The Moors regarded the Spaniard as 'a very good renegade' and held council to draw up a plan of action. They realized that the Samorim's covetousness would drive him to accept the King of Portugal's presents. Their object was consequently to find a means of setting him against the Portuguese, whom they knew to be proud and resolute people. The plainest way was to try their patience and cause them to commit errors that would call for reprisals. This could be achieved by selling them articles of poor quality or spoiled goods at the highest price. They would also persuade the Gozil to vex them with intentional discourtesies, delays, and innumerable obstacles, so that they should take offence. Meanwhile, the Gozil and the financial officer would seek to depict the Portuguese to the Samorim as presumptuous folk who were never satisfied and always demanded more than they were given and had recourse to force to seize whatever was withheld from them. The officials would have to use their wits in order to sow distrust in the Samorim's mind, and later play on his fears, gradually provoking his anger so that when the moment came to wipe out the Portuguese, the King should believe that they themselves were responsible for the affray in which they would meet their end.

As soon as Alonso Pérez had gone, Vasco da Gama summoned Nicolau Coelho to the flagship, together with the masters and pilots. He told them what had passed and asked for their advice. They all agreed on one point: that the *capitão-mór* should in no circumstances go ashore, since his life would be in jeopardy and if that were lost, so would they all be, and all their efforts and hardships would be wasted. Therefore, on the day the Samorim summoned the captain-general of the fleet, someone else must replace him and pretend to be the King's ambassador.

When Gama had heard them, he replied:

'My lord brother and friends, when I embarked on this ship and undertook this mission, I offered my life and soul to God in the hope that He would aid me in the accomplishment of my duty, if He thought fit. I tell you in all sincerity then that even if at this moment I were before Lisbon harbour I would rather slay myself with my own hands than enter it and appear before the King without bearing him the fruits of the undertaking he has charged me with. And since I have made this decision in my heart, my life means nothing to me any more. If I feared death and allowed another to do what it is my duty to accomplish, I should indeed cut a sorry figure. Rest assured, then, that I shall go ashore without any hesitation, for all this is in God's hands.'

A pregnant silence reigned on the deck of the *St Gabriel*. Gama's expression softened as his gaze rested on his brother, Coelho and all the men, officers, pilots, boatswains, seamen and soldiers, who had served him so well.

'My lord brother and all my friends,' he went on, 'I beg you now in the name of Our Lord Jesus Christ not to stint your endeavours to attain our end, whatever the perils that may threaten me, even if I perish. By whatever means you may think fit, I bid you load these ships with whatever goods you can obtain in order to exhibit them to the King. If you cannot succeed in this, you must return empty-handed and tell the King what we have done. If the winds are against you, you must sail along the coast and discover as many places as you can, taking note of them all and seeking to obtain pepper and spices and other articles to take to the King. Take nothing by force on land or sea, for we must not allow the lies of the Moors to assume the colour of truth. They say that we are robbers and spies, and that we shall end by seizing their lands by force. We are neither robbers nor spies: as to the conquest of this land, we pray that God may grant it as a favour to our lord the King. Furthermore I tell you this: all these things which I have enjoined on you as a friend, I now order you to observe by virtue of the power that has been conferred on me as commander of these ships.'

Neither Paulo da Gama nor the others present found any objection to this firm and noble speech: in the name of all the officers, pilots, masters, seamen and soldiers, Paulo told the captain of the fleet that they were prepared to rely on God's will and placed their lives in his hands.

❧ 18 ❧

In The Samorim's Palace

VASCO now sent an official message to the Samorim, confirming that the Portuguese would make no purchase in the town of Calicut until a treaty of peace and friendship should have been concluded, and declaring that he was prepared to remain on board his ships until the treaty was signed and he should have performed the mission with which his King had entrusted him.

The Ṣamorim was doubtful and sought the opinion of his advisers. The Gozil and the fiscal officer suggested: 'Say that before you decide if you should receive their embassy, you must hear a person of rank set forth clearly the object of their visit.' This course had been suggested by the Moors, and by it the two officials hoped to provoke the Portuguese captain to some expression of impatience.

The Samorim hesitated for three days before accepting this counsel. He bade Davane, who was on shore with João Martins, to accompany one of the *naïrs*, a cousin of Gozil, who was to take his reply to the *St Gabriel*. When Gama saw their boat approaching, he hastily had the decks strewn with cloths and the presents intended for the Samorim laid out, while some of the seamen pretended to be polishing them. When he had received the *naïr* with the greatest courtesy and heard the King's message, Vasco took Nicolau Coelho to one side.

'I wish you to go and meet the Samorim,' he said. 'Tell him that I am ready to send men ashore to buy the stores we need provided that the King of Calicut undertakes that they come to no harm, that they receive the same treatment as other foreign merchants, and are not cheated over the price or quality of what they buy. They must be allowed the use of boats every day to bring whatever they purchase to our ships. They will pay the same duties to the Samorim as other foreign merchants. Finally, I want to have a contract with the Samorim for permission to buy and sell according to the customs of the country. This is to be a permanent understanding, to which the King of Calicut will give his oath and he will set it out in writing and send it me with his signature attached. Tell him that as soon as the captain-general of the fleet is in possession of this contract, a factor will be sent ashore with our goods. If the factor informs me that all the conditions of the contract are adhered to word for word, I shall go ashore as soon as a person of rank is sent aboard my flagship as a hostage. I shall deliver the presents that have been sent to the Samorim, and thereafter I shall execute my duties as the ambassador of my lord the King of Portugal.'

While Gama was giving Coelho these instructions, the *naïr's* gaze was fixed on the array of presents laid on the cloths and glittering in the sun. Gama succeeded in impressing him by offering him a silk cap and a fine knife-box.

As the *naïr* returned ashore with the messenger from the Christian captain, a crowd gathered on the beach to meet their boat. The Gozil, surrounded by his guard of two hundred *naïrs*, rose from the mat on which he had been sitting and greeted Coelho with a deep bow, inviting him to sit beside him until the *naïr* should return from the royal palace. There followed a long wait, for the Samorim caused the cousin of the Gozil to describe in detail everything he had seen on the ship, and especially the presents destined for him. The sun had already fallen below the horizon when the *naïr* returned with a disappointing reply: the Samorim was very busy, and could not receive the Portuguese captain until the following day.

Coelho followed the instructions of his commander and received this news with a smiling face. He asked for a boat so as to return to his ship, but the Gozil refused on the pretext that the sea was too rough for him to put out in the dark. Coelho made no reply and resigned himself patiently to his ill-fortune. Finally the Gozil rose and had him escorted to the house of a rich Hindu where he was regaled on rice served on fig-leaves, with roast and boiled chicken and figs. After this, richly decorated mats were brought for him to lie on, and he tried to sleep.

'The Spaniard, who had observed all that had passed,' writes Corrêa, 'waited until far into the night and then made his way to the house where Coelho was lodged. When Coelho got up in the night, the man called him and recommended him to disguise his feelings as best he could, since all these vexations were put upon him merely to provoke him and, if he lost his temper, he would soon find himself worsted. After secretly imparting this advice, the Spaniard disappeared into the night.'

When day came, Coelho was led to the gate of the palace in the midst of a great throng, and greeted with much honour by the dispenser of justice. The Samorim was indisposed and regretted that he could not give audience. He begged Coelho to deliver the message of the Portuguese commander to the Hindu official.

Coelho courteously replied that his instructions were that the message should be delivered only to the Samorim in person, and to no other. If the Samorim was unable to grant him an audience, he would return to his ship and reappear when the King might be in the mood to receive him.

The official insisted, but Coelho remained calm and firm. When he asked for a boat in order to return to his ship, the Samorim suddenly forgot his diplomatic illness and gave orders that the Portuguese captain was to be brought before him. When he had heard Gama's message, he bade Coelho await his answer at the palace gate, but Coelho gently replied that his commander's orders were that he should receive the Samorim's message from his own mouth. As he stood there without budging and seemed determined not to give way, the Samorim muttered that he granted all the requests made by the captain-general and gave orders for a suitable answer to be sent.

There followed a lengthy interval, and while Coelho still held his ground, the grand Brahman brought a palm-leaf writing tablet covered with all kinds of signs. The Brahman placed a small cord which he wore across his chest between his thumbs, and holding his hands together swore that the leaf had been signed by the Samorim's own hand and that it contained his acceptance of all the captain-general's requests. After he had questioned the factor Davane, who stood at his side, Coelho took the leaf, kissed it, touched his forehead with it, and placed it in his bosom. As the two were walking back to the shore, the Spaniard furtively crossed their path and slipped a letter for Vasco da Gama into Davane's hand. 'You should celebrate the return of your captain in order to do honour to the bringer of a letter signed by the Samorim,' the letter said. 'Send only a small quantity of goods on shore each day, and have whatever you have bought taken aboard each evening. Send Davane with your factor, and also João Martins and another man. Bid them make no complaints, not to haggle and to accept whatever they are offered without dispute.'

On receiving this letter, Gama at once had the *St Gabriel* be-flagged, and ordered the trumpets to sound and the cannon to be fired. All this amazed and astonished the people of Calicut. Then, resigning himself to God's will, he sent his secretary Diogo Dias ashore as factor, with Pero de Braga to assist him, and João Martins, Davane and Malemo Cana, the King of Melindi's pilot, in their company. The five men took with them samples which were intended for the purpose of settling the general conditions of trade: they took a hundredweight of coral and the same quantity of vermilion, a cask of quicksilver, a hundred pounds of copper and some gold and silver coins, and carried a table covered with a green cloth and a pair of wooden scales. They were instructed not to haggle or dispute anything, but to appear satisfied with everything, without showing displeasure, even if they were forced to appear simple in the eyes of the natives. These recommendations were not wasted, for Diogo Dias and his friends were offered, at the instigation of the Moors, the worst qualities of pepper and spices, and given short weight and asked high prices. They adhered faithfully to the captain-general's instructions, and paid all they were asked without complaint or protest.

The fiscal officer shamelessly turned these unusual conditions to account, prudently leaving a small part of his excess profits for the Samorim, of whose greed he was well aware. But he failed to set aside any part of the catch for his good friend the Gozil, who was accordingly aggrieved. Furthermore, the Moors, who were sharp enough to see through Vasco da Gama's tactics, threatened the Gozil that they would withhold their subsidies if he did not contrive to frighten his master by telling him that the trade of the Portuguese was only a pretext to gather information about the defences of Calicut and that they intended to come back in force and conquer it. The Gozil acceded to their requirements and went to the Samorim, who also called the fiscal officer. The latter said that he had no fault to find with people who took everything and paid without dispute.

'That proves what I say!' exclaimed the Gozil. 'If these Portuguese were real merchants, they would not accept bad goods at double their proper value. These Christians are not traders at all. They are soldiers and they have come here to destroy our kingdom. They must be annihilated, and we must burn their ships so that none of them can return to their own country and reveal the way they have discovered across the ocean!'

The Samorim was afraid of losing the presents he coveted, and decided to defer making a decision until he had received the King of Portugal's ambassador.

'Obedient to God's will,' says Corrêa, the devoted Pérez waited until darkness fell and then went in the guise of a beggar to inform Diogo Dias of all these intrigues. He urged the factor to recommend the captain-general to refuse to come ashore without receiving a proper hostage, and he, Pérez, undertook to ascertain that the person offered was suitable.

Thus forewarned, Gama told the Samorim's messenger who had come aboard the *St Gabriel* to settle the day of the audience, that he required a hostage of rank as a guarantee for his safety. The Samorim was pressed for a decision and warned three of his *naïrs* for the duty. Gozil was alarmed to find that one of these was his own nephew. He tried to persuade his master to alter his decision, but the King replied that he would find a way of recovering the hostages as soon as the King of Portugal's ambassador was at his mercy.

The three *naïrs*, with gold bangles on their wrists and gold rings in their ears, were taken to Diogo Dias. The factor was anxious to delay receiving them until he had had Pérez's assurance about their rank, and said that he must receive them from the Samorim's hand. But Pérez soon informed him that, following the custom of the country, the Gozil prized his nephew more than if he were his own son. No better hostage could be found to guarantee the safety of the captain-general.

Having seen to the comfort of the esteemed nephew and one of his companions, Gama decided that the third hostage should accompany him on his visit to the Samorim. He chose twelve gentlemen to form his retinue and bade them all dress in their finest clothes. Some of the soldiers, dressed in rich garments and carrying trumpets decked with red and white silk pennants bearing the armillary sphere embroidered in gold thread, clambered into a barge to escort the *capitão-mór*. The splendid uniform that Gama himself was to wear for his appearance before the King of Calicut was carefully folded and placed in a chest.

As they approached the shore, Gama ordered the rowers to raise their oars. He was anxious not to expose his ambassadorial dignity to the slights that Nicolau Coelho had had to suffer in silence, and first sent the *naïr* and the interpreter ashore to obtain confirmation that the Samorim was disposed to receive him without delay. This was a wise precaution, for the two men returned saying that the Samorim had been kept in the country, and asked that the captain-general should await his return at Calicut. Gama remained unperturbed and begged the *naïr* to inform his master that the King of Portugal's ambassador would remain on his ship awaiting the day when it would be convenient for the Samorim to receive him: he then turned about and went back on board the *St Gabriel*.

The Gozil, visibly put out in his schemes, told Diogo Dias that the commander of the fleet had been much to blame in disobeying the Samorim's orders, and received the sharp retort that the *capitão-mór* received his orders from the King of Portugal, his lord, and no other. Dias added that the sun was near setting and that the universal usage of courts required that an ambassador should be received in full daylight, with all the ceremony the circumstance demanded. Fearing for the safety of his nephew, the Gozil persuaded the Samorim to open the gates of his palace to the haughty Portuguese captain on the following day.

'When the Samorim's message arrived,' says João de Barros, 'Vasco da Gama went ashore with twelve reliable men. He was received on the shore by a noble official called the Catual, escorted by two hundred men on foot, some to carry baggage and others, armed with swords and round shields, forming the escort. More men carried on their shoulders the litter in which the Catual lay, for the people in this land of Malabar have no beasts of burden.'

The Catual was a sort of vice-marshal of the court and he had brought a second palanquin for Gama, who was invited to mount. The native porters went at such a brisk pace that the dozen Portuguese selected to accompany their commander, unused to walking after their long months at sea, could not catch up with them until the evening, when they reached the place where they were to spend the night.

Next day they stopped before a magnificent Hindu temple. Under its dome there were images before which the people of the country prostrated themselves. The Portuguese, still supposing that these were distant disciples of St Thomas, imitated them, to the great satisfaction of the natives. In the next town, another Catual of higher rank than the first came out to meet Gama and saluted him gallantly, in the midst of soldiers, disposed in good order, and musicians. The captain-general of the fleet was requested to enter a finer and richer palanquin, and resumed his journey.

Gama had first expressed the desire to be taken to Diogo Dias' factory on the pretext of donning the robes prepared for his embassy, though in fact in order that his secretary might give him the latest news of the situation. The twelve gentlemen of his escort only came up with him very belatedly. Their progress on the sandy road had been slow, and they were later impeded by the great crowds which gathered to see them. When he emerged from the factory, says Corrêa, the captain-general 'was wearing a long sleeved cloak of brown satin lined with smooth brocade, and under it a short tunic of blue satin, and white breeches. On his head he had a soft-brimmed cap of blue velvet decked with a white plume held by a rich brooch. An enamelled chain hung across his chest while a gold-chased dagger hung from his richly garnished belt. His page was in purple satin, and before him, led by Diogo Dias, went the twelve gentlemen, all handsome figures and splendidly arrayed. They marched in single file and each of them carried a present for the Samorim, consisting of a piece of fine scarlet, a piece of yellow satin, a chair covered with brocade and decorated with silver-gilt nails, a crimson satin cushion, a foot-cushion of purple satin, a basin and ewer of wrought and gilded silver, and a large mirror with gilded and painted doors, fifty silk caps decorated with buttons and each covered with a crimson silk veil decorated with thread of gold, and finally fifty gilded cases, each decorated with silver studs and containing a Flemish knife. The gentlemen carrying the presents were preceded by trumpeters who played with all their might.'

The crowd was so dense that the procession had difficulty in proceeding. Diogo Dias was already greeting the Samorim before Gama could reach the gate of the palace. The King of Calicut was so impatient to see the presents that he did not wait for the arrival of the ambassador to have them displayed. One of the *naïrs*, doubtless suborned by the Moors, sneered loudly: the King of Portugal must be very poor, if these few things were all he could offer to the King of Calicut! A little gold would have been better. The man was not altogether at fault, for the poorest of his master's robes was worth far more than the whole present sent by King Manoel.

Amidst the crowd of Hindus who pressed around him, Gama had had no difficulty in picking out certain persons who carried short broadswords and wore shields on their arms, observing him intently: these were the Moors, on the look-out for an opportunity to stir up a riot. But Gama pretended to be unaware of the danger that threatened his every step, and advanced with majestic and dignified strides, waiting for the *naïrs* to clear a way for him when the crowd became too thick. At once the throng cleared of its own volition, as though filled with sudden awe. This was occasioned by the appearance at the palace gate of the great Catual, who among other prorogatives, enjoyed the right of summarily beheading anyone who entered the Samorim's apartments without his permission.

He led Gama into an outer court, and the curious mob pushed in behind him. Before the *naïrs* could restore order, a skirmish had begun and a man had been killed and several more injured. A second court, this time roofed and surrounded by a handsome colonnade, opened on to a vast hall in which the Samorim sat under a white canopy 'with very fine and subtle decorations'. Corrêa says that he was already seated on the brocaded chair which Diogo Dias had been forced to hand over without waiting for the captain-general's arrival, but it seems more probable that the oriental potentate was reclining on a divan covered with rich silks, as João de Barros says.

'His skin was very dark,' says Corrêa. 'He was naked except from the navel to the knees. This part of his body was covered with white cloths, one of which, like a scarf, ended in a point threaded with gold rings encrusted with great rubies. His left arm was clasped above the elbow by three large linked bangles all covered with precious stones, and that in the centre with especially large ones, undoubtedly of great value. From it there hung a diamond as big as an inch long, of extraordinary brilliance and quite priceless. About his neck the Samorim wore a chain of pearls almost as big as walnuts: it fell in two swaths done to his navel. Above this necklace he wore a shorter chain of gold, from which was suspended a heart-shaped medallion, surrounded by pearls even larger than those of the chain and filled with rubies: in the midst of the heart was a very beautiful green stone as large as a bean. The Spaniard later told Vasco da Gama that this was of great value and was called an emerald. Like the diamond of the armband and another great pearl fixed in the Samorim's hair, it belonged to the ancient treasure of the Kings of Calicut. The Samorim had long black hair knotted on the top of his head. A string of pearls, like those of his necklace, was turned round the knot, and at the end of the string there was one pear-shaped one bigger than all the rest. The King's ears were pierced and decorated with numerous rings of small round pieces of gold.'

In the presence of this dazzling apparition, who seemed to have come out of the Arabian Nights, the 'piece of yellow satin', and even the scarlet, cut a poor figure. To the right and left of the Samorim stood two pages, dark and naked except for silk loincloths. The first of these carried a red shield decorated with gold and precious stones and with a golden armband: in his right hand he gripped a sword an ell long and a span broad with a pommel garnished with gold and stones and festooned with pearls. The other page held a broad-brimmed gold cup into which the King spat his betel: it was prepared for him by his great Brahman from a leaf like that of the orange, mingled with salt, chalk and pieces of areca-nut. This mixture reddens the mouth and sweetens the breath.

The Samorim made not the slightest motion when Gama arrived. Only after some time did he nod almost imperceptibly towards the great Brahman, clad in white, who awaited the order to present the King of Portugal's ambassador. The Brahman took Gama by the hand and led him towards his master, who bowed slightly from the waist in response to Gama's profound obeisances. He then raised his right arm and touched Gama's right hand with the tip of his fingers, beckoning him to sit on the steps of the dais below his couch. But Gama remained standing and at once began to address him, his words being translated by the interpreter and João Martins.

'Most powerful sire,' he said, 'you are the most powerful ruler of all India, and all the rest are beneath your feet. The great King of Portugal, my master, has heard of your greatness, the fame of which girdles the whole earth, and is possessed of a great desire to know you and to make a treaty of friendship with you, as with a brother. He has therefore sent his ships to visit you in peace and friendship with wares of his own country to dispose of in yours, and desires to acquire the produce of your country, especially pepper and spices, which are not found in Portugal.'

The Samorim replied in a few words which João Martins hesitated to translate for the captain-general's ear. 'You say you come from a very powerful kingdom,' said the King, 'yet the gifts you have brought me from your ruler are of trifling value!'

Gama showed no discomfiture at this slighting remark, but replied confidently that the three ships formed only the smallest part of a great fleet that had been dispersed by storm. The King of Portugal's presents had been on another ship, he said, and those now displayed consisted only of his own personal offering.

'And I am to inform you,' he continued, 'that the King of Portugal, my master, will send so many ships laden with so much merchandise and bearing so much money that they will buy everything that is to be sold in Calicut. As a guarantee of the truth of these words, I deliver you this letter signed with the King's hand and sealed with his seal: within you will find words of peace and truth, addressed to you in virtue of the treaty of friendship he has bidden me conclude with you.'

He then kissed King Manoel's letter and placed it against his forehead, after which he knelt on one knee and delivered it to the Samorim, who received it and placed it with both hands against his breast as a sign of love. Having broken the seal, he gazed at it fixedly and then handed it to the fiscal officer to be translated.

'Can't you give me the golden statue you have on your ship?' he asked.

Gama was disconcerted for a moment.

'It is not a gold statue, but only gilded,' he answered. 'It is the statue of the Virgin Mary, and I shall never be separated from it, for Our Lady has guided me across the ocean and will lead me back to my own country.'

In the Samorim's Palace

The Samorim's features bore an expression of great disappointment. However, he authorized Gama to ask his fiscal officer for all the goods he could carry on his ships and to allow his crews to come ashore and visit the town of Calicut and amuse themselves without receiving any harm from anyone. In proof of the truth of his words, he called the Gozil and gave orders that his words were to be proclaimed by criers through the town. Then the Samorim dismissed the captain-general, after having promised him the honour of a further audience.

The great Catual, with the Gozil and the fiscal officer at his side, escorted Gama with due ceremony to the gate of his factory where they took leave amidst many courtesies. Gama spent the night with his companions, and next day sent his trumpeters aboard with a letter for his brother and Nicolau Coelho.

The Great Catual

THE day did not end without an unexpected visit, that of the fiscal officer, who arrived at the factory followed by a whole caravan of presents. Gama received twenty pieces of fine cotton worked with silver and known in Calicut as *beirame*, twenty pieces of even finer cotton called *sinabafos*, ten pieces of silk of various colours, four blocks of gum benjamin so heavy that a man could hardly carry them, fifty bags of musk in a jar of fine porcelain and six large bowls and six more deep dishes of porcelain. Since Fernão Gomes had been happy to receive from Afonso V the right to acquire a single civet-cat a year during his tenure of the contract for the Guinea trade, and benjamin was a much sought-after drug, the present was regarded as truly worthy of a king; and this must have been Gama's own opinion as he thanked the official in King Manoel's name. When he was told that all the presents were intended for his own personal use, and that the Samorim would later entrust him with a present which the King of Portugal might find to his taste, Gama realized that the King of Calicut had effectively indicated how little he prized what he had been given. The musk and benjamin alone were worth a thousand times more than all the objects Gama had handed over on behalf of his King.

Meanwhile the Gozil had caused criers to announce throughout the town that the Samorim ordered his subjects to do the people from the Portuguese ships no harm and that they must be supplied with whatever they needed. Vasco da Gama then had the scales set up outside the factory; the place was cleared and tidied and a shelter of palm-leaves was made. Benches were set out, and the merchants came and sat there: the Moors came with them too, to spy on the activities of the Portuguese. Each evening the spices and other goods were paid for according to their weight, and next day they were loaded on boats for carriage to the ships. This continued for a number of days and Gama bade Davane take presents to the Catual, the Gozil and the fiscal officer. But the Gozil's hatred of Gama only increased, for envy led him to imagine that the fiscal officer was more favoured than himself in these transactions. When the Moors promised him a large sum of money if he succeeded in getting rid of the Portuguese, he was therefore well disposed to listen: the Catual received the same offer from them and assured them of his collaboration.

He shortly afterwards came to visit Gama and told him that the Samorim desired to receive him again as he had promised, and begged him to come to him in the country. The *capitão-mór* rejoiced at this news and trustingly entered the palanquin sent by the Catual. He was accompanied by Martins and several others, and they had not yet left Calicut when the Spaniard approached Martins and whispered in his ear: 'Suffer and say nothing.' Only when the party was already outside the town was it possible to pass on this message to Gama, who asked Martins to warn all his companions closely to follow the advice.

The sun had already set and the Catual's men continued to march on through fields and woods. Night was upon them when they stopped in the midst of a thick forest in front of a wretched house, where Gama and his men were invited to spend the night on rough mats after a meagre meal. Next day the journey was resumed under the heat of a scorching sun, and they at last reached a river where two boats were waiting. Following Pérez's advice, the Portuguese affected to make light of the adventure and made not the slightest demur. They climbed aboard the boats as if going for an excursion, and made no objection when they were asked to land on the bare bank and given only boiled rice to eat. Although he was convinced that his last hour had come, Gama pretended to be delighted by the unexpected trip and allowed himself to be shut in a poor hovel without making any protest. Next day he was led by the *naïr* to the Catual, who dwelt not far away and had had Martins brought to serve as interpreter.

'A ship has put in at Calicut from Kilwa and Mozambique,' said the Catual. 'Those on board tell us that the Portuguese are pirates who merely pretend to engage in trade the better to spy on towns which they intend later to attack and rob. The Samorim has given orders for your ships to be seized and the crews to be held under arrest until they confess. You must obey his orders, and since you are their chief, you must be the first to confess.'

As if the whole thing were only a jest, Vasco da Gama said lightly that he would confess all that and much more, but only to the Samorim, and to no one else. He would say nothing at all to the Catual.

Thus thwarted, the Catual took Martins aside and tried to draw him into admissions that might be turned against the Portuguese. To use a phrase that Rabelais was to employ, he might as well have 'tried to get farts out a of dead ass'. At length the Catual wearied of the struggle, and convinced that the faithful interpreter was a complete imbecile, left him alone.

Gama thought that they were a great distance from Calicut, but they had come scarcely two leagues, and all the comings and goings of the last three days had had no purpose but to unnerve him. On finding that he had not succeeded, the Catual then had recourse to a different method. Expecting to meet with a refusal which would enable him to denounce the Portuguese to the Samorim for bad faith, he demanded that Gama should at once have all the merchandise still on the ships set ashore. He was astonished when Gama accepted without difficulty, and even asked the Catual to send the two boats on which he and his companions had arrived to his brother Paulo with a letter. This, however, contained a concealed warning that he was to keep a strict watch on the hostages.

The two boats returned just as Gama had promised, but they were not sufficient to contain all the goods. The Catual sent off more barges but their masters came back empty-handed. Paulo da Gama and Nicolau Coelho, they reported, had refused to hand anything over without written orders from the captain-general. Gama pretended to be furiously angry on receiving this message and declared that he himself would go aboard and see that the rest of the goods were laden on ten large craft which he asked the Catual to obtain. He added that if all the goods were not sold, he would offer the residue to the Catual and other officials. This prospect appeared to please the Catual, though he was not disposed to allow his prisoner to escape. A written order would suffice, he said, and all those on shore could return to their ships, except the indispensable interpreter, Martins, and two men, whom Gama might choose.

Gama concealed his disappointment, but wrote the instructions the Catual demanded. However, he sent word to his brother by the men who were released that even if all the remaining goods were loaded on the barges, the Catual would still keep him in his power.

'He therefore besought his brother,' writes Corrêa, 'in the name of God and the blood that ran in both their veins, to offer presents to the hostages and send them courteously ashore if it turned out that the Catual still persisted in preventing him from returning to the ship. He added that if, even after the release of the hostages, he was still held captive, his brother should raise anchor and set sail for Portugal and report to their lord the King the results of the mission he had entrusted to Gama. If he himself were killed, nothing would be lost, but if the ships did not return to Portugal with news of the great discovery, they would lose something so important that it would be hard to render account for it to God. There was nothing for Paulo da Gama to do but to leave at the earliest possible moment. If he were to remain much longer he would be killed and his ships and merchandise seized, for the Moors had now many ships in the port and were only waiting for the pretext to attack and destroy the Portuguese ships.'

Paulo da Gama sent back the barges without unloading any goods. In a letter to his brother he said that every officer and man under their command preferred to go down with their ships rather than abandon their captain-general, and he, Paulo da Gama, would not accept his brother's orders to the contrary. He asked Gama to leave no doubt in the Catual's mind that if he persisted in holding their commander against his will, all the ships in the port of Calicut would be sunk and the Samorim's capital would be destroyed.

The Catual desired nothing better. Bidding the Gozil to place a strong guard over Gama, Diogo Dias, Pero de Braga, João Martins and the two other Portuguese still on shore, he hurried to report the insolent threat of the Portuguese captain to the Samorim, spicing his account with a number of lies designed to arouse the monarch's ire. In his wrath, the Samorim gave orders for the confiscation of all the goods in the factory, and was on the verge of giving the Catual orders to put Gama and his companions to death when the great Brahman intervened and was supported by the fiscal officer.

'My lord, do not do that, for you have no reason for it,' said the holy man. 'Even if what the Catual says is true, the strangers have not so far done any harm. They have on the contrary behaved peaceably and well, and have brought you the finest present you have ever received from the hands of strangers. Leave them in peace, and if they behave amiss, then do as you will.'

The argument drawn from King Manoel's present may have made the Samorim smile. But he had confidence in the wisdom of the Brahman, and by temperament he inclined to caution rather than to extreme measures. Since he had the captain-general in his power, he decided to await events. However, he kept the goods he had already seized.

Paulo da Gama retired to sleep on his problem, and woke up with a solution for it. Summoning his companions early next day, he told them:

'To sail away and desert my brother whom I love more than my own life is a thing beyond my powers. I know that if I were to do it I should die of shame and grief before we ever touched Portugal. But I know my brother's stubbornness, and I know too that he would rather die a hundred times than leave our lord the King in ignorance of the discovery we have made. I have pondered these matters all night long, wondering what was the best course to take, and I perceive that my mistake was in giving way to a justifiable resentment and having recourse to force. There is only one possible course of action, to release the hostages and offer them rich presents. I believe that in this way we shall foil the designs of the Moors and that only good will come of it. Even if my brother and his companions are not freed when we return the hostages, at least it is less likely that they will come to harm.'

All those present accepted the argument, and Nicolau Coelho said:

'If you wish, I will land with the hostages and with God's favour will remain with the captain-general and share his fate in case the Samorim gives way to the Moors and refuses to set him free.'

Then Paulo da Gama summoned the two hostages. He asked them if they were aware that their lives depended on that of the King of Portugal's ambassador and that he might have them beheaded if Vasco da

Gama came to any harm. They replied that they were aware of this.

Paulo da Gama then told them of the plot devised by the Catual, adding:

'Since the Samorim is served by traitors who have no fear of their master, we can no longer place our trust in him. I shall therefore leave Calicut and return to Portugal, since we are no longer safe here. You can tell the Samorim and his false servants that he may do what he wishes with the Portuguese who are still on shore. But let him bear in mind my words to you, for I know that you are noble and I urge you to consider your own honour. The Samorim has trifled with you by making you hostages for his word, which he has not kept. Tell him that the King of Portugal is so loyal to his servants that for love of a single Portuguese who is wronged he will send to the very ends of the earth to avenge him. In this case his vengeance is certain, for his ambassador has come in all peace and goodwill to offer the Samorim a rich present and his friendship, and the Samorim, acting like a man without honour, has broken his word and betrayed his trust, things that could never be expected of a great king whose fame had reached our ears. Tell the Samorim that now, wherever we go we shall recount the tale of his baseness and treachery, and we shall speak of him as a king false to his word and faithless to strangers who came to him offering peace—very different in these matters from the good and noble King of Melindi. Now I must go. But let the Samorim and his false servants look to the treatment they dispense to the Portuguese retained in Calicut against their will: I swear to you by the head of the King of Portugal, my master, that we shall make them pay a hundredfold for every one of their misdeeds.'

After these words, Paulo da Gama presented each of the *naïrs* with a red silk cap, a case of Flemish knives, three ells of crimson satin and a gold coin. Then he gave orders for the sails to be raised.

The *naïrs* were perplexed and begged him not to depart until they had spoken to the Samorim. But Paulo da Gama replied that he could wait no longer, now that he knew that Calicut was governed by a treacherous and perjurous king. And while the boat with the two hostages on board made for the shore, the ship was turned towards the open sea. However, the wind off the land was a weak one and the ships were forced to anchor a league off shore.

⟩ 20 ⟨

The Crossroads of Destiny

IT was August 29, 1498. Nearly fourteen months had elapsed since the *St Gabriel*, *St Raphael* and *Bérrio* had left Lisbon. More than half of those who had cried 'Farewell, Farewell' in response to the weeping throng on the Restelo beach were dead or in a state of extreme exhaustion. Now, the captain-general of the fleet and five of his companions were in the hands of the Catual, and he had been bribed by the Moors of Calicut who desired to kill them. These Moors had many well-armed ships in the port with full complements of warlike men thirsting to attack the Portuguese vessels. How could Paulo da Gama, who had only a handful of sound seamen and soldiers, hope to resist the enemy if battle were forced upon him?

The plan of the Moors was remarkably simple: if the intruders who had discovered the sea-way from Lisbon to India could be exterminated, years would pass before any other Portuguese vessel made its appearance in these waters, or for that matter any other ship from the west, for the fame of their failure would for long discourage such Christians as might be tempted to imitate them. Moreover, the Moors were well situated to realize that the Christian camp was divided everywhere against itself. It would be easy for them to find allies, or accomplices, among those who patiently awaited in Alexandria or Tripoli in Syria the arrival of the caravans that assured wealth and power to Venice, Genoa, Florence and other towns. Moreover, the threat of competition which now for the first time hung over an area hitherto completely monopolized by the ships of Islam would at once turn the way-stations of east Africa into so many defence-points, and similar fortifications would also spring up at the mouth of the Red Sea and the Persian Gulf, in the Gulf of Cambaya and on the western coast of India itself. Sofala,

Quelimane, Mozambique, Kilwa, Mombasa, Melindi (whose chivalrous King would soon be reduced to order), Mogadishu, Aden, Socotra, Muscat, Ormuz, Diu, Damão, Goa, Mangalor, Cranganor, Cananor, Calicut, Cochin, Coulão, Trivanderam, all the places where the Moors were influential, would be turned into fortresses ready to repulse with a storm of cannon-fire any ships so foolhardy as to round the African cape and threaten the exclusive control of a sea that was to be closed permanently to strangers. The proud Venetians would be only too glad to obtain cannon for the producers who fed the commerce on which their supremacy was built, thus preserving the right to boast of their city as 'the Dominant'.

Let it not be objected that these were merely vain misgivings. Ten years later—after Venice had asked the Pope to intervene with King Manoel and persuade him to help the Republic in its war against the Turks, the Ten advised the Sultan of Cairo to wage war to the knife against the Portuguese as they were on the verge of gaining the mastery of the Indian ocean. Venice would buy timber on their behalf in Turkey and be responsible for its delivery in Alexandria; she would send shipwrights, caulkers and cannon-founders to help to build and equip large ships, producing the plans and finding the naval architects.

Who can say what the world would have been like today if a handful of Portuguese had given way to the threats of a distant Hindu monarch on that August 29, 1498? Less than half a century had passed since the capture of Constantinople, and it had sufficed to permit the Turks to conquer Serbia and Bosnia, to enslave Greece, to annexe Walachia, to subdue Karamania and the Crimea, to humiliate Venice, enter Transylvania, besiege Rhodes, subject Albania and the Epirus and reduce the whole of Asia Minor. In 1520 Selim I cast the Ottoman mantle over Egypt and Kurdistan. His successor Sulaiman the Magnificent would take Belgrade, seize Rhodes and the neighbouring islands, invade Hungary, annex Tunis and Algiers, after having laid siege to Vienna, and his ships would threaten Malta. If the discovery of the sea-way to India had come to nothing, the resources of the padishah and of the Sultan of Cairo, each of which laid heavy duties on goods in transit, would not have been reduced and no hostile influence on the right flank of Egypt would have been brought into being to handicap the movements of the Ottoman empire and ruin Muslim power in the Indies. There is every reason to suppose that Venice would have adopted a conciliatory policy towards Islam in order to retain its privileges— Francis I of France did not hesitate to seek an alliance with the Turks against the House of Austria—and the outcome of the battle of Lepanto, in which the ships of the Serene Republic fought side by side with those of Pius V and Spain, might have been different.

In his remarkable *Balance Sheet of History*, M. René Grousset has brilliantly summarized the situation.

'. . . The origin of the great voyages of discovery lies in the failure of the crusades. With the collapse of the Frankish colonies in Syria, the sultans of Egypt held the exclusive monopoly of the trade of the Indian Ocean, and their abuse of it drove the seamen of the far west to seek a direct way to the Indies by the Cape of Good Hope.

'A comparison of dates is significant. In 1498 the first Ottoman troops entered Venetia near Vicenza, but Vasco da Gama reached Calicut. In 1503 Turkey seized Modena, Coron and Lepanto from Venice; but in 1509 the Portuguese viceroy Francisco de Almeida, having destroyed the combined fleets of the Sultan of Egypt and the Samorim of Calicut, made himself master of the Indian Ocean. In 1522 Sulaiman the Magnificent seized Rhodes; but in 1527 the Portuguese dispersed the fleet of the Shah of Gujerat. In 1532 the Turks ravaged Austria; but in 1537 the fleet they sent to help Gujerat was scattered by João de Castro.

'Thus at the moment when the Ottoman empire was unleashing the most formidable series of attacks directed by Asia at the heart of Europe, the west had reached Asia by the sea-route and taken the vast continent in the rear, attacking the Muslim world behind its breastplate. The moment was moreover singularly appropriate for this venture. In the first half of the fourteenth century India had formed a vast Muslim sultanate which it would have been useless to attack: by the end of the fifteenth century, this empire had long since crumbled away and the peninsula was in a state of unparalleled anarchy. The western coast of the Dekkan in particular, in whose ports the Portuguese had staked their claim, was divided among various rival Muslim kingdoms: Gujerat, Khandash, Ahmednagar, Bijapur, not to mention their common enemy, the Hindu kingdom of Bijarranagan. Once the fleets of the Shah of Gujerat and Samorim of

Calicut (the only ones of any consequence) had been destroyed, none of these states, which were quite lacking in sea-faring traditions, was capable of resisting the Portuguese, whose artillery gave them an overwhelming superiority. Furthermore, the Portuguese viceroys ably turned the masses of the Hindu population against the Indo-Muslim princes and also revived the latent Christianity of the old Nestorian communities of the Malabar coast. This far-sighted policy bore fruit. The occupation of Goa, the chief port of the sultanate of Bijapur, by Albuquerque in 1510, presaged the establishment of the first European sea-power in the Indies.'

'The Portuguese,' M. Grousset adds, 'were perfectly conscious of the historical significance of their work. In the face of the vastness of Asia, they felt themselves to represent Europe and were fully aware of the dignity conferred on them by this role.' On that day of August 29, 1498, which might bring them life or death and their country greatness or the ruin of its hopes, Paulo da Gama and his companions, separated from their own country by the immense barrier of Africa and the perils of the sea, stood alone for the west, in three Portuguese ships lying motionless before a silent, hostile and threatening shore. They remembered the oath their captain-general had taken to their lord King Manoel, and were resolved to keep the standard of Christ 'for ever unfurled and never folded, before Moors and before gentiles, or any other people they might find on their way'. As Vasco da Gama and his companions prepared to die, they resolved to preserve the Cross and defend it to the last drop of their blood against the dangers of water, fire or steel.

21

The Victory of The Will

WHEN the two *naïrs* released by Paulo da Gama were brought before the Samorim and his officers, they delivered the message with which they had been entrusted, and added:

'Lord, tell us the day and hour you have chosen to put to death the captain of the fleet and his companions and at that day and hour we will come and kill ourselves in your presence. You offered us as an earnest of your sincerity, and we were willing that our heads should be sacrificed, for they were the guarantee of your honour. But if you are false to your word, all that remains is for you to deprive us of our lives. And, lord, we beseech you to reflect on the gravity of the injury you have done your own honour. The Portuguese have done no harm in your kingdom; on the contrary they had brought a present in earnest of peace and friendship.'

The fiscal officer and the Gozil added their support. The first of these knew that he had almost ruined himself by having defended the Portuguese, and realized that his own fate was linked with their security, while the Gozil had been bitterly reproached by the nephew whom he loved better than his own son, who felt deeply the shame that had been put upon him and was resolved to die unless the Portuguese were spared.

Informed that the *St Gabriel*, *St Raphael* and *Bérrio* had put to sea without doing any damage, despite the assertions of the Catual, the Samorim ordered the Moorish factor Davane to be brought before him. Throwing himself at his feet, Davane cried: 'Lord, lay a great and exemplary punishment on those who have advised you to do such injury to your own honour by urging you to betray your royal word!'

'Then,' says Corrêa, 'the Samorim ordered Vasco da Gama to be brought.' He assured Gama that he had been misled and deceived, and deluded by lies into believing that the Portuguese had evil intentions. But he now knew the truth, and would punish the guilty in accordance with the degree of their guilt. He said also that Vasco da Gama could go, and that he and his companions were free.

Gama retorted coldly:

'Do what befits your honour. I am only a stranger in this land. But heed my words: if you, King of Calicut, do not act as a great king should, your fame will be lost.'

Far from being incensed by these hard words, the Samorim begged the *capitão-mór* to accept as a token of his friendship a magnificent trinket of rubies and pearls, and a number of fine veils of silk and cotton. As he dismissed him, he begged Gama's pardon for all the disagreeable experiences to which the Portuguese had been so unjustly subjected, and promised that if the captain-general returned to Calicut he should see how the Samorim punished those who falsely gave him evil counsel.

When Gama and his companions arrived on board, his brother Paulo clasped him in his arms and hugged him to his bosom, while all present wept for joy. Alonso Pérez had come with him and told the whole story of the plot woven by the Moors, the officials and the Samorim. Before sending him ashore, loaded with splendid presents, Gama gave him a letter in which he had written in his own hand: 'Gentlemen of Portugal: This Spaniard, Alonso Pérez by name, is our true friend. You may rely upon him in everything, for I have found the loyalty of a good and faithful Christian in his heart.' This paper, bearing the captain-general's signature, caused the excellent Pérez more joy than all his presents.

'Tell the Moors on my behalf,' said Gama as they parted, 'that they will see me again in these regions. Tell them that they will reap the consequences of the harm they have done to the Portuguese. Tell them too that they will live to rue the day, for the consequences will be no less than the destruction of their power and trade in India. Bid them stamp these words in their memories and remember them on the day when those things come to pass as I have said.'

No sooner had Pérez returned to Calicut than the Samorim summoned him, and bade him tell all he knew about the Moors, his own officials and the Portuguese. The Spaniard did so, 'and very readily'. Disturbed by the extent of his error, the Samorim at once sent a messenger in a boat to beg Gama to bring his ships back into the harbour of Calicut, so that he, the Samorim, might see that they were laden with good spices and the wares seized from the factory. Gama refused. Dismissing the messenger, he bade him tell his master that, on his return to Portugal, he would report faithfully to the King all the events of his stay at Calicut. 'Tell the Samorim,' he concluded loftily, 'that I shall be sure to inform the King my master of his repentance.'

A fresh breeze was now blowing. The ships put to sea, and all the Portuguese, kneeling with their leader, gave thanks to God for having delivered them from so great a peril. They asked Our Lord Jesus Christ to bring them, out of His mercy, safe and sound to the port of Lisbon, so that the King might know through them of the sea-way to India and the wealth and customs of its peoples. It was September 10th.

22

Cananor

THE ruler of the neighbouring kingdom of Cananor had received from reliable informants news of the doings of the Portuguese in Calicut, and was fully aware of the conduct of the Samorim towards them and of the plots stirred up against them by the Moors. When the Moors of Cananor and their associates tried to set him against Gama and his companions, he refused to listen to their lies and abruptly threatened to cut their heads off. If it was true, he declared, that the power of the Moors was threatened by the Portuguese, he himself had every reason to seek the friendship of a people so feared at such a great distance from their own country. In this he was following the counsel of his soothsayers, who foretold that the Portuguese would destroy their enemies by both land and sea.

As soon as he had learned that the fleet had left the port of Calicut, he sent boats along the coast, fearing that Gama's ships might not stop at Cananor, and gave them orders to watch the sea by day and night. As soon as the three ships were sighted, the King sent out a *parao*, a large and fully manned vessel, carrying a *naïr* who delivered the following message: 'The King of Cananor, his master, besought the captains for love of their lord, the King of Portugal, not to pass Cananor without casting anchor, for the King of Cananor already knew of their misadventures at Calicut, which he deeply regretted.'

Gaspar Corrêa says that the *capitâo-mór* had hardly been informed of this request when a swarm of boats laden with water-jars, firewood, figs, poultry, coconuts, dried fish, butter, and palm oil arrived from Cananor. The people on these craft told the Portuguese that even if they would not visit Cananor, they should at least accept these articles, which were offered in all sincerity and would be useful to them in the course of their journey: But if they were interested in trade, they would do well to put in at Cananor, whose King would see that they obtained whatever they needed at better prices and in better quality than what they had bought in Calicut. The King, their master, they said, had no dearer wish than to conclude a treaty of peace and friendship with the Portuguese.

The ships were beflagged and put into the port. As soon as they had dropped anchor, they saluted the town with a salvo of artillery, which rejoiced the ears of the King. He himself was waiting on the shore and sent his chief minister to greet Gama. The Portuguese commander expressed his satisfaction and declared that he would be glad to satisfy the King's requests, except that he would not go ashore, since he was forbidden to do so until a treaty of peace and friendship should have been concluded. In order to meet the King's wishes, he drew up a list of such goods as he needed to complete his cargo. On the following day so much was brought out in *paraos* that part of it had to be returned since the ships could carry no more.

Won over by the honesty and generosity of the King, Gama sent ashore so much coral, vermillion, quicksilver, copper and brass-ware, that the King thought he had received much more than he had given. Moreover, Coelho went to deliver a present consisting of a piece of scarlet, another of black satin velvet, a third of crimson damask, a large silver basin containing thirty scarlet caps, fifty richly decorated knife-cases and a large gilded mirror. Gama rewarded the King's secretary who brought the goods to the ships with two caps, two knife-cases and five ells of scarlet cloth.

The King of Cananor was so anxious to meet Gama that he found a means of doing so without constraining the Portuguese to disobey his feigned orders. A crowd of workmen built a 'sort of jetty of wood, which projected into the sea the length of a crossbow-shot. It was so narrow that two men could not walk abreast along it. At its end a small and handsome wooden pavilion was constructed. When it was finished, the King entered the pavilion with six or seven of his retainers and summoned the Portuguese commander to visit him, for in this way his boats could not touch the shore.'

The shore was covered with a great crowd, and the royal musicians played loud and long. Gama and his brother, clad in splendid garments and reclining on rich coverings in beflagged boats, set out to the sound of trumpets and the thunder of cannon-fire, to comply with the King's gracious and ingenious invitation. As they reached the wooden house in which the King sat in bejewelled splendour, the two captains rose and uncovered. The King also rose, beaming with joy. He took the hands of Gama and his brother and made them sit on either side of him, looking from one to the other with an air of great friendliness. Then with the aid of the interpreters, Paulo da Gama rose and said:

'Lord, you now know who we are and how God has brought us hither. I shall only say that we have seen with our own eyes that you are truly a great king and one incapable of the falseness of the Samorim. And since you have proved your generosity and sincerity by your actions, we shall be happy to conclude a certain and permanent treaty of peace and friendship between you and our lord and master the King of Portugal, whose goodness and loyalty is such that when such treaties are made he becomes at once like a brother to his allies, and their friends become his friends and their enemies his enemies.'

'My heart is filled with the greatest joy it has ever felt,' replied the King of Cananor, 'and my whole being is full of the peace and friendship I desire to exchange with your King. We shall make the treaty as you propose, and I shall sign it after my own fashion.'

'God alone can be certain that this port of Cananor will be revisited again by Portuguese ships,' said Paulo da Gama. 'That is in His hands, for we are only sailors and our lives are always at the mercy of the perils of the high seas. But by our God who is in heaven and by the head of our King, we promise you, my brother and I, who are both sons of the same father, that if ever other Portuguese ships come to these regions of India, they will enter this port and bring you letters to confirm and establish the peace and brotherhood between our King and you, which shall last as you desire. In token and proof of this alliance, we give you this sword, for such is the custom of our King when he has made a treaty of friendship. Whoever breaks such a treaty loses his honour as if he were to break this sword.'

The King of Cananor took an oath by his own hand and by the eyes and bosom of his mother that these words, promises and assurances delivered on behalf of the King of Portugal were confirmed forever as his own. He gave orders that his scribes were to

prepare a golden leaf with all these things written down and sub-
scribed by himself and his ministers.

Whilst the treaty was being drawn up, this generous prince told
Vasco and Paulo da Gama:

'The Samorim has written to me to express his regret at the misadventures you have suffered in his kingdom. He knows that he has
been ill advised and is determined to chastise the guilty.'

'I do not know if he speaks the truth,' said Gama. 'For my part,
I have put these things out of my mind, but the day will come when
his regrets will certainly be greater than they are at present.'

The treaty, inscribed on a golden leaf, was brought and read
before the two captains. When the King had signed it, he entrusted
to the two brothers, for delivery to King Manoel, a large golden
necklace decorated with very precious stones, with ten gold rings
set with stones and twenty pieces of fine cotton. And he took his
departure, assuring them of his loyal friendship.

23

The Jew of Granada

DAVANE, the Moorish trader, had decided to settle in Cananor. Gama did not allow this man who had served him so loyally and faithfully to depart without bestowing on him a sum of money and rich presents and also a letter in his own hand assuring all Portuguese captains who might appear there that Davane, a native of Cambaya, was a good, faithful and true friend, and should always be treated as such by King Manoel's subjects. Then the ships set sail and left the coast, covering a distance of forty or fifty leagues. But then the wind dropped and finally died out altogether, leaving the fleet becalmed. Gama could not conceal his vexation, and the pilots advised him to return whence he had come rather than labour the ships and exhaust the supply of water, for it was still too early for the monsoon. 'It would be shameful for us to return ashore!' Gama exclaimed. 'The people of Cananor would say that we were ignorant of seamanship.'

Ibn Majid, the pilot from Melindi, made a proposal.

'Let us not return to Cananor. We can lie off an island I know, where there is a good anchorage not far from the mainland. There we shall have fresh water and fuel, and shall be sheltered from all winds as we wait for the monsoon.'

The *capitâo-mór* resigned himself to this plan. Taking advantage of the first breath of wind, the ships returned towards the shore, where they found a favourable breeze which carried them slowly towards the islands. They passed a great many boats, and the pilots urged the captains to seize them, since they were laden with valuable goods. But Gama refused, saying: 'Our ships are well laden with what we came to India to seek. We are not thieves and we will not take what does not belong to us.'

He feared that the pillar of St Gabriel, which Diogo Dias had set up at the entrance to the port of Calicut, might have been pulled down by the angry Moors. He had only one left, called Santa Maria, and it was now erected on the island shown him by the pilot. It was September 15, 1498. The island and those around it have kept the holy name of the Virgin: the St Mary Islands lie off the Malabar coast.

The ships' hulls were now greatly in need of scraping and caulking, and ibn Majid told Gama that this work could be easily carried out before the monsoon began to blow at the anchorage of Anshediva, meaning 'Five Isles' in the language of the country and now known as Angediva or Anquedive. They reached this place on September 20, and the captain-general decided to stop at the largest of them which had a sheltered anchorage and plenty of fresh springs.

Opposite the islands is the mouth of a river called the Cintacora, from which the craft of native fishermen appeared every morning, passing before Angediva, scarcely a league from the mainland. When they saw the Portuguese ships, however, the fishermen avoided them, and it was impossible for the crews to buy their fish. Some other ships anchored near the islands to take on fresh water and fuel, never guessing the Portuguese were in the bay. When their shore-party suddenly beheld the strangers and their vessels, they were filled with terror. But Gama sent his Moorish pirate to them, and he reassured them. When the natives saw that the Portuguese meant them no harm, they took courage and brought them chickens, figs and coconuts and were delighted to receive caps and knives in exchange. They then sent boats to tell the fishermen that the strangers were harmless. From that day onward, plenty of fish was brought, and it was paid for so liberally in silver coin that the fishermen brought other supplies and even cloth, and made friends with the crews.

'Now there was on that coast at Onor, facing these islands, a pirate named Timoja,' says João de Barros. 'He was in the future to become a good friend of the Portuguese. As soon as he knew that the fleet had arrived at Angediva and that the seamen were strangers, he conceived the idea of attacking them by means of a subterfuge. He fastened together eight large rowing-boats and covered them over with foliage, so that the result resembled a great raft laden with greenery and floating on the water. When Gama saw this strange object approaching his ships, he asked the friendly Hindus what it was. They replied that it must be an invention of the pirate Timoja, who dwelt at Onor and thought of such contrivances. Vasco da Gama therefore ordered his brother and Nicolau Coelho to greet this suspicious visitation with cannon-fire, and as a result the boats, which had been fastened together under the screen of foliage, hastily separated and fled to the shore. But our people captured one of them which contained rice and other provisions.'

It soon became known along the whole Malabar coast that the Portuguese ships were resting and carrying out repairs at Angediva, and this news reached Goa, which was only twelve leagues away.

Yusuf Adil Khan, the sultan of Bijapur, had an excellent port in Goa. It stood on an island between the mouths of two large rivers, and possessed a large fleet of small sailing-ships. These were so well armed that they could force passing ships to put in at the port and pay tribute. The sultan's troops and crews were officered by Arabs, Persians, Turks and Levantines, who together made a strong and unified force. Curious to know more about the vessels from the distant lands of Christendom that lay in the bay of Angediva, the Sultan summoned his captain-general, who was a Jew born in Granada. He had been exiled from his native city during his youth, and had gone off wandering from land to land until he reached Turkey, whence he went to visit Mecca and so passed on to India. Yusuf had the greatest confidence in him and readily accepted his advice.

'These strangers are Portuguese,' the Granadine told him. 'Their land lies at the limit of the Christian world. I have always heard that they are good warriors, that they work hard and that they are very loyal to their masters. I advise you to do all you can to induce them to enter your service. If you wish I myself will go and visit their ships, and arrange to speak to their captains.'

This idea pleased the Sabayo (the title commonly accorded Yusuf on the Dekkan coast), and the Jew went off on a small foist, a light fast boat with sails and oars, taking with him eight larger ships, all strongly armed and carrying troops ready to make war on the Portuguese if the need arose. He arranged his journey so as to reach Angediva under cover of night and unperceived by anyone. He and the eight larger foists hid themselves among the islands at the mouth of the river Cintacora.

When he thought that the night was sufficiently advanced, he got into a small boat that silently took him to Angediva, where he ascertained that the three ships did come from Portugal, as he had informed his master. At daybreak, he went out openly in his small foist for the purpose of meeting the Portuguese and determining their numbers and the strength of their armament. He hoped to induce their captains to make for Goa, where they could readily be reduced to obedience.

But unknown to him, the Hindu fishermen had watched his manoeuvres and seen him hide the foists in the mouth of their river. They had recognized these vessels as part of the fleet of the Moor Sabayo, and guessed that they had come to attack their Portuguese friends. Thus forewarned, Gama thanked them warmly for their loyalty and rewarded them as they deserved.

The watchmen soon announced the appearance of a small foist, which, as Gaspar Corrêa says, 'seemed to be passing that way by chance'. On board was a dignified man with a flowing beard and snow-white hair. He pulled up within hailing distance of where the ships lay side by side and cried out in Spanish: 'May God protect these ships and my lords, their captains, and all who sail in them!'

At his behest, his oarsmen also shouted, and the Portuguese replied by sounding their trumpets. The Jew then approached closer, and said:

'My lords captains, promise me my safety and permit me to come aboard your ships to hear news of my own country and I will give you such information as you need. Since God has brought you here, may it be for your good and mine also! I have been forty years a captive, and now heaven has vouchsafed to show me these ships from Spain where I was born!'

He was told that he could come on board and would be received with the honour due to his rank, for the Portuguese did no one any harm unless they were molested. Gama and his brother received him courteously on the *St Gabriel* and asked him in what part of Spain he was born, and by what route he had come to a region so distant from the place of his birth. The Jew spoke a great deal and the captains seemed delighted with his replies, while some of his oarsmen, who had accompanied him, gazed about them in astonishment at what they saw. Finally, the captain-general summoned Coelho, who was on board the *Bérrio*, saying that he too must make the visitor's acquaintance.

Coelho approached with several of his men from the side on which the foist lay. At this moment Gama himself rose, and this was the signal for his men to move. In a moment the Jew was surrounded and overpowered, and the rowers in the foist threw themselves in the sea, but a boat put out and captured them one after another. During this time the Jew complained loudly. 'Oh, my lords captains, may God aid me and you too! I have trusted your word, and here am I bound and a captive!'

'Jew,' replied Gama harshly, 'you treacherously asked for your safety to be assured and you have received no more than your deserts.'

Coelho had now rounded up the rowers who had remained in the foist and brought them aboard the flagship, and they were placed in irons along with those who had been taken from the water. Then Gama gave orders for the Jew to be stripped and flogged, saying: 'I am punishing you for the treachery in your heart in hiding your foists in the islands. By the life of the King of Portugal my master, I swear to kill you with whips and boiling oil if you do not confess the whole truth.'

'Lord,' said the Granadine humbly, 'I know that I deserve death. But have pity on me and my white beard, and I will tell you all.'

Gama made a sign and he was unbound and given his garments. When he had clothed himself, he told the story of the plot he had contrived against the Portuguese with the approval of his master, the Moor Sabayo, lord of Goa. When he had finished, the captain-general of the fleet told him that unless he handed over all the foists hidden among the islands at the mouth of the river, he, Vasco da Gama, would have him flayed alive. 'Order and I will obey; I am in your hands, my lord,' said the Jew.

The ships' boats were now manned with twenty men apiece and their masters and pilots, and armed with small cannon and the captain-general got into the small foist and made the Jew, with his hands lashed behind his back and his ankles in irons, lie by his side. When it was quite dark, they set out for the mouth of the river Cintacora, and Gama told the Jew: 'When we are near the foists, you shall speak to your men in such a way as not to alarm them or put them on their guard, otherwise I shall have you killed.' The Jew protested simply: 'Lord, all this I will do if you will spare my life.'

The small foist sailed ahead of the ships' boats, and it was soon hailed by a sentry: 'Who goes there?' The Jew replied, 'I am here and I have some kinsmen with me.' The foist continued to move forward until Gama gave the war cry of the Portuguese: 'Santiago! St George!' It was answered by a din of confused shouts and explosions, as his men leapt aboard the large foists flinging before them burning pots of gunpowder. The Sabayo's men, roughly roused from their slumbers, were seized with panic and thought from all the noise and cries that their attackers were far more numerous. Seeking safety in flight, they leapt into the water, while the Portuguese leapt from ship to ship, ruthlessly hunting down those who were swimming in the water or clinging to rocks. Dawn was now beginning to break, and the sky lightened: the whole incident had been so well planned that not a man on the foists escaped. Having put them in chains and attached their vessels to their own boats, the Portuguese returned to Angediva with shouts of joy.

The foists were armed with iron guns and were well laden with rice, coconuts, dried fish, spears, long swords and large shields of light wood covered with polished leather. They also found large bows, which Corrêa remarks were 'like those of the English, with reed arrows with long, broad points'. Gama had the guns thrown in the sea, and some of the ships broken up for fuel. At this moment the fishermen arrived in their small craft. They were too afraid of the Sabayo's vengeance to take possession of the abandoned foists, but they did not hesitate to appropriate what they could.

Twelve of the strongest prisoners were taken aboard each ship to man the pumps. All the rest were executed on the spot, in the presence of the fishermen, who were told that these men were punished for having sought to kill the Portuguese without any cause.

The cruelty of this punishment is revolting, but such was the brutality of war in those days: its only merit lies in its openness: in times nearer our own nations believed to be civilized have committed worse crimes. Moreover, the name of Moor aroused a special hatred in the heart of Christians, and particularly in the Spains, where the presence of Muslims had been so long and violently experienced. Gama may also have felt that the survival of a single witness would expose the fishermen whose loyalty to the Portuguese had frustrated the plot to the vengeance of the Sabayo.

The Jew awaited his turn in mortal terror, believing that he too was about to be executed with the rest; but Gama merely had him placed in the hold. The monsoon had now arrived and soon after the ships set sail. Unlike the outward journey, the voyage to the east African coast was extremely difficult and took three months. On the way no less than thirty bodies of seamen and soldiers who had fallen victims to scurvy were flung into the sea. Their gums painfully swollen, their rotting flesh falling away in shreds, their legs monstrously bloated and incapable of sustaining the weight of their bodies, the survivors implored the captain to turn back and seek the coast of India. There were scarcely a dozen sound men left on each of the ships when Gama, following the advice of his brother and Coelho, yielded to their pleas. But at that moment a breath of wind filled the sails and brought with it the hope that they might yet see their own country.

✣ 24 ✣

The End of the 'St Raphael'

THEY reached the port of Melindi on January 7, 1499. With the consent of the captain-general, the pilot ibn Majid hailed a boat and went ashore 'to beg the King to reward him for the great joy we brought him'. The good King's joy was indeed so great that he at once desired to come down to the strand to receive the captains.

'They,' says Corrêa, 'had the boats launched and went towards the shore. As soon as they touched ground, they leapt out and hastened towards the King whose impatience was such that he had come down to greet them and his feet were already in the water.'

He led them back to his palace, where he embraced them each in turn. 'Sire,' Paulo da Gama told him, 'the truth of your royal heart set us on the right road. Thanks to you, we at last found what we had sought for so long, and if God permits us to return safely to Portugal, the credit will be yours.'

As the pilots came to kiss the King's feet, he added:

'We desire to ask a great favour of you. Give us these pilots who have taken us to Calicut and others as skilled as they. They know the art of navigating this sea, which our own sailors do not. On our outward journey, when we had rounded the great cape we experienced so many storms that the land was invisible to us, and as we could not observe the configuration of the shore, we shall have difficulty in finding the way back without incurring great danger. If you will give us pilots from your country, they will show us the way by sea to the great cape, and when we have rounded it, we shall show them how to sail the seas we know and they do not. They shall see Portugal and our King, and when they come back they will tell you the truth about what they have seen.'

'It seems that you have divined the wishes of my heart!' exclaimed

242

the King of Melindi. 'I have already spoken to the best pilots I can find. I entrust them to your protection, beseeching you to take good care of them, for they have confided their weeping wives and children to me, and I have given my oath for their security.'

'Sire,' promised Vasco and Paulo together, 'we shall respect your oath even to the death.'

The captain-general then had two hundred gold cruzados brought from the *St Gabriel* and handed them to the King asking him to distribute them among the pilots' wives.

In the presence of his ministers and the chief lords of his kingdom the good King entrusted Gama with a letter addressed to King Manoel. Like that of the King of Cananor, it was written on a gold leaf. It told the King all that had passed between his captains and the ruler of Melindi and recorded their mutual promises, confirming that of the ruler with a solemn oath. It was accompanied by the gift of a superb necklace of gold embellished with many pearls and precious stones. The ruler also showed that he had not forgotten the Queen, and kindly provided for her a finely carved chest inlaid with gold and ivory, and filled with veils of silk threaded with gold and so fine that the Portuguese had never beheld anything like them. The chest also contained twenty gold rings set with precious stones. The captains, for their part, each received trinkets of gold and precious stones, rings and fine textiles. When they had bidden the liberal prince farewell and had just returned to their ships, they were surprised to see two boats approach escorting a third in which the King's first minister appeared. He had come to announce that the other two boats contained packages of articles for the pilots, masters, soldiers and crew. The good King of Melindi did not want them to leave his shores without carrying a token of remembrance. The packages contained fine cloths and woollens. Moreover, the minister added, the King had forgotten to hand over something for the Queen of Portugal. 'This,' says Corrêa, 'was a piece of amber half an ell in length and as thick as a man's body at the waist; it was set in silver.'

Vasco da Gama and his brother would not let the boats return without filling them with what remained of the European merchandise. Corrêa includes the list, which shows that, despite the extreme weariness which overwhelmed them after so long and difficult a crossing, the captains and secretaries still kept their accounts in order: '. . . ten chests of coral, much amber, vermillion, quicksilver, pieces of brocade, velvet, satin, damask, scarlet, coloured Rouen stuffs, a chest filled with mirrors, knives, red caps, strings of coloured beads, gilded glassware and two hundred ingots óf copper'. The minister received his share of the presents, with which he seemed highly satisfied. As his boat moved away from the ships, followed by the two barges laden to bursting with wares for the King, the captains ordered their men to cheer and blow their trumpets loud enough to make themselves heard on shore. The poor wretches could not have had much breath left, but they obeyed with a will: it was not often that a King troubled to make himself agreeable to them.

The good prince had a quick ear and he heard them. He at once called out the merchants of the town and bade them send to the beach a hundred pieces of Mecca velvet of many colours and exquisite fineness together with the same quantity of satin and damask. It was all produced in next to no time and sent to the ships with a messenger bidden to tell the captains that since these pieces were too poor for their own use they might like to distribute them among their servants and crew to have made into clothes on their arrival in Portugal. The seamen and soldiers had scarcely recovered from their astonishment at this new liberality on the part of the King when another crowd of boats put out bringing provisions and a thousand articles for the journey, including a great jar of preserved ginger. The messenger who brought this last delivery enjoined the captains, on the King's behalf, not to forget to take this remedy whenever they felt cold at sea. He added that his master's comment on the gifts that had been sent to him was: 'I am too poor even to be able to repay such generosity!' Marvellous King of Melindi!

The pilots sent by this model ruler had already appeared on board with their baggage. They were warmly welcomed by their Portuguese colleagues, and on the next day, St Sebastian's day, they anchored off shore. On each of the ships a priest said Mass amidst general emotion. These weary voyagers, who had undergone such perils and toils, so many sufferings and griefs, and seen so many of their fellows die, sent up fervent prayers to heaven, 'Begging our Lord with many tears and great devotion to bring them safely to Portugal out of the greatness of his mercy.'

One of the religious was João Figueira, who had travelled on the flagship and set down day by day for his own pleasure the incidents of the voyage. When they reached Melindi, he fell so ill that he was already holding the mortal candle in his hands when the captain-general came to his bedside. 'Thinking that he was about to die,' says Corrêa, 'he handed Vasco da Gama a notebook in which he had set down everything that had occurred until that day. Gama was delighted with it, and when they left Melindi and the priest João Figueira was restored to health, the captain-general begged him to continue to write this detailed account of the voyage. Several copies were made of his notes, and I found many fragments of one of them in the house of Afonso de Albuquerque among some old papers, while I, Gaspar Corrêa, was secretary to this great captain. And on reaching these papers, I included as much as I could. . . .'

When Mass had been said, the sails were raised. On each of the three ships the helm was entrusted to one of the King of Melindi's pilots. 'If they said: Tomorrow we shall see such a land, or such a river, or such an island, they were always proved right.'

But it was soon realized that the crews, decimated by sickness, were insufficient for their duties. If a storm had happened to complicate the conditions in which they were navigating the result would have been disastrous. Prudently, though his heart was filled with despair at the sacrifice, Gama decided that he must part with the most battered of the three ships and divided its crew among the other two. Two days after their departure they passed Mombasa without putting in, but they halted at a group of islands lying in shallow waters, and Gama ordered everything that could be turned to account to be removed from the *St Raphael*—cannon, sails, spars, rope, iron, and wood from the helm. Its cargo was placed on board the *St Gabriel* and the *Bérrio*, and the ship was burnt. The figure of the Archangel which had protected Paulo da Gama's ship can still be seen in the Naval Museum in Lisbon. In our opinion it is wrongly described as a figure-head: this was evidently a figure like that which the Abyssinians at Mozambique had venerated on board the *St Gabriel*.

Gama bestowed the name of 'Baixos de São Rafael' on the place, which is now known as the Karange Islands, and sailed on on January 27. On February 1, the flagship and the *Bérrio* passed Mozambique in view of the islet of St George where they had set up a pillar ten months before. The Moorish pilots bade the masters reduce sail during the night and keep careful watch, since from the Sofala river there often blew 'so furious a wind that it swept trees and cattle before it and drove them into the sea'. But the ships made good progress, for strong currents carried them southward. On March 3 they beheld the Angra de São Bras, the furthest point reached by Bartolomeu Dias. Gama decided to halt there, so that his crew might relax before rounding the Cape of Good Hope. They left again ten days later; on March 20, they were in the Atlantic, where the south-east trade-winds filled their sails and drove them briskly northward.

❧ 25 ❦

The Monstrance of Belém

'THEY now crowded on all sail,' says Corrêa, 'and leaving the Cape
of Good Hope behind, they realized that they were approaching their
own land. Then they were filled with great joy and fell in one
another's arms. Kneeling, they raised their arms to heaven, and
thanked God for the gladness he had brought them.'

Vasco da Gama ordered the pilot, the boatswain and the three
seamen who had been guilty of stirring up mutiny on the outward
journey to be brought before him.

'What have you to say for yourselves now?' he asked them. 'You
should be filled with shame at the thought that you were so frightened that you wanted to turn back and set me in irons! If I had not
prevented you, you would have robbed us of the joy of having
rendered this great service to God and our lord, the King, who will
reward us generously for our toils and troubles and hardships.'

The poor wretches, who had paid so dearly for a few moments of
weakness, did not know what to say. One of the seamen, called João
da Almeijoeira, did have the courage to speak up and his short
speech was not without ingenuity.

'Sir,' said he with humble and with a contrite air. 'We have acted
according to our nature, and you have acted according to yours. On
a day of joy, such as today, can you not find it in your heart to
spare us?'

'I spare you,' the captain-general replied, 'and I swear to you that
I hold no grudge against you in my heart. But I have made a vow to
take you two, pilot and boatswain in irons to the King. When he has
seen you come before him in that fashion, he will think you have
been punished enough, and you shall receive the rewards I will beseech him to bestow on you and your children. This I promise you.

247

You shall come from the King's palace as free men, and when you are released from your irons you shall keep them to remind you for the rest of your days of the perilous journey you have gloriously completed.'

It might be thought that Pero de Alenquer and Gonçalo Alvares would have preferred to do without this memory. Gama's inflexibility seems in our eyes severe. Doubtless, in addition to the vow he mentioned, the discoverer of the sea-way to India had a thought for the future: the voyage he was just completing was only the first of a long series of expeditions which would also face storms and dangers of all kinds. Without a strict discipline which must be founded on implicit respect and fear of the captain's authority, such undertakings were foredoomed to failure. The infliction of public shame in the presence of the King on two men who, in virtue of their special responsibilities, should have been more than all the rest above any idea of mutiny, would discourage others from following their example. Nevertheless, it would have been agreeable if the great Vasco da Gama had shown more magnanimity that day.

'When they reached the Equator,' says Corrêa, 'they met with dead calms and showers, and realized that they lay off the coast of Guinea. They were then buffeted by contrary winds that blew from the Straits of Gibraltar. The pilots sailed out to sea as far as they could, sailing on a bowline, while the sea-water began to come in and it was impossible to forsake the pumps for a single moment. In that region they saw that the sea was full of reddish weeds with leaves like osiers and they called it the Sargasso Sea, a name it still retains. At last the Portuguese pilots saw the pole-star at the same height as in Portugal. . . .'

Paulo da Gama had been ill since they had rounded the Cape and his condition had grown steadily worse later: his brother scarcely left his bedside. When they put in at the island of Santiago in the Cape Verdes, the *capitão-mór* sent Nicolau Coelho on ahead to inform the King of the fortunate conclusion of their expedition. João de Sá, Paulo's second-in-command on the *St Raphael*, was put in charge of the flagship with orders to bring her to Lisbon. Gama himself freighted a caravel which was faster than the *St Gabriel*, and, placing his brother on board, set sail in the hope of reaching the Azores in time to save him.

It has been said that Coelho was anxious to appear in the King's presence before Gama and left without waiting for orders, in the hope of receiving the credit for the success of the expedition. King Manoel would certainly not have appreciated any such proof of lack of discipline, and there is nothing to confirm the assertion, which can only be regarded as a gratuitous reflection on a good and courageous captain, who never in any circumstances displayed less than absolute loyalty to his leader. He cast anchor in the Tagus on July 10, 1499, two years, almost to the day, since he had left Lisbon. A few weeks later he was followed by the *St Gabriel*, which anchored in the river in the middle of August. The great enterprise begun eighty-four years earlier with the conquest of Ceuta was brought to a dazzling climax as the old century died.

Paulo da Gama was taken ashore as soon as the caravel entered the port of Angra on Terceira in the Azores. Gaspar Corrêa tells us that his life 'lasted only that day'. He was buried in the monastery of São Francisco, 'with all the honours due to him, and was accompanied by his brother and all the notables in the town and many of the people. Vasco da Gama mourned from the bottom of his heart the loss of a brother he loved and cherished so deeply, and his grief at losing him was so great that he forgot his joy at returning to his country.'

A man of great modesty, who had always implicitly obeyed the captain-general's orders, though Vasco was his junior, Paulo da Gama had throughout the long voyage shown his understanding of men and affairs, and given ample proof of his loyalty. The *capitão-mór* was sunk in deep abjection. 'He was sad and disheartened by the loss of his brother, and his grief made the return very different from what he had hoped, for the glory, reward and honour that awaited him after so great a discovery now seemed little enough to him. But he gave thanks to God and offered up his grief, for it was in the service of God and his King that he endured it.'

A merchant of Angra called Artur Rodrigues had a caravel laden with goods for the Algarve and ready to sail when Gama arrived. He was naturally inquisitive, and asked the crew whence they came. 'From India,' was the answer. Rodrigues was quick-witted, and soon proved it.

'He did not wait to learn more, and forgetting the Algarve, he sailed straight for Lisbon, which he reached four days later, anchoring in the bay of Cascais at the mouth of the Tagus. He leapt into a small boat and went ashore, leaving his son on the ship with orders not to let anyone go ashore or speak to anyone about the ship from India. Learning that the King was at Sintra, Artur Rodrigues hastened thither. He arrived at one in the morning, and as the King had just sat down to sup, he was at once ushered into the presence. He kissed the King's hand and said: 'Sire, I kiss your Highness' hand in gratitude for the reward you will give me for the good news I have brought. I have come from the island of Terceira, where four days' since two ships arrived from India.'

'The King,' adds Corrêa, 'waited to hear no more: he immediately left the table and went to the palace chapel where he prayed for a long time.'

Gaspar Corrêa wrote 'two ships'. His account of the facts are here, as in various other incidents of the immortal voyage, in contradiction with the version that now seems definitely established and to which we have adhered. In his version, it was not the *St Raphael*, but the *Bérrio* which was destroyed, not on the return, but on the outward journey, on account of the poor state of its hull, and the destruction took place at the Rio dos Bons Sinais: the *St Gabriel* and *St Raphael* sailed to the Azores to make their triumphal entry at Lisbon together. This apotheosis must, however, be abandoned, and it is clear that Corrêa was mistaken.

On the contrary it seems likely that the light caravel chartered by Vasco da Gama reached the Azores several days before the *Bérrio* appeared in the Tagus, and thus gave the astute Rodrigues time to forestall Coelho. The tomb of Paulo da Gama disappeared when the church of São Francisco was rebuilt, and the exact date of his death, which would have thrown some light on the subject, cannot be ascertained. All we can say is that the anecdote told by Corrêa is as probable as it is curious. 'Without delay,' the chronicler says, 'the King knighted Artur Rodrigues and made his son a page in his household, giving the man a hundred gold cruzados. He at once announced that he would leave for Lisbon on the following day, for he realized that other ships would soon arrive from Terceira with more detailed news.'

Gama's caravel is thought to have anchored off the Restelo on

August 29. His friends who rushed to welcome him recommended him not to reveal his grief to the King, and he therefore took off his mourning and put on a fine coloured cloak and a round cap 'which gave him a grand air with his long flowing beard which he had not cut since he left Lisbon'. Jorge de Vasconcelos had been sent by King Manoel to confirm the arrangements for his reception. He 'besought the captain to think of the glory of the great discovery our Lord had permitted him to make and weigh his good fortune against his grief, for the first would compensate for the second, and he might thus postpone his sorrow and mourning, for which the King would be much obliged'.

Followed by an enormous concourse, the whole court had come down to the Restelo to salute the conqueror. As Gama walked between the Count of Borba and Bishop Calcadilha, Gama saw the King rise to receive him. He knelt and hugged the monarch's knees, then kissed his hand, and said: 'Sire, the moment has come when all my cares are over and my happiness is complete, since God has brought me back to your Highness' presence with my mission accomplished.'

'Welcome!' replied the King. 'My pleasure at seeing you is the greatest that could be imagined. Since God has heard your prayer and granted that you should live to see the conclusion of this great feat, he will also permit you to live to enjoy the rewards you shall receive for so great a service as you have rendered me.'

Gama again kissed the King's hand in gratitude for these words, and Dom Manoel continued:

'I beg you, as you love me, to be consoled for the death of your brother, since our Lord has willed that the whole honour of this discovery should fall to you, just as I myself had placed all my faith and hopes in you. I give thanks to God for the great glory which He has granted me this day through your hands. But although your brother is dead, he will have lost none of the honour that is his due, nor of the rewards I have reserved for him. Similarly I shall honour and reward all others who have lost their lives in this undertaking.'

The King then mounted his horse to ride to the palace of the Alcacova and asked Gama to accompany him. On their arrival he led him to the Queen's apartments, and she received him with great kindness. Before leaving the King and Queen, Gama promised to return the following day to tell the tale of his voyage. He then returned home, escorted by a cheering multitude.

With his usual single-mindedness, Gama had already advised the King that he would send his pilot and boatswain to the palace laden with chains. The King made it clear that this demonstration was quite unnecessary and replied evasively that he gave Gama full authority to bring the men to justice or set them free. Gama then summoned Pero de Alenquer and Gonçalo Alvares and told them:

'His Highness has bidden me punish you or pardon you as I think fit. Since you have suffered in expiation of your wrongs I pardon you. And now, as I promised, I shall give you the reward of your services: you may go in peace to meet your wives and families, for you will find more tranquillity and joy among them now than if you had returned to Portugal as fugitives who had been afraid of the storms and had brought your captain in chains, as your intention was!'

The two men fell to their knees, saying: 'Sir, may God repay you for your mercy to us!'

'Next morning Gama went to the palace and found his Highness dressing. King Manoel received him smilingly and with many kind words, and said: "You have not slept late, Dom Vasco da Gama!" The commander fell on one knee, and kissed the King's hand for the honour he had done him by granting him the style of Dom. The King confirmed that it would descend to all his heirs, and after talking with him at length, accompanied him to Mass.'

Coelho soon arrived followed by the great chest containing the precious textiles, jewels and the letters written by the Kings of Cananor and Melindi on leaves of gold, and the great piece of amber set in a silver stand, 'which the Queen greatly admired', the musk, the benjamin and the Chinese porcelains brought from Calicut. 'Sire,' said Gama to the King, 'Nicolau Coelho has borne a heavy share in the cares, burdens and hardships of this expedition, and he deserves your reward.'

The greatest nobles of the land were present, intent on hearing the story of the voyages, which Dom Vasco related 'with great sobriety'. They all congratulated the King, and said that they envied the greatness of the feat, in comparison with which all their high dignities seemed as nothing. King Manoel gave orders that the pilots of Melindi should be shown all the beauties of the kingdom. 'Watching everything with great attention and taking notes in writing', the pilots saw 'the King and Queen surrounded by the splendour of the court on its festivities, the royal parties, the King's dinner, the bull-baiting, the tournaments, the churches, the royal palaces and the monastery of Batalha'. Our modern offices of propaganda, or 'information' as they are now discreetly called, have invented nothing.

The King complimented Dom Vasco on his success in the affair at Angediva and then presented him with all the prisoners he had brought back. They were so well treated by their new master that they all adopted Christianity, led by the Granadine Jew. This astute old man chose to be known henceforth as Gaspar da Gama: it may be doubted if he prepared himself for baptism by confessing his treachery as a result of which all his seamen and soldiers except those who had been taken aboard to man the pumps on the Portuguese ships had swung from a rope's end at Angediva. Corrêa tells us that the King 'often conversed with him, for he was greatly interested in the things of the east which this man described. And he dealt very liberally with him, presenting him with garments from his wardrobe and horses from his stable, and the Jew also received servants from among Dom Vasco's captives'. He may well have felt his popularity assured when he became familiarly known in Lisbon as 'Gaspar of the Indies'.

Meanwhile, the officials of the House of Mina (which, as we have seen, was to become the House of Mina and India) reckoned up the royal accounts. Setting on one side of the balance the cost of the ships, the value of the merchandise they had taken for barter, the pay of the officers and men, and allowing for the rewards the King had promised, and on the other, the sums received for the pepper and other spices brought from India, they found that 'for each hundred the profit was six hundred'. This was a very handsome return, and as a result of it King Manoel was able to send Dom Vasco twenty thousand gold cruzados (each worth considerably more than a pound today), together with ten hundredweight of each of the 'drugs', which he was 'to give to his friends', as well as the right to invest each year 'two hundred gold cruzados of his own money for the purchase of cinnamon at Cananor', it being understood that this spice might be loaded on any royal ship without paying any dues 'so long as India should last'. The captain-general of the fleet also received a pension from the Crown of a thousand cruzados a year, and the revenues of the town of Sines, where he had been born. But this last award was not to the liking of the Order of Santiago, which had hitherto enjoyed this source of income and refused to give it up. In order to console Dom Vasco the King awarded him the title of Count of Vidigueira.

The heirs of Paulo da Gama received half of what had been given to the captain-general. King Manoel also generously rewarded Nicolau Coelho and the secretaries and other officers, pilots, boatswains, seamen and soldiers. All, living or dead, received their share. 'With their pay and the royal rewards,' says Corrêa, 'they all became rich and counted themselves very fortunate,' as did their heirs and successors.

On the orders of the King, the Bishop of Guarda accompanied Dom Vasco on a solemn visit to the chapel of Our Lady of Guadalupe, not far from Sagres. The Virgin before whose feet Prince Henry had laid his strivings, his disappointments, his faith and his hopes, received the collar of gold and precious stones presented by the King of Cananor. A royal manna was showered on the religious houses, which were asked to give thanks to God for the great benefits He had granted the Portuguese. Throughout the whole kingdom, from humble homes and sumptuous palaces alike, a great thanksgiving was sent up to heaven.

Nor was the hermitage of the Restelo forgotten. Already three years earlier King Manoel had asked Pope Alexander VI for authority to replace the modest chapel of Our Lady of Bethlehem, where Gama and his companions had prayed the night before their fleet set sail, by a magnificent monastery, likewise dedicated to Our Lady and now known as the Convent of the Hieronymites at Belém or 'os Jeronimos'. The centuries have added to the splendour of its stonework which represents the maritime epic of the Portuguese people. In it the goldsmith Gil Vicente placed the marvellous monstrance made with the first gold received from the east, and there repose the mortal remains of Vasco da Gama, facing the monument to the illustrious singer of his glory, Luis de Camoens.

DATE DUE			